MY BOOK

LUCILLE

LAWSON

TWO PLAYS
FOR PURITANS

THE DEVIL'S
DISCIPLE

CÆSAR AND
CLEOPATRA

GEORGE BERNARD SHAW

TWO PLAYS FOR PURITANS

drawings
by
George Him

THE HERITAGE PRESS

NEW YORK

Acknowledgment is made to
the Public Trustee and
the Society of Authors, London.
The special contents of this
edition are copyright © 1966 by
The George Macy Companies, Inc.

Contents

PREFACE

SINCE I gave my Plays, Pleasant and Unpleasant, to the
world two years ago, many things have happened to me. I
had then just entered on the fourth year of my activity as
a critic of the London theatres. They very nearly killed
me. I had survived seven years of London's music, four
or five years of London's pictures, and about as much of
its current literature, wrestling critically with them with all
my force and skill. After that, the criticism of the theatre
came to me as a huge relief in point of bodily exertion.
The difference between the leisure of a Persian cat and the
labor of a cockney cab horse is not greater than the difference between the official weekly or fortnightly playgoings
of the theatre critic and the restless daily rushing to and fro
of the music critic, from the stroke of three in the afternoon, when the concerts begin, to the stroke of twelve at
night, when the opera ends. The pictures were nearly as
bad. An Alpinist once, noticing the massive soles of my
boots, asked me whether I climbed mountains. No, I re-
plied: these boots are for the hard floors of the London
galleries. Yet I once dealt with music and pictures together in the spare time of an active young revolutionist,
and wrote plays and books and other toilsome things into

vii

the bargain. But the theatre struck me down like the veriest weakling. I sank under it like a baby fed on starch. My very bones began to perish, so that I had to get them planed and gouged by accomplished surgeons. I fell from heights and broke my limbs in pieces. The doctors said: This man has not eaten meat for twenty years: he must eat it or die. I said: This man has been going to the London theatres for three years; and the soul of him has become inane and is feeding unnaturally on his body. And I was right. I did not change my diet; but I had myself carried up into a mountain where there was no theatre; and there I began to revive. Too weak to work, I wrote books and plays: hence the second and third plays in this volume.* And now I am stronger than I have been at any moment since my feet first carried me as a critic across the fatal threshold of a London playhouse.

Why was this? What is the matter with the theatre, that a strong man can die of it? Well, the answer will make a long story; but it must be told. And, to begin, why have I just called the theatre a playhouse? The well-fed Englishman, though he lives and dies a schoolboy, cannot play. He cannot even play cricket or football: he has to work at them: that is why he beats the foreigner who plays at them. To him playing means playing the fool. He can hunt and shoot and travel and fight: he can, when special holiday festivity is suggested to him, eat and drink, dice and drab, smoke and lounge. But play he cannot. The moment you make his theatre a place of amusement instead of a place of edification, you make it, not a real playhouse, but a place of excitement for the sportsman and the sensualist.

However, this well-fed grown-up-schoolboy Englishman counts for little in the modern metropolitan audience. In the long lines of waiting playgoers lining the pavements outside our fashionable theatres every evening, the men are only the currants in the dumpling. Women are in the majority; and women and men alike belong to that least robust of all our social classes, the class which earns from eighteen to thirty shillings a week in sedentary employment, and lives in a dull lodging or with its intolerably prosaic families. These people preserve the innocence of the theatre: they have neither the philosopher's impatience to get to realities (reality being the one thing they want to es-

---

* *Captain Brassbound's Conversion* was the third play in the original volume for which Shaw wrote this Preface.

cape from), nor the longing of the sportsman for violent action, nor the fullfed, experienced, disillusioned sensuality of the rich man, whether he be gentleman or sporting publican. They read a good deal, and are at home in the fool's paradise of popular romance. They love the pretty man and the pretty woman, and will have both of them fashionably dressed and exquisitely idle, posing against backgrounds of drawingroom and dainty garden; in love, but sentimentally, romantically; always ladylike and gentlemanlike. Jejunely insipid, all this, to the stalls, which are paid for (when they *are* paid for) by people who have their own dresses and drawingrooms, and know them to be a mere masquerade behind which there is nothing romantic, and little that is interesting to most of the masqueraders except the clandestine play of natural licentiousness.

The stalls cannot be fully understood without taking into account the absence of the rich evangelical English merchant and his family, and the presence of the rich Jewish merchant and *his* family. I can see no validity whatever in the view that the influence of the rich Jews on the theatre is any worse than the influence of the rich of any other race. Other qualities being equal, men become rich in commerce in proportion to the intensity and exclusiveness of their desire for money. It may be a misfortune that the purchasing power of men who value money above art, philosophy, and the welfare of the whole community, should enable them to influence the theatre (and everything else in the market); but there is no reason to suppose that their influence is any nobler when they imagine themselves Christians than when they know themselves Jews. All that can fairly be said of the Jewish influence on the theatre is that it is exotic, and is not only a customer's influence but a financier's influence: so much so, that the way is smoothest for those plays and those performers that appeal specially to the Jewish taste. English influence on the theatre, as far as the stalls are concerned, does not exist, because the rich purchasing-powerful Englishman prefers politics and church-going: his soul is too stubborn to be purged by an avowed make-believe. When he wants sensuality he practises it: he does not play with voluptuous or romantic ideas. From the play of ideas – and the drama can never be anything more – he demands edification, and will not pay for anything else in that arena. Consequently the box office will never become an English influence until the theatre turns from the drama of romance and sensuality to the drama of edification.

Turning from the stalls to the whole auditorium, consider what is implied by the fact that the prices (all much too high, by the way) range from half a guinea to a shilling, the ages from eighteen to eighty, whilst every age, and nearly every price, represents a different taste. Is it not clear that this diversity in the audience makes it impossible to gratify every one of its units by the same luxury, since in that domain of infinite caprice, one man's meat is another man's poison, one age's longing another age's loathing? And yet that is just what the theatres kept trying to do almost all the time I was doomed to attend them. On the other hand, to interest people of divers ages, classes and temperaments by some generally momentous subject of thought, as the politicians and preachers do, would seem the most obvious course in the world. And yet the theatres avoided that as a ruinous eccentricity. Their wiseacres persisted in assuming that all men have the same tastes, fancies, and qualities of passion; that no two have the same interests; and that most playgoers have no interests at all. This being precisely contrary to the obvious facts, it followed that the majority of the plays produced were failures, recognizable as such before the end of the first act by the very wiseacres aforementioned, who, quite incapable of understanding the lesson, would thereupon set to work to obtain and produce a play applying their theory still more strictly, with proportionately more disastrous results. The sums of money I saw thus transferred from the pockets of theatrical speculators and syndicates to those of wig-makers, costumiers, scene painters, carpenters, doorkeepers, actors, theatre landlords, and all the other people for whose exclusive benefit most London theatres seem to exist, would have kept a theatre devoted exclusively to the highest drama open all the year round. If the Browning and Shelley Societies were fools, as the wiseacres said they were, for producing Strafford, Colombe's Birthday, and The Cenci; if the Independent Theatre, the New Century Theatre, and the Stage Society are impracticable faddists for producing the plays of Ibsen and Maeterlinck, then what epithet is contemptuous enough for the people who produce the would-be popular plays?

The actor-managers were far more successful, because

they produced plays that at least pleased themselves, whereas the others, with a false theory of how to please everybody, produced plays that pleased nobody. But their occasional personal successes in voluptuous plays, and, in any case, their careful concealment of failure, confirmed the prevalent error, which was only exposed fully when the plays had to stand or fall openly by their own merits. Even Shakespear was played with his brains cut out. In 1896, when Sir Henry Irving was disabled by an accident at a moment when Miss Ellen Terry was too ill to appear, the theatre had to be closed after a brief attempt to rely on the attraction of a Shakespearean play performed by the stock company. This may have been Shakespear's fault: indeed Sir Henry later on complained that he had lost a princely sum by Shakespear. But Shakespear's reply to this, if he were able to make it, would be that the princely sum was spent, not on his dramatic poetry, but on a gorgeous stage ritualism superimposed on reckless mutilations of his text, the whole being addressed to a public as to which nothing is certain except that its natural bias is towards reverence for Shakespear and dislike and distrust of ritualism. No doubt the Lyceum ritual appealed to a far more cultivated sensuousness and imaginativeness than the musical farces in which our stage Abbots of Misrule pontificated (with the same financially disastrous result); but in both there was the same intentional brainlessness, founded on the same theory that the public did not want brains, did not want to think, did not want anything but pleasure at the theatre. Unfortunately, this theory happens to be true of a certain section of the public. This section, being courted by the theatres, went to them and drove the other people out. It then discovered, as any expert could have foreseen, that the theatre cannot compete in mere pleasuremongering either with the other arts or with matter-of-fact gallantry. Stage pictures are the worst pictures, stage music the worst music, stage scenery the worst scenery within reach of the Londoner. The leading lady or gentleman may be as tempting to the admirer in the pit as the dishes in a cookshop window are to the penniless tramp on the pavement; but people do not, I presume, go to the theatre to be merely tantalized.

The breakdown on the last point was conclusive. For when the managers tried to put their principle of pleasing everybody into practice, Necessity, ever ironical towards

Folly, had driven them to seek a universal pleasure to appeal to. And since many have no ear for music or eye for color, the search for universality inevitably flung the managers back on the instinct of sex as the avenue to all hearts. Of course the appeal was a vapid failure. Speaking for my own sex, I can say that the leading lady was not to everybody's taste: her pretty face often became ugly when she tried to make it expressive; her voice lost its charm (if it ever had any) when she had nothing sincere to say; and the stalls, from racial prejudice, were apt to insist on more Rebecca and less Rowena than the pit cared for. It may seem strange, even monstrous, that a man should feel a constant attachment to the hideous witches in Macbeth, and yet yawn at the prospect of spending another evening in the contemplation of a beauteous young leading lady with voluptuous contours and longlashed eyes, painted and dressed to perfection in the latest fashions. But that is just what happened to me in the theatre.

I did not find that matters were improved by the lady pretending to be "a woman with a past," violently oversexed, or the play being called a problem play, even when the manager, and sometimes, I suspect, the very author, firmly believed the word problem to be the latest euphemism for what Justice Shallow called a bona roba, and certainly would not either of them have staked a farthing on the interest of a genuine problem. In fact these so-called problem plays invariably depended for their dramatic interest on foregone conclusions of the most heartwearying conventionality concerning sexual morality. The authors had no problematic views: all they wanted was to capture some of the fascination of Ibsen. It seemed to them that most of Ibsen's heroines were naughty ladies. And they tried to produce Ibsen plays by making their heroines naughty. But they took great care to make them pretty and expensively dressed. Thus the pseudo-Ibsen play was nothing but the ordinary sensuous ritual of the stage become as frankly pornographic as good manners allowed.

I found that the whole business of stage sensuousness, whether as Lyceum Shakespear, musical farce, or sham Ibsen, finally disgusted me, not because I was Pharisaical, or intolerantly refined, but because I was bored; and boredom is a condition which makes men as susceptible to disgust and irritation as headache makes them to noise and glare. Being a man, I have my share of the masculine silliness and vulgarity on the subject of sex which so astonishes women, to whom sex is a serious matter. I am not an Archbishop, and do not pretend to pass my life on one plane or in one mood, and that the highest: on the contrary, I am, I protest, as accessible to the humors of The Rogue's Comedy or The Rake's Progress as to the pious decencies of The Sign of the Cross. Thus Falstaff, coarser than any of the men in our loosest plays, does not bore me: Doll Tearsheet, more abandoned than any of the women, does not shock me. I think that Romeo and Juliet would be a poorer play if it were robbed of the solitary fragment it has preserved for us of the conversation of the husband of Juliet's nurse. No: my disgust was not mere thinskinned prudery. When my moral sense revolted, as it often did to the very fibres, it was invariably at the nauseous compliances of the theatre with conventional virtue. If I despised the musical farces, it was because they never had the courage of their vices. With all their labored efforts to keep up an understanding of furtive naughtiness between the low comedian on the stage and the drunken undergraduate in the stalls, they insisted all the time on their virtue and patriotism and loyalty as pitifully as a poor girl of the pavement will pretend to be a clergyman's daughter. True, I may have been offended when a manager, catering for me with coarse frankness as a slave dealer caters for a Pasha, invited me to forget the common bond of humanity between me and his company by demanding nothing from them but a gloatably voluptuous appearance. But this extreme is never reached at our better theatres. The shop assistants, the typists, the clerks, who, as I have said, preserve the innocence of the theatre, would not dare to let themselves be pleased by it. Even if they did, they would not get it from the managers, who, when they are brought to the only logical conclusion from their principle of making the theatre a temple of pleasure, indignantly refuse to change the dramatic profession for Mrs Warren's. For that is what all this demand for pleasure at the theatre finally comes to; and the answer to it is, not that people ought not to desire sensuous pleasure (they cannot help it) but that the theatre cannot give it to them, even to the extent permitted by the honor and conscience of the best managers, because a theatre is so far from being a pleasant or even a comfortable place that only by making us forget ourselves can it prevent us from realizing its inconveniences. A play that does not do this for the pleasure-seeker allows him to discover that he has chosen a disagreeable and expensive way of spending the evening. He wants to drink, to smoke, to change the spectacle, to get rid of the middle-aged actor and actress who are boring him, and to see shapely young dancing girls and acrobats doing more amusing things in a more plastic manner. In short, he wants the music hall; and he goes there, leaving the managers astonished at this unexpected but quite inevitable result of the attempt to please him. Whereas, had he been enthralled by the play, even with horror, instead of himself enthralling with the dread of his displeasure the manager, the author and the actors, all had been well. And so we must conclude that the theatre is a place which people can only endure when they forget themselves: that is, when their attention is entirely captured, their interest thoroughly roused, their sympathies raised to the eagerest readiness, and their selfishness utterly annihilated. Imagine, then, the result of conducting theatres on the principle of appealing exclusively to the instinct of self-gratification in people without power of attention, without interests, without sympathy, in short, without brains or heart. That is how they were conducted whilst I was writing about them; and that is how they nearly killed me.

Yet the managers mean well. Their self-respect is in excess rather than in defect; for they are in full reaction against the Bohemianism of past generations of actors, and so bent on compelling social recognition by a blameless respectability, that the drama, neglected in the struggle, is only just beginning to stir feebly after standing stock-still in England from Robertson's time in the sixties until the first actor was knighted in the nineties. The manager may not want good plays; but he does not want bad plays: he wants nice ones. Nice plays, with nice dresses, nice drawingrooms and nice people, are indispensable: to be ungenteel is worse than to fail. I use the word ungenteel purposely; for the stage presents life on thirty pounds a day, not as it is, but as it is conceived by the earners of thirty shillings a week. The real thing would shock the audience exactly as the manners of the public school and university shock a Board of Guardians. In just the same way, the plays which constitute the genuine aristocracy of modern dramatic literature shock the reverence for gentility which governs our theatres today. For instance, the objection to

Ibsen is not really an objection to his philosophy: it is a protest against the fact that his characters do not behave as ladies and gentlemen are popularly supposed to behave. If you adore Hedda Gabler in real life, if you envy her and feel that nothing but your poverty prevents you from being as exquisite a creature, if you know that the accident of matrimony (say with an officer of the guards who falls in love with you across the counter whilst you are reckoning the words in his telegram) may at any moment put you in her place, Ibsen's exposure of the worthlessness and meanness of her life is cruel and blasphemous to you. This point of view is not caught by the clever ladies of Hedda's own class, who recognize the portrait, applaud its painter, and think the fuss against Ibsen means nothing more than the conventional disapproval of her discussions of a *ménage à trois* with Judge Brack. A little experience of popular plays would soon convince these clever ladies that a heroine who atones in the last act by committing suicide may do all the things that Hedda only talked about, without a word of remonstrance from the press or the public. It is not murder, not adultery, not rapine that is objected to: quite the contrary. It is an unladylike attitude towards life: in other words, a disparagement of the social ideals of the poorer middle class and of the vast reinforcements it has had from the working class during the last twenty years. Let but the attitude of the author be gentlemanlike, and his heroines may do what they please. Mrs Tanqueray was received with delight by the public: Saint Teresa would have been hissed off the same stage for her contempt for the ideal represented by a carriage, a fashionable dressmaker, and a dozen servants.

Here, then, is a pretty problem for the manager. He is convinced that plays must depend for their dramatic force on appeals to the sex instinct; and yet he owes it to his own newly conquered social position that they shall be perfectly genteel plays, fit for churchgoers. The sex instinct must therefore proceed upon genteel assumptions. Impossible! you will exclaim. But you are wrong: nothing is more astonishing than the extent to which, in real life, the sex instinct does so proceed, even when the consequence is its lifelong starvation. Few of us have vitality enough to make any of our instincts imperious: we can be made to live on pretences, as the masterful minority well know. But the timid majority, if it rules nowhere else, at least rules in the theatre: fitly enough too, because on the stage pretence is all that can exist. Life has its realities behind its shows: the theatre has nothing but its shows. But can the theatre make a show of lovers' endearments? A thousand times no: perish the thought of such unladylike, ungentlemanlike exhibitions. You can have fights, rescues, conflagrations, trials-at-law, avalanches, murders and executions all directly simulated on the stage if you will. But any such realistic treatment of the incidents of sex is quite out of the question. The singer, the dramatic dancer, the exquisite declaimer of impassioned poesy, the rare artist who, bringing something of the art of all three to the ordinary work of the theatre, can enthral an audience by the expression of dramatic feeling alone, may take love for a theme on the stage; but the prosaic walking gentleman of our fashionable theatres, realistically simulating the incidents of life, cannot touch it without indecorum.

Can any dilemma be more complete? Love is assumed to be the only theme that touches all your audience infallibly, young and old, rich and poor. And yet love is the one subject that the drawingroom drama dare not present.

Out of this dilemma, which is a very old one, has come the romantic play: that is, the play in which love is carefully kept off the stage, whilst it is alleged as the motive of all the actions presented to the audience. The result is, to me at least, an intolerable perversion of human conduct. There are two classes of stories that seem to me to be not only fundamentally false but sordidly base. One is the pseudo-religious story, in which the hero or heroine does good on strictly commercial grounds, reluctantly exercising a little virtue on earth in consideration of receiving in return an exorbitant payment in heaven: much as if an odalisque were to allow a cadi to whip her for a couple of millions in gold. The other is the romance in which the hero, also rigidly commercial, will do nothing except for the sake of the heroine. Surely this is as depressing as it is unreal. Compare with it the treatment of love, frankly indecent according to our notions, in oriental fiction. In The Arabian Nights we have a series of stories, some of them very good ones, in which no sort of decorum is observed. The result is that they are infinitely more instructive and enjoyable than our romances, because love is treated in them as naturally as any other passion. There is no cast iron convention as to its effects; no false association of general depravity of character with its corporealities or of general elevation with its sentimentalities; no pretence that a man or woman cannot be courageous and kind and friendly unless infatuatedly in love with somebody (is no poet manly enough to sing The Old Maids of England?): rather, indeed, an insistence on the blinding and narrowing power of lovesickness to make princely heroes unhappy and unfortunate. These tales expose, further, the delusion that the interest of this most capricious, most transient, most easily baffled of all instincts, is inexhaustible, and that the field of the English romancer has been cruelly narrowed by the restrictions under which he is permitted to deal with it. The Arabian storyteller, relieved of all such restrictions, heaps character on character, adventure on adventure, marvel on marvel; whilst the English novelist, like the starving tramp who can think of nothing but his hunger, seems to be unable to escape from the obsession of sex, and will rewrite the very gospels because the originals are not written in the sensuously ecstatic style. At the instance of Martin Luther we long ago gave up imposing celibacy on our priests; but we still impose it on our art, with the very undesirable and unexpected result that no editor, publisher, or manager, will now accept a story or produce a play without "love interest" in it. Take, for a recent example, Mr H. G. Wells's War of the Worlds, a tale of the invasion of the earth by the inhabitants of the planet Mars: a capital story, not to be laid down until finished. Love interest is impossible on its scientific plane: nothing could be more impertinent and irritating. Yet Mr Wells has had to pretend that the hero is in love with a young lady manufactured for the purpose, and to imply that it is on her account alone that he feels concerned about the apparently inevitable destruction of the human race by the Martians. Another example. An American novelist, recently deceased, made a hit some years ago by compiling a Bostonian Utopia from the prospectuses of the little bands of devout Communists who have from time to time, since the days of Fourier and Owen, tried to establish millennial colonies outside our commercial civilization. Even in this economic Utopia we find the inevitable love affair. The hero, waking up in a distant future from a miraculous sleep, meets a Boston young lady, provided expressly for him to fall in love with. Women have by that time given up wearing skirts; but she, to spare his delicacy, gets one out of a museum of antiquities to wear in his presence until he is hardened to the customs of the new age. When I came to that touching incident, I became as Paolo and Francesca: "in that book I read no more." I will not multiply examples: if such unendurable follies occur in the sort of story made by working out a meteorologic or economic hypothesis, the extent to which it is carried in sentimental romances needs no expatiation.

The worst of it is that since man's intellectual consciousness of himself is derived from the descriptions of him in books, a persistent misrepresentation of humanity in literature gets finally accepted and acted upon. If every mirror reflected our noses twice their natural size, we should live and die in the faith that we were all Punches; and we should scout a true mirror as the work of a fool, madman, or jester. Nay, I believe we should, by Lamarckian adaptation, enlarge our noses to the admired size; for I have noticed that when a certain type of feature appears in painting and is admired as beautiful, it presently becomes common in nature; so that the Beatrices and Francescas in the picture galleries of one generation, to whom minor poets address verses entitled To My Lady, come to life as the parlormaids and waitresses of the next. If the conventions of romance are only insisted on long enough and uniformly enough (a condition guaranteed by the uniformity of human folly and vanity), then, for the huge School Board-taught masses who read romance and nothing else, these conventions will become the laws of personal honor. Jealousy, which is either an egotistical meanness or a specific mania, will become obligatory; and ruin, ostracism, breaking up of homes, duelling, murder, suicide and infanticide will be produced (often have been produced, in fact) by incidents which, if left to the operation of natural and right feeling, would produce nothing worse than an hour's soon-forgotten fuss. Men will be slain needlessly on the field of battle because officers conceive it to be their first duty to make romantic exhibitions of conspicuous gallantry. The squire who has never spared an hour from the hunting field to do a little public work on a parish council will be cheered as a patriot because he is willing to kill and get killed for the sake of conferring himself as an institution on other countries. In the courts cases will be argued, not on juridical but on romantic principles; and vindictive damages and vindictive sentences, with the acceptance of nonsensical, and the repudiation or suppression of sensible testimony, will destroy the very sense of law. Kaisers, generals, judges, and prime ministers will set the example of playing to the gallery. Finally the people, now that their Board School literacy enables every penman to play on their romantic illusions, will be led by the nose far more completely than they ever were by playing on their former ignorance and superstition. Nay, why should I say will be? they *are*. Ten years of cheap reading have changed the English from the most stolid nation in Europe to the most theatrical and hysterical.

Is it clear now, why the theatre was insufferable to me; why it left its black mark on my bones as it has left its black mark on the character of the nation; why I call the Puritans to rescue it again as they rescued it before when its foolish pursuit of pleasure sunk it in "profaneness and immorality"? I have, I think, always been a Puritan in my attitude towards Art. I am as fond of fine music and handsome building as Milton was, or Cromwell, or Bunyan; but if I found that they were becoming the instruments of a systematic idolatry of sensuousness, I would hold it good statesmanship to blow every cathedral in the world to pieces with dynamite, organ and all, without the least heed to the screams of the art critics and cultured voluptuaries. And when I see that the nineteenth century has crowned the idolatry of Art with the deification of Love, so that every poet is supposed to have pierced to the holy of holies when he has announced that Love is the Supreme, or the Enough, or the All, I feel that Art was safer in the hands of the most fanatical of Cromwell's major generals than it will be if ever it gets into mine. The pleasures of the senses I can sympathize with and share; but the substitution of sensuous ecstasy for intellectual activity and honesty is the very devil. It has already brought us to Flogging Bills in Parliament, and, by reaction, to androgynous heroes on the stage; and if the infection spreads until the democratic attitude becomes thoroughly Romanticist, the country will become unbearable for all realists, Philistine or Platonic. When it comes to that, the brute force of the strong-minded Bismarckian man of action, impatient of humbug, will combine with the subtlety and spiritual energy of the man of thought whom shams cannot illude or interest. That combination will be on one side; and Romanticism will be on the other. In which event, so much the worse for Romanticism, which will come down even if it has to drag Democracy down with it. For all institutions have in the long run to live by the nature of things, and not by imagination.

ON DIABOLONIAN ETHICS

THERE is a foolish opinion prevalent that an author should allow his works to speak for themselves, and that he who appends and prefixes explanations to them is likely to be as bad an artist as the painter cited by Cervantes, who wrote under his picture This is a Cock, lest there should be any mistake about it. The pat retort to this thoughtless comparison is that the painter invariably does so label his picture. What is a Royal Academy catalogue but a series of statements that This is The Vale of Rest, This is The School of Athens, This is Chill October, This is The Prince of Wales, and so on? The reason most dramatists do not publish their plays with prefaces is that they cannot write them, the business of intellectually conscious philosopher and skilled critic being no part of the playwright's craft. Naturally, making a virtue of their incapacity, they either repudiate prefaces as shameful, or else, with a modest air, request some popular critic to supply one, as much as to say, Were I to tell the truth about myself I must needs seem vainglorious: were I to tell less than the truth I should do myself an injustice and deceive my readers. As to the critic thus called in from the outside, what can he do but imply that his friend's transcendant ability as a dramatist is surpassed only by his beautiful nature as a man? Now what I say is, why should I get another man to praise me when I can praise myself? I have no disabilities to plead: produce me your best critic, and I will criticize his head off. As to philosophy, I taught my critics the little they know in my Quintessence of Ibsenism; and now they turn their guns—the guns I loaded for them—on me, and proclaim that I write as if mankind had intellect without will, or heart, as they call it. Ingrates: who was it that directed your attention to the distinction between Will and Intellect? Not Schopenhauer, I think, but Shaw.

Again, they tell me that So-and-So, who does not write prefaces, is no charlatan. Well, I am. I first caught the ear of the British public on a cart in Hyde Park, to the blaring of brass bands, and this not at all as a reluctant sacrifice of my instinct of privacy to political necessity, but because, like all dramatists and mimes of genuine vocation, I am a natural-born mountebank. I am well aware that the ordinary British citizen requires a profession of shame from all mountebanks by way of homage to the sanctity of the ignoble private life to which he is condemned by his incapacity for public life. Thus Shakespear, after proclaiming that Not marble nor the gilded monuments of Princes should outlive his powerful rhyme, would apologize, in the approved taste, for making himself a motley to the view; and the British citizen has ever since quoted the apology and ignored the fanfare. When an actress writes her memoirs, she impresses on you in every chapter how cruelly it tried her feelings to exhibit her person to the public gaze; but she does not forget to decorate the book with a dozen portraits of herself. I really cannot respond to this demand for mock-modesty. I am ashamed neither of my work nor of the way it is done. I like explaining its merits to the huge majority who dont know good work from bad. It does them good; and it does me good, curing me of nervousness, laziness, and snobbishness. I write prefaces as Dryden did, and treatises as Wagner, because I *can;* and I would give half a dozen of Shakespear's plays for one of the prefaces he ought to have written. I leave the delicacies of retirement to those who are gentlemen first and literary workmen afterwards. The cart and trumpet for me.

This is all very well; but the trumpet is an instrument that grows on one; and sometimes my blasts have been so strident that even those who are most annoyed by them have mistaken the novelty of my shamelessness for novelty in my plays and opinions. Take, for instance, the first play in this volume, entitled The Devil's Disciple. It does not contain a single even passably novel incident. Every old patron of the Adelphi pit would, were he not beglamored in a way presently to be explained, recognize the reading of the will, the oppressed orphan finding a protector, the arrest, the heroic sacrifice, the court martial, the scaffold, the reprieve at the last moment, as he recognizes beefsteak pudding on the bill of fare at his restaurant. Yet when the play was produced in 1897 in New York by Mr Richard Mansfield, with a success that proves either that the melodrama was built on very safe old lines, or that the American public is composed exclusively of men of genius, the critics, though one said one thing and another another as to the play's merits, yet all agreed that it was novel – *original*, as they put it – to the verge of audacious eccentricity.

Now this, if it applies to the incidents, plot, construction, and general professional and technical qualities of the play, is nonsense; for the truth is, I am in these matters a very old-fashioned playwright. When a good deal of the same talk, both hostile and friendly, was provoked by my last volume of plays, Mr Robert Buchanan, a dramatist who knows what I know and remembers what I remember of the history of the stage, pointed out that the stage tricks by which I gave the younger generation of playgoers an exquisite sense of quaint unexpectedness, had done duty years ago in Cool as a Cucumber, Used Up, and many forgotten farces and comedies of the Byron-Robertson school, in which the imperturbably impudent comedian, afterwards shelved by the reaction to brainless sentimentality, was a stock figure. It is always so more or less: the novelties of one generation are only the resuscitated fashions of the generation before last.

But the stage tricks of The Devil's Disciple are not, like some of those of Arms and the Man, the forgotten ones of the sixties, but the hackneyed ones of our own time. Why, then, were they not recognized? Partly, no doubt, because of my trumpet and cartwheel declamation. The critics were the victims of the long course of hypnotic suggestion by which G.B.S. the journalist manufactured an unconventional reputation for Bernard Shaw the author. In England as elsewhere the spontaneous recognition of really original work begins with a mere handful of people, and propagates itself so slowly that it has become a commonplace to say that genius, demanding bread, is given a stone after its possessor's death. The remedy for this is sedulous advertisement. Accordingly, I have advertised myself so well that I find myself, whilst still in middle life, almost as legendary a person as the Flying Dutchman. Critics, like other people, see what they look for, not what is actually before them. In my plays they look for my legendary qualities, and find originality and brilliancy in my most hackneyed claptraps. Were I to republish Buckstone's Wreck Ashore as my latest comedy, it would be hailed as a masterpiece of perverse paradox and scintillating satire. Not, of course, by the really able critics – for example, you, my friend, now reading this sentence. The illusion that makes *you* think me so original is far subtler than that. The Devil's

Disciple has, in truth, a genuine novelty in it. Only, that novelty is not any invention of my own, but simply the novelty of the advanced thought of my day. As such, it will assuredly lose its gloss with the lapse of time, and leave The Devil's Disciple exposed as the threadbare popular melodrama it technically is.

Let me explain (for, as Mr A. B. Walkley has pointed out in his disquisitions on Frames of Mind, I am nothing if not explanatory). Dick Dudgeon, the devil's disciple, is a Puritan of the Puritans. He is brought up in a household where the Puritan religion has died, and become, in its corruption, an excuse for his mother's master passion of hatred in all its phases of cruelty and envy. This corruption has already been dramatized for us by Charles Dickens in his picture of the Clennam household in Little Dorrit: Mrs Dudgeon being a replica of Mrs Clennam with certain circumstantial variations, and perhaps a touch of the same author's Mrs Gargery in Great Expectations. In such a home the young Puritan finds himself starved of religion, which is the most clamorous need of his nature. With all his mother's indomitable selffulness, but with Pity instead of Hatred as his master passion, he pities the devil; takes his side; and champions him, like a true Covenanter, against the world. He thus becomes, like all genuinely religious men, a reprobate and an outcast. Once this is understood, the play becomes straightforwardly simple.

The Diabolonian position is new to the London playgoer of today, but not to lovers of serious literature. From Prometheus to the Wagnerian Siegfried, some enemy of the gods, unterrified champion of those oppressed by them, has always towered among the heroes of the loftiest poetry. Our newest idol, the Superman, celebrating the death of godhead, may be younger than the hills; but he is as old as the shepherds. Two and a half centuries ago our greatest English dramatizer of life, John Bunyan, ended one of his stories with the remark that there is a way to hell even from the gates of heaven, and so led us to the equally true proposition that there is a way to heaven even from the gates of hell. A century ago William Blake was, like Dick Dudgeon, an avowed Diabolonian: he called his angels devils and his devils angels. His devil is a Redeemer. Let those who have praised my originality in conceiving Dick Dudgeon's strange religion read Blake's Marriage of Heaven and Hell; and I shall be fortunate if they do not

rail at me for a plagiarist. But they need not go back to
Blake and Bunyan. Have they not heard the recent fuss
about Nietzsche and his Good and Evil Turned Inside
Out? Mr Robert Buchanan has actually written a long
poem of which the Devil is the merciful hero, which poem
was in my hands before a word of The Devil's Disciple
was written. There never was a play more certain to be
written than The Devil's Disciple at the end of the nineteenth century. The age was visibly pregnant with it.

I grieve to have to add that my old friends and col-
leagues the London critics for the most part showed no
sort of connoisseurship either in Puritanism or in Diabo-
lonianism when the play was performed for a few weeks at
a suburban theatre (Kennington) in October 1899 by Mr
Murray Carson. They took Mrs Dudgeon at her own val-
uation as a religious woman because she was detestably
disagreeable. And they took Dick as a blackguard, on her
authority, because he was neither detestable nor disagreeable. But they presently found themselves in a dilemma.
Why should a blackguard save another man's life, and that
man no friend of his, at the risk of his own? Clearly, said
the critics, because he is redeemed by love. All wicked heroes are, on the stage: that is the romantic metaphysic. Unfortunately for this explanation (which I do not profess to
understand) it turned out in the third act that Dick was a
Puritan in this respect also: a man impassioned only for
saving grace, and not to be led or turned by wife or
mother, Church or State, pride of life or lust of the flesh.
In the lovely home of the courageous, affectionate, practi-
cal minister who marries a pretty wife twenty years
younger than himself, and turns soldier in an instant to
save the man who has saved him, Dick looks round and
understands the charm and the peace and the sanctity, but
knows that such material comforts are not for him. When
the woman nursed in that atmosphere falls in love with
him and concludes (like the critics, who somehow always
agree with my sentimental heroines) that he risked his life
for her sake, he tells her the obvious truth that he would
have done as much for any stranger – that the law of his
own nature, and no interest nor lust whatsoever, forbad
him to cry out that the hangman's noose should be taken
off his neck only to be put on another man's.

But then, said the critics, where is the motive? *Why* did
Dick save Anderson? On the stage, it appears, people do

things for reasons. Off the stage they dont: that is why your penny-in-the-slot heroes, who only work when you drop a motive into them, are so oppressively automatic and uninteresting. The saving of life at the risk of the saver's own is not a common thing; but modern populations are so vast that even the most uncommon things are recorded once a week or oftener. Not one of my critics but has seen a hundred times in his paper how some policeman or fireman or nursemaid has received a medal, or the compliments of a magistrate, or perhaps a public funeral, for risking his or her life to save another's. Has he ever seen it added that the saved was the husband of the woman the saver loved, or was that woman herself, or was even known to the saver as much as by sight? Never. When we want to read of the deeds that are done for love, whither do we turn? To the murder column; and there we are rarely disappointed.

Need I repeat that the theatre critic's professional routine so discourages any association between real life and the stage, that he soon loses the natural habit of referring to the one to explain the other? The critic who discovered a romantic motive for Dick's sacrifice was no mere literary dreamer, but a clever barrister. He pointed out that Dick Dudgeon clearly did adore Mrs Anderson; that it was for her sake that he offered his life to save her beloved husband; and that his explicit denial of his passion was the splendid mendacity of a gentleman whose respect for a married woman, and duty to her absent husband, sealed his passion-palpitating lips. From the moment that this fatally plausible explanation was launched, my play became my critic's play, not mine. Thenceforth Dick Dudgeon every night confirmed the critic by stealing behind Judith, and mutely attesting his passion by surreptitiously imprinting a heartbroken kiss on a stray lock of her hair whilst he uttered the barren denial. As for me, I was just then wandering about the streets of Constantinople, unaware of all these doings. When I returned all was over. My personal relations with the critic and the actor forbad me to curse them. I had not even the chance of publicly forgiving them. They meant well by me; but if they ever write a play, may I be there to explain!

As to the other plays in this volume, the application of my
title is less obvious, since neither Julius Cæsar, Cleopatra
nor Lady Cicely Waynflete* have any external political
connexion with Puritanism. The very name of Cleopatra
suggests at once a tragedy of Circe, with the horrible difference that whereas the ancient myth rightly represents
Circe as turning heroes into hogs, the modern romantic
convention would represent her as turning hogs into
heroes. Shakespear's Antony and Cleopatra must needs be
as intolerable to the true Puritan as it is vaguely distressing
to the ordinary healthy citizen, because, after giving a
faithful picture of the soldier broken down by debauchery,
and the typical wanton in whose arms such men perish,
Shakespear finally strains all his huge command of rhetoric and stage pathos to give a theatrical sublimity to the
wretched end of the business, and to persuade foolish
spectators that the world was well lost by the twain. Such
falsehood is not to be borne except by the real Cleopatras
and Antonys (they are to be found in every public house)
who would no doubt be glad enough to be transfigured by
some poet as immortal lovers. Woe to the poet who stoops
to such folly! The lot of the man who sees life truly and
thinks about it romantically is Despair. How well we know
the cries of that despair! Vanity of vanities, all is vanity!
moans the Preacher, when life has at last taught him that
Nature will not dance to his moralist-made tunes. Thackeray, scores of centuries later, is still baying the moon in
the same terms. Out, out, brief candle! cries Shakespear, in
his tragedy of the modern literary man as murderer and
witch consulter. Surely the time is past for patience with
writers who, having to choose between giving up life in
despair and discarding the trumpery moral kitchen scales
in which they try to weigh the universe, superstitiously
stick to the scales, and spend the rest of the lives they pretend to despise in breaking men's spirits. But even in pessi-
mism there is a choice between intellectual honesty and
dishonesty. Hogarth drew the rake and the harlot without
glorifying their end. Swift, accepting our system of morals
and religion, delivered the inevitable verdict of that system
on us through the mouth of the king of Brobdingnag, and
described man as the Yahoo, shocking his superior the
horse by his every action. Strindberg, the only living gen-

* Lady Cicely is an important character in *Captain Brassbound's
Conversion.*

xxvi

uine Shakespearean dramatist, shows that the female Yahoo, measured by romantic standards, is viler than her
male dupe and slave. I respect these resolute tragicomedi-
ans: they are logical and faithful: they force you to face the
fact that you must either accept their conclusions as valid
(in which case it is cowardly to continue living) or admit
that your way of judging conduct is absurd. But when
your Shakespears and Thackerays huddle up the matter at
the end by killing somebody and covering your eyes with
the undertaker's handkerchief, duly onioned with some pathetic phrase, as The flight of angels sing thee to thy rest,
or Adsum, or the like, I have no respect for them at all:
such maudlin tricks may impose on tea-drunkards, not
on me.

Besides, I have a technical objection to making sexual
infatuation a tragic theme. Experience proves that it is only
effective in the comic spirit. We can bear to see Mrs
Quickly pawning her plate for love of Falstaff, but not Antony running away from the battle of Actium for love of
Cleopatra. Let realism have its demonstration, comedy its
criticism, or even bawdry its horselaugh at the expense of
sexual infatuation, if it must; but to ask us to subject our
souls to its ruinous glamor, to worship it, deify it, and imply that it alone makes our life worth living, is nothing but
folly gone mad erotically – a thing compared to which Falstaff's unbeglamored drinking and drabbing is respectable
and rightminded. Whoever, then, expects to find Cleopatra a Circe and Cæsar a hog in these pages, had better
lay down my book and be spared a disappointment.

In Cæsar, I have used another character with which
Shakespear has been beforehand. But Shakespear, who
knew human weakness so well, never knew human strength
of the Cæsarian type. His Cæsar is an admitted failure: his
Lear is a masterpiece. The tragedy of disillusion and
doubt, of the agonized struggle for a foothold on the quick-
sand made by an acute observation striving to verify its
vain attribution of morality and respectability to Nature, of
the faithless will and the keen eyes that the faithless will is
too weak to blind: all this will give you a Hamlet or a Macbeth, and win you great applause from literary gentlemen;
but it will not give you a Julius Cæsar. Cæsar was not in
Shakespear, nor in the epoch, now fast waning, which he
inaugurated. It cost Shakespear no pang to write Cæsar
down for the merely technical purpose of writing Brutus

up. And what a Brutus! A perfect Girondin, mirrored in Shakespear's art two hundred years before the real thing came to maturity and talked and stalked and had its head duly cut off by the coarser Antonys and Octaviuses of its time, who at least knew the difference between life and rhetoric.

It will be said that these remarks can bear no other construction than an offer of my Cæsar to the public as an improvement on Shakespear's. And in fact, that is their precise purport. But here let me give a friendly warning to those scribes who have so often exclaimed against my criticisms of Shakespear as blasphemies against a hitherto unquestioned Perfection and Infallibility. Such criticisms are no more new than the creed of my Diabolonian Puritan or my revival of the humors of Cool as a Cucumber. Too much surprise at them betrays an acquaintance with Shakespear criticism so limited as not to include even the prefaces of Dr Johnson and the utterances of Napoleon. I have merely repeated in the dialect of my own time and in the light of its philosophy what they said in the dialect and light of theirs. Do not be misled by the Shakespear fanciers who, ever since his own time, have delighted in his plays just as they might have delighted in a particular breed of pigeons if they had never learnt to read. His genuine critics, from Ben Jonson to Mr Frank Harris, have always kept as far on this side idolatry as I.

As to our ordinary uncritical citizens, they have been slowly trudging forward these three centuries to the point which Shakespear reached at a bound in Elizabeth's time. Today most of them have arrived there or thereabouts, with the result that his plays are at last beginning to be performed as he wrote them; and the long line of disgraceful farces, melodramas, and stage pageants which actor-managers, from Garrick and Cibber to our own contemporaries, have hacked out of his plays as peasants have hacked huts out of the Coliseum, are beginning to vanish from the stage. It is a significant fact that the mutilators of Shakespear, who never could be persuaded that Shakespear knew his business better than they, have ever been the most fanatical of his worshippers. The late Augustin Daly thought no price too extravagant for an addition to his collection of Shakespear relics; but in arranging Shakespear's plays for the stage, he proceeded on the assumption that Shakespear was a botcher and he an artist. I am far too good a Shakespearean ever to forgive Sir Henry Irving for producing a version of King Lear so mutilated that the numerous critics who had never read the play could not follow the story of Gloster. Both these idolaters of the Bard must have thought Mr Forbes Robertson mad because he restored Fortinbras to the stage and played as much of Hamlet as there was time for instead of as little. And the instant success of the experiment probably altered their minds no further than to make them think the public mad. Mr Benson actually gives the play complete at two sittings, causing the aforesaid numerous critics to remark with naïve surprise that Polonius is a complete and interesting character. It was the age of gross ignorance of Shakespear and incapacity for his works that produced the indiscriminate eulogies with which we are familiar. It was the revival of genuine criticism of those works that coincided with the movement for giving genuine instead of spurious and silly representations of his plays. So much for Bardolatry!

It does not follow, however, that the right to criticize Shakespear involves the power of writing better plays. And in fact – do not be surprised at my modesty – I do not profess to write better plays. The writing of practicable stage plays does not present an infinite scope to human talent; and the dramatists who magnify its difficulties are humbugs. The summit of their art has been attained again and again. No man will ever write a better tragedy than Lear, a better comedy than Le Festin de Pierre or Peer Gynt, a better opera than Don Giovanni, a better music drama than The Niblung's Ring, or, for the matter of that, better fashionable plays and melodramas than are now being turned out by writers whom nobody dreams of mocking with the word immortal. It is the philosophy, the outlook on life, that changes, not the craft of the playwright. A generation that is thoroughly moralized and patriotized, that conceives virtuous indignation as spiritually nutritious, that murders the murderer and robs the thief, that grovels before all sorts of ideals, social, military, ecclesiastical, royal and divine, may be, from my point of view, steeped in error; but it need not want for as good plays as the hand of man can produce. Only, those plays will be neither written nor relished by men in whose philosophy guilt and innocence, and consequently revenge and idolatry, have no meaning. Such men must rewrite all the old plays in terms of their own philosophy; and that is why, as Mr Stuart-

Glennie has pointed out, there can be no new drama without a new philosophy. To which I may add that there can be no Shakespear or Goethe without one either, nor two Shakespears in one philosophic epoch, since, as I have said, the first great comer in that epoch reaps the whole harvest and reduces those who come after to the rank of mere gleaners, or, worse than that, fools who go laboriously through all the motions of the reaper and binder in an empty field. What is the use of writing plays or painting frescoes if you have nothing more to say or show than was said and shown by Shakespear, Michael Angelo, and Raphael? If these had not seen things differently, for better or worse, from the dramatic poets of the Townley mysteries, or from Giotto, they could not have produced their works: no, not though their skill of pen and hand had been double what it was. After them there was no need (and *need* alone nerves men to face the persecution in the teeth of which new art is brought to birth) to redo the already done, until in due time, when their philosophy wore itself out, a new race of nineteenth century poets and critics, from Byron to William Morris, began, first to speak coldly of Shakespear and Raphael, and then to rediscover, in the medieval art which these Renascence masters had superseded, certain forgotten elements which were germinating again for the new harvest. What is more, they began to discover that the technical skill of the masters was by no means superlative. Indeed, I defy anyone to prove that the great epoch makers in fine art have owed their position to their technical skill. It is true that when we search for examples of a prodigious command of language and of graphic line, we can think of nobody better than Shakespear and Michael Angelo. But both of them laid their arts waste for centuries by leading later artists to seek greatness in copying their technique. The technique was acquired, refined on, and surpassed over and over again; but the supremacy of the two great exemplars remained undisputed. As a matter of easily observable fact, every generation produces men of extraordinary special faculty, artistic, mathematical and linguistic, who for lack of new ideas, or indeed of any ideas worth mentioning, achieve no distinction outside music halls and class rooms, although they can do things easily that the great epoch makers did clumsily or not at all. The contempt of the academic pedant for the original artist is often founded on a genuine superiority of technical knowledge and aptitude: he is sometimes a better anatomical draughtsman than Raphael, a better hand at triple counterpoint than Beethoven, a better versifier than Byron. Nay, this is true not merely of pedants, but of men who have produced works of art of some note. If technical facility were the secret of greatness in art, Mr Swinburne would be greater than Browning and Byron rolled into one, Stevenson greater than Scott or Dickens, Mendelssohn than Wagner, Maclise than Madox Brown. Besides, new ideas make their technique as water makes its channel; and the technician without ideas is as useless as the canal constructor without water, though he may do very skilfully what the Mississippi does very rudely. To clinch the argument, you have only to observe that the epoch maker himself has generally begun working professionally before his new ideas have mastered him sufficiently to insist on constant expression by his art. In such cases you are compelled to admit that if he had by chance died earlier, his greatness would have remained unachieved, although his technical qualifications would have been well enough established. The early imitative works of great men are usually conspicuously inferior to the best works of their forerunners. Imagine Wagner dying after composing Rienzi, or Shelly after Zastrozzi! Would any competent critic then have rated Wagner's technical aptitude as high as Rossini's, Spontini's, or Meyerbeer's; or Shelley's as high as Moore's? Turn the problem another way: does anyone suppose that if Shakespear had conceived Goethe's or Ibsen's ideas, he would have expressed them any worse than Goethe or Ibsen? Human faculty being what it is, is it likely that in our time any advance, except in external conditions, will take place in the arts of expression sufficient to enable an author, without making himself ridiculous, to undertake to say what he has to say better than Homer or Shakespear? But the humblest author, and much more a rather arrogant one like myself, may profess to have something to say by this time that neither Homer nor Shakespear said. And the playgoer may reasonably ask to have historical events and persons presented to him in the light of his own time, even though Homer and Shakespear have already shown them in the light of their time. For example, Homer presented Achilles and Ajax as heroes to the world in the Iliads. In due time came Shakespear, who said, virtually: I really cannot accept this spoiled child and this brawny fool as great men merely because Homer flattered them in playing to the Greek gallery. Consequently we have, in Troilus and Cressida, the verdict of Shakespear's epoch (our own) on the pair. This did not in the least involve any pretence on Shakespear's part to be a greater poet than Homer.

When Shakespear in turn came to deal with Henry V and Julius Cæsar, he did so according to his own essentially knightly conception of a great statesman-commander. But in the XIX century comes the German historian Mommsen, who also takes Cæsar for his hero, and explains the immense difference in scope between the perfect knight Vercingetorix and his great conqueror Julius Cæsar. In this country, Carlyle, with his vein of peasant inspiration, apprehended the sort of greatness that places the true hero of history so far beyond the mere *preux chevalier*, whose fanatical personal honor, gallantry and self-sacrifice, are founded on a passion for death born of inability to bear the weight of a life that will not grant ideal conditions to the liver. This one ray of perception became Carlyle's whole stock-in-trade; and it sufficed to make a literary master of him. In due time, when Mommsen is an old man, and Carlyle dead, come I, and dramatize the by-this-time familiar distinction in Arms and the Man, with its comedic conflict between the knightly Bulgarian and the Mommsenite Swiss captain. Whereupon a great many playgoers who have not yet read Shakespear, much less Mommsen and Carlyle, raise a shriek of concern for their knightly ideal as if nobody had ever questioned its sufficiency since the middle ages. Let them thank me for educating them so far. And let them allow me to set forth Cæsar in the same modern light, taking the same liberty with Shakespear as he with Homer, and with no thought of pretending to express the Mommsenite view of Cæsar any better than Shakespear expressed a view which was not even Plutarchian, and must, I fear, be referred to the tradition in stage conquerors established by Marlowe's Tamerlane as much as to even the chivalrous conception of heroism dramatized in Henry V.

For my own part, I can avouch that such powers of invention, humor and stage ingenuity as I have been able to exercise in Plays, Pleasant and Unpleasant, and in these Plays for Puritans, availed me not at all until I saw the old facts in a new light. Technically, I do not find myself able to proceed otherwise than as former playwrights have done. True, my plays have the latest mechanical improvements: the action is not carried on by impossible soliloquies and asides; and my people get on and off the stage without requiring four doors to a room which in real life would have only one. But my stories are the old stories; my characters are the familiar harlequin and columbine, clown and pantaloon (note the harlequin's leap in the third act of Cæsar and Cleopatra); my stage tricks and suspenses and thrills and jests are the ones in vogue when I was a boy, by which time my grandfather was tired of them. To the young people who make their acquaintance for the first time in my plays, they may be as novel as Cyrano's nose to those who have never seen Punch; whilst to older playgoers the unexpectedness of my attempt to substitute natural history for conventional ethics and romantic logic may so transfigure the eternal stage puppets and their inevitable dilemmas as to make their identification impossible for the moment. If so, so much the better for me: I shall perhaps enjoy a few years of immortality. But the whirligig of time will soon bring my audiences to my own point of view; and then the next Shakespear that comes along will turn these petty tentatives of mine into masterpieces final for their epoch. By that time my twentieth century characteristics will pass unnoticed as a matter of course, whilst the eighteenth century artificiality that marks the work of every literary Irishman of my generation will seem antiquated and silly. It is a dangerous thing to be hailed at once, as a few rash admirers have hailed me, as above all things original: what the world calls originality is only an unaccustomed method of tickling it. Meyerbeer seemed prodigiously original to the Parisians when he first burst on them. Today, he is only the crow who followed Beethoven's plough. I am a crow who have followed many ploughs. No doubt I seem prodigiously clever to those who have never hopped, hungry and curious, across the fields of philosophy, politics and art. Karl Marx said of Stuart Mill that his eminence was due to the flatness of the surrounding country. In these days of Board Schools, universal reading, cheap newspapers, and the inevitable ensuing demand for notabilities of all sorts, literary, military, political and fashionable, to write paragraphs about, that sort of eminence is within the reach of very moderate ability. Reputations are cheap nowadays. Even were they dear, it would still be impossible for any public-spirited citizen of the world to hope that his reputation might endure; for this would be to hope that the flood of general enlightenment may never rise above his miserable high-water-mark. I hate to think that Shakespear has lasted 300 years, though he got no further than Koheleth the Preacher, who died many centuries before him; or that Plato, more than 2000 years old, is still ahead of our voters. We must hurry on: we must get rid of reputations: they are weeds in the soil of ignorance. Cultivate that soil, and they will flower more beautifully, but only as annuals. If this preface will at all help to get rid of mine, the writing of it will have been well worth the pains.

G.B.S.

THE DEVIL'S DIS-CIPLE

ACT I

At the most wretched hour between a black night and a wintry morning in the year 1777, Mrs Dudgeon, of New Hampshire, is sitting up in the kitchen and general dwelling room of her farm house on the outskirts of the town of Websterbridge. She is not a prepossessing woman. No woman looks her best after sitting up all night; and Mrs Dudgeon's face, even at its best, is grimly trenched by the channels into which the barren forms and observances of a dead Puritanism can pen a bitter temper and a fierce pride. She is an elderly matron who has worked hard and got nothing by it except dominion and detestation in her sordid home, and an unquestioned reputation for piety and respectability among her neighbors, to whom drink and debauchery are still so much more tempting than religion and recti-tude, that they conceive goodness simply as self-denial. This conception is easily extended to others-denial, and finally generalized as covering anything disagreeable. So Mrs Dudgeon, being exceedingly disagreeable, is held to be exceedingly good. Short of flat felony, she enjoys complete license except for amiable weaknesses of any sort, and is consequently, without knowing it, the most licentious woman in the parish on the strength of never having broken the seventh commandment or missed a Sunday at the Presbyterian church.

The year 1777 is the one in which the passions roused by the breaking-off of the American colonies from England, more by their own weight than their own will, boiled up to shooting point, the shooting being idealized to the English mind as suppression of rebellion and maintenance of British dominion, and to the American as defence of liberty, resistance to tyranny, and self-sacrifice on the altar of the Rights of Man. Into the merits of these idealizations it is not here necessary to inquire: suffice it to say, without prejudice, that they have convinced both Americans and English that the most highminded course for them to pursue is to kill as many of one another as possible, and that military operations to that end are in full swing, morally supported by confident requests from the clergy of both sides for the blessing of God on their arms.

Under such circumstances many other women besides this disagreeable Mrs Dudgeon find themselves sitting up all night waiting for news. Like her, too, they fall asleep towards morning at the risk of nodding themselves into the kitchen fire. Mrs Dudgeon sleeps with a shawl over her head, and her feet on a broad fender of iron laths, the step of the domestic altar of the fireplace, with its huge hobs and boiler, and its hinged arm above the smoky mantel-shelf for roasting. The plain kitchen table is opposite the fire, at her elbow, with a candle on it in a tin sconce. Her chair, like all the others in the room, is uncushioned and unpainted; but as it has a round railed back and a seat conventionally moulded to the sitter's curves, it is comparatively a chair of state. The room has three doors, one on the same side as the fireplace, near the corner, leading to the best bedroom; one, at the opposite end of the opposite wall, leading to the scullery and washhouse; and the house-door, with its latch, heavy lock, and clumsy wooden bar, in the front wall, between the window in its middle and the corner next the bedroom door. Between the door and the window a rack of pegs suggests to the deductive observer that the men of the house are all away, as there are no hats or coats on them. On the other side of the window the clock hangs on a nail, with its white wooden dial, black iron weights, and brass pendulum. Between the clock and the corner, a big cupboard, locked, stands on a dwarf dresser full of common crockery.

On the side opposite the fireplace, between the door and the corner, a shamelessly ugly black horsehair sofa stands against the wall. An inspection of its stridulous surface shews that Mrs Dudgeon is not alone. A girl of

4

sixteen or seventeen has fallen asleep on it. She is a wild, timid looking creature with black hair and tanned skin. Her frock, a scanty garment, is rent, weather-stained, berrystained, and by no means scrupulously clean. It hangs on her with a freedom which, taken with her brown legs and bare feet, suggests no great stock of underclothing.

Suddenly there comes a tapping at the door, not loud enough to wake the sleepers. Then knocking, which disturbs Mrs Dudgeon a little. Finally the latch is tried, whereupon she springs up at once.

MRS DUDGEON [*threateningly*] Well, why dont you open the door? [*She sees that the girl is asleep, and immediately raises a clamor of heartfelt vexation*]. Well, dear, dear me! Now this is – [*shaking her*] wake up, wake up: do you hear?

THE GIRL [*sitting up*] What is it?

MRS DUDGEON Wake up; and be ashamed of yourself, you unfeeling sinful girl, falling asleep like that, and your father hardly cold in his grave.

THE GIRL [*half asleep still*] I didnt mean to. I dropped off –

MRS DUDGEON [*cutting her short*] Oh yes, youve plenty of excuses, I daresay. Dropped off! [*Fiercely, as the knocking recommences*] Why dont you get up and let your uncle in? after me waiting up all night for him! [*She pushes her rudely off the sofa*]. There: I'll open the door: much good you are to wait up. Go and mend that fire a bit.

The girl, cowed and wretched, goes to the fire and puts a log on. Mrs Dudgeon unbars the door and opens it, letting into the stuffy kitchen a little of the freshness and a great deal of the chill of the dawn, also her second son Christy, a fattish, stupid, fair-haired, roundfaced man of about 22, muffled in a plaid shawl and grey overcoat. He hurries, shivering, to the fire, leaving Mrs Dudgeon to shut the door.

CHRISTY [*at the fire*] F – f – f! but it *is* cold. [*Seeing the girl, and staring lumpishly at her*] Why, who are you?

THE GIRL [*shyly*] Essie.

MRS DUDGEON Oh, you may well ask. [*To Essie*] Go to your room, child, and lie down, since you havnt feeling enough to keep you awake. Your history isnt fit for your own ears to hear.

ESSIE I –

MRS DUDGEON [*peremptorily*] Dont answer me, Miss; but shew your obedience by doing what I tell you. [*Essie, almost in tears, crosses the room to the door near the sofa*]. And dont forget your prayers. [*Essie goes out*]. She'd have gone to bed last night just as if nothing had happened if I'd let her.

CHRISTY [*phlegmatically*] Well, she cant be expected to feel Uncle Peter's death like one of the family.

MRS DUDGEON What are you talking about, child? Isnt she his daughter – the punishment of his wickedness and shame? [*She assaults her chair by sitting down*].

CHRISTY [*staring*] Uncle Peter's daughter!

MRS DUDGEON Why else should she be here? D'ye think Ive not had enough trouble and care put upon me bringing up my own girls, let alone you and your good-for-nothing brother, without having your uncle's bastards –

CHRISTY [*interrupting her with an apprehensive glance at the door by which Essie went out*] Sh! She may hear you.

MRS DUDGEON [*raising her voice*] Let her hear me. People who fear God dont fear to give the devil's work its right name. [*Christy, soullessly indifferent to the strife of Good and Evil, stares at the fire, warming himself*]. Well, how long are you going to stare there like a stuck pig? What news have you for me?

CHRISTY [*taking off his hat and shawl and going to the rack to hang them up*] The minister is to break the news to you. He'll be here presently.

MRS DUDGEON Break what news?

CHRISTY [*standing on tiptoe, from boyish habit, to hang his hat up, though he is quite tall enough to reach the peg, and speaking with callous placidity, considering the nature of the announcement*] Father's dead too.

MRS DUDGEON [*stupent*] Your *father*!

CHRISTY [*sulkily, coming back to the fire and warming himself again, attending much more to the fire than to his mother*] Well, it's not my fault. When we got to

Nevinstown we found him ill in bed. He didnt know
us at first. The minister sat up with him and sent me
away. He died in the night.

MRS DUDGEON [*bursting into dry angry tears*] Well, I do think this is
hard on me – very hard on me. His brother, that was
a disgrace to us all his life, gets hanged on the public
gallows as a rebel; and your father, instead of staying
at home where his duty was, with his own family,
goes after him and dies, leaving everything on my
shoulders. After sending this girl to me to take care of,
too! [*She plucks her shawl vexedly over her ears*]. It's
sinful, so it is: downright sinful.

CHRISTY [*with a slow, bovine cheerfulness, after a pause*] I think
it's going to be a fine morning, after all.

MRS DUDGEON [*railing at him*] A fine morning! And your father
newly dead! Wheres your feelings, child?

CHRISTY [*obstinately*] Well, I didnt mean any harm. I suppose
a man may make a remark about the weather even if
his father's dead.

MRS DUDGEON [*bitterly*] A nice comfort my children are to me! One
son a fool, and the other a lost sinner thats left his
home to live with smugglers and gypsies and villains,
the scum of the earth!

Someone knocks.

CHRISTY [*without moving*] That's the minister.

MRS DUDGEON [*sharply*] Well, arnt you going to let Mr Anderson in?

*Christy goes sheepishly to the door. Mrs Dudgeon buries
her face in her hands, as it is her duty as a widow to be
overcome with grief. Christy opens the door, and admits
the minister, Anthony Anderson, a shrewd, genial, ready
Presbyterian divine of about 50, with something of the
authority of his profession in his bearing. But it is an altogether secular authority, sweetened by a conciliatory,
sensible manner not at all suggestive of a quite thorough-
going other-worldliness. He is a strong, healthy man too,
with a thick sanguine neck; and his keen, cheerful mouth
cuts into somewhat fleshy corners. No doubt an excellent
parson, but still a man capable of making the most of
this world, and perhaps a little apologetically conscious
of getting on better with it than a sound Presbyterian
ought.*

ANDERSON [*to Christy, at the door, looking at Mrs Dudgeon whilst he takes off his cloak*] Have you told her?

CHRISTY She made me. [*He shuts the door; yawns; and loafs across to the sofa, where he sits down and presently drops off to sleep*].

Anderson looks compassionately at Mrs Dudgeon. Then he hangs his cloak and hat on the rack. Mrs Dudgeon dries her eyes and looks up at him.

ANDERSON Sister: the Lord has laid his hand very heavily upon you.

MRS DUDGEON [*with intensely recalcitrant resignation*] It's His will, I suppose; and I must bow to it. But I do think it hard. What call had Timothy to go to Springtown, and remind everybody that he belonged to a man that was being hanged? – and [*spitefully*] that deserved it, if ever a man did.

ANDERSON [*gently*] They were brothers, Mrs Dudgeon.

MRS DUDGEON Timothy never acknowledged him as his brother after we were married: he had too much respect for me to insult me with such a brother. Would such a selfish wretch as Peter have come thirty miles to see Timothy hanged, do you think? Not thirty yards, not he. However, I must bear my cross as best I may: least said is soonest mended.

ANDERSON [*very grave, coming down to the fire to stand with his back to it*] Your eldest son was present at the execution, Mrs Dudgeon.

MRS DUDGEON [*disagreeably surprised*] Richard?

ANDERSON [*nodding*] Yes.

MRS DUDGEON [*vindictively*] Let it be a warning to him. He may end that way himself, the wicked, dissolute, godless – [*she suddenly stops; her voice fails; and she asks, with evident dread*] Did Timothy see him?

ANDERSON Yes.

MRS DUDGEON [*holding her breath*] Well?

ANDERSON He only saw him in the crowd: they did not speak. [*Mrs Dudgeon, greatly relieved, exhales the pent up breath and sits at her ease again*]. Your husband was greatly touched and impressed by his brother's awful death. [*Mrs Dudgeon sneers. Anderson breaks off*

9

to demand with some indignation] Well, wasnt it only natural, Mrs Dudgeon? He softened towards his prodigal son in that moment. He sent for him to come to see him.

MRS DUDGEON [*her alarm renewed*] Sent for Richard!

ANDERSON Yes; but Richard would not come. He sent his father a message; but I'm sorry to say it was a wicked message – an awful message.

MRS DUDGEON What was it?

ANDERSON That he would stand by his wicked uncle, and stand against his good parents, in this world and the next.

MRS DUDGEON [*implacably*] He will be punished for it. He will be punished for it – in both worlds.

ANDERSON That is not in our hands, Mrs Dudgeon.

MRS DUDGEON Did I say it was, Mr Anderson? We are told that the wicked shall be punished. Why should we do our duty and keep God's law if there is to be no difference made between us and those who follow their own likings and dislikings, and make a jest of us and of their Maker's word?

ANDERSON Well, Richard's earthly father has been merciful to him; and his heavenly judge is the father of us all.

MRS DUDGEON [*forgetting herself*] Richard's earthly father was a softheaded –

ANDERSON [*shocked*] Oh!

MRS DUDGEON [*with a touch of shame*] Well, I am Richard's mother. If I am against him who has any right to be for him? [*Trying to conciliate him*] Wont you sit down, Mr Anderson? I should have asked you before; but I'm so troubled.

ANDERSON Thank you. [*He takes a chair from beside the fireplace, and turns it so that he can sit comfortably at the fire. When he is seated he adds, in the tone of a man who knows that he is opening a difficult subject*] Has Christy told you about the new will?

MRS DUDGEON [*all her fears returning*] The new will! Did Timothy –? [*She breaks off, gasping, unable to complete the question*].

ANDERSON Yes. In his last hours he changed his mind.

MRS DUDGEON [*white with intense rage*] And you let him rob me?

ANDERSON   I had no power to prevent him giving what was his to his own son.

MRS DUDGEON   He had nothing of his own. His money was the money I brought him as my marriage portion. It was for me to deal with my own money and my own son. He dare not have done it if I had been with him; and well he knew it. That was why he stole away like a thief to take advantage of the law to rob me by making a new will behind my back. The more shame on you, Mr Anderson, – you, a minister of the gospel – to act as his accomplice in such a crime.

ANDERSON   [*rising*] I will take no offence at what you say in the first bitterness of your grief.

MRS DUDGEON   [*contemptuously*] Grief!

ANDERSON   Well, of your disappointment, if you can find it in your heart to think that the better word.

MRS DUDGEON   My heart! *My* heart! And since when, pray, have *you* begun to hold up our hearts as trustworthy guides for us?

ANDERSON   [*rather guiltily*] I – er –

MRS DUDGEON   [*vehemently*] Dont lie, Mr Anderson. We are told that the heart of man is deceitful above all things, and desperately wicked. My heart belonged, not to Timothy, but to that poor wretched brother of his that has just ended his days with a rope round his neck – aye, to Peter Dudgeon. You know it: old Eli Hawkins, the man to whose pulpit you succeeded, though you are not worthy to loose his shoe latchet, told it you when he gave over our souls into your charge. He warned me and strengthened me against my heart, and made me marry a Godfearing man – as he thought. What else but that discipline has made me the woman I am? And you, you, who followed your heart in your marriage, you talk to me of what I find in my heart. Go home to your pretty wife, man; and leave me to my prayers. [*She turns from him and leans with her elbows on the table, brooding over her wrongs and taking no further notice of him*].

ANDERSON   [*willing enough to escape*] The Lord forbid that I should come between you and the source of all comfort! [*He goes to the rack for his coat and hat*].

MRS DUDGEON [*without looking at him*] The Lord will know what to forbid and what to allow without your help.

ANDERSON And whom to forgive, I hope – Eli Hawkins and myself, if we have ever set up our preaching against His law. [*He fastens his cloak, and is now ready to go*]. Just one word – on necessary business, Mrs Dudgeon. There is the reading of the will to be gone through; and Richard has a right to be present. He is in the town; but he has the grace to say that he does not want to force himself in here.

MRS DUDGEON He *shall* come here. Does he expect us to leave his father's house for his convenience? Let them all come, and come quickly, and go quickly. They shall not make the will an excuse to shirk half their day's work. I shall be ready, never fear.

ANDERSON [*coming back a step or two*] Mrs Dudgeon: I used to have some little influence with you. When did I lose it?

MRS DUDGEON [*still without turning to him*] When you married for love. Now youre answered.

ANDERSON Yes: I am answered. [*He goes out, musing*].

MRS DUDGEON [*to herself, thinking of her husband*] Thief! Thief!! [*She shakes herself angrily out of her chair; throws back the shawl from her head; and sets to work to prepare the room for the reading of the will, beginning by replacing Anderson's chair against the wall, and pushing back her own to the window. Then she calls, in her hard, driving, wrathful way*] Christy. [*No answer: he is fast asleep*]. Christy. [*She shakes him roughly*]. Get up out of that; and be ashamed of yourself – sleeping, and your father dead! [*She returns to the table; puts the candle on the mantelshelf; and takes from the table drawer a red table cloth which she spreads*].

CHRISTY [*rising reluctantly*] Well, do you suppose we are never going to sleep until we are out of mourning?

MRS DUDGEON I want none of your sulks. Here: help me to set this table. [*They place the table in the middle of the room, with Christy's end towards the fireplace and Mrs Dudgeon's towards the sofa. Christy drops the table as soon as possible, and goes to the fire, leaving his mother to make the final adjustments of its position*]. We shall have the minister back here with the lawyer and all the family to read the will before you have done toasting yourself. Go and wake that girl; and then light the stove in the shed: you cant have your breakfast here. And mind you wash yourself, and make yourself fit to receive the company. [*She punctuates these orders by going to the cupboard; unlocking it; and producing a decanter of wine, which has no doubt stood there untouched since the last state occasion in the family, and some glasses, which she sets on the table. Also two green ware plates, on one of which she puts a barnbrack with a knife beside it. On the other she shakes some biscuits out of a tin, putting back one or two, and counting the rest*]. Now mind: there are ten biscuits there: let there be ten there when I come back after dressing myself. And keep your fingers off the raisins in that cake. And tell Essie the same. I suppose I can trust you to bring in the case of stuffed birds without breaking the glass? [*She replaces the tin in the cupboard, which she locks, pocketing the key carefully*].

CHRISTY [*lingering at the fire*] Youd better put the inkstand instead, for the lawyer.

RS DUDGEON Thats no answer to make to me, sir. Go and do as youre told. [*Christy turns sullenly to obey*]. Stop: take down that shutter before you go, and let the daylight in: you cant expect me to do all the heavy work of the house with a great heavy lout like you idling about.

13

Christy takes the window bar out of its clamps, and puts it aside; then opens the shutter, shewing the grey morning. Mrs Dudgeon takes the sconce from the mantelshelf; blows out the candle; extinguishes the snuff by pinching it with her fingers, first licking them for the purpose; and replaces the sconce on the shelf.

CHRISTY [*looking through the window*] Here's the minister's wife.

MRS DUDGEON [*displeased*] What! Is she coming here?

CHRISTY Yes.

MRS DUDGEON What does she want troubling me at this hour, before I'm properly dressed to receive people?

CHRISTY Youd better ask her.

MRS DUDGEON [*threateningly*] *Youd* better keep a civil tongue in your head. [*He goes sulkily towards the door. She comes after him, plying him with instructions*]. Tell that girl to come to me as soon as she's had her breakfast. And tell her to make herself fit to be seen before the people. [*Christy goes out and slams the door in her face*]. Nice manners, that! [*Someone knocks at the house door: she turns and cries inhospitably*] Come in. [*Judith Anderson, the minister's wife, comes in. Judith is more than twenty years younger than her husband, though she will never be as young as he in vitality. She is pretty and proper and ladylike, and has been admired and petted into an opinion of herself sufficiently favorable to give her a self-assurance which serves her instead of strength. She has a pretty taste in dress, and in her face the pretty lines of a sentimental character formed by dreams. Even her little self-complacency is pretty, like a child's vanity. Rather a pathetic creature to any sympathetic observer who knows how rough a place the world is. One feels, on the whole, that Anderson might have chosen worse, and that she, needing protection, could not have chosen better*]. Oh, it's you, is it, Mrs Anderson?

JUDITH [*very politely – almost patronizingly*] Yes. Can I do anything for you, Mrs Dudgeon? Can I help to get the place ready before they come to read the will?

MRS DUDGEON [*stiffly*] Thank you, Mrs Anderson, my house is always ready for anyone to come into.

14

JUDITH [*with complacent amiability*] Yes, indeed it is. Perhaps you had rather I did not intrude on you just now.

MRS DUDGEON Oh, one more or less will make no difference this morning, Mrs Anderson. Now that youre here, youd better stay. If you wouldnt mind shutting the door! [*Judith smiles, implying "How stupid of me!" and shuts it with an exasperating air of doing something pretty and becoming*]. Thats better. I must go and tidy myself a bit. I suppose you dont mind stopping here to receive anyone that comes until I'm ready.

JUDITH [*graciously giving her leave*] Oh yes, certainly. Leave them to me, Mrs Dudgeon; and take your time. [*She hangs her cloak and bonnet on the rack*].

MRS DUDGEON [*half sneering*] I thought that would be more in your way than getting the house ready. [*Essie comes back*]. Oh, here *you* are! [*Severely*] Come here: let me see you. [*Essie timidly goes to her. Mrs Dudgeon takes her roughly by the arm and pulls her round to inspect the results of her attempt to clean and tidy herself – results which shew little practice and less conviction*]. Mm! Thats what you call doing your hair properly, I suppose. It's easy to see what you are, and how you were brought up. [*She throws her arm away, and goes on, peremptorily*] Now you listen to me and do as youre told. You sit down there in the corner by the fire; and when the company comes dont dare to speak until youre spoken to. [*Essie creeps away to the fireplace*]. Your father's people had better see you and know youre there: theyre as much bound to keep you from starvation as I am. At any rate they might help. But let me have no chattering and making free with them, as if you were their equal. Do you hear?

ESSIE Yes.

MRS DUDGEON Well, then go and do as youre told. [*Essie sits down miserably on the corner of the fender furthest from the door*]. Never mind her, Mrs Anderson: you know who she is and what she is. If she gives you any trouble, just tell me; and I'll settle accounts with her. [*Mrs Dudgeon goes into the bedroom, shutting the door sharply behind her as if even it had to be made to do its duty with a ruthless hand*].

JUDITH [*patronizing Essie, and arranging the cake and wine*

15

on the table more becomingly] You must not mind if your aunt is strict with you. She is a very good woman, and desires your good too.

ESSIE [*in listless misery*] Yes.

JUDITH [*annoyed with Essie for her failure to be consoled and edified, and to appreciate the kindly condescension of the remark*] You are not going to be sullen, I hope, Essie.

ESSIE No.

JUDITH Thats a good girl! [*She places a couple of chairs at the table with their backs to the window, with a pleasant sense of being a more thoughtful housekeeper than Mrs Dudgeon*]. Do you know any of your father's relatives?

ESSIE No. They wouldnt have anything to do with him: they were too religious. Father used to talk about Dick Dudgeon; but I never saw him.

JUDITH [*ostentatiously shocked*] Dick Dudgeon! Essie: do you wish to be a really respectable and grateful girl, and to make a place for yourself here by steady good conduct?

ESSIE [*very half-heartedly*] Yes.

JUDITH Then you must never mention the name of Richard Dudgeon – never even think about him. He is a bad man.

ESSIE What has he done?

JUDITH You must not ask questions about him, Essie. You are too young to know what it is to be a bad man. But he is a smuggler; and he lives with gypsies; and he has no love for his mother and his family; and he

wrestles and plays games on Sunday instead of going to church. Never let him into your presence, if you can help it, Essie; and try to keep yourself and all womanhood unspotted by contact with such men.

ESSIE   Yes.

JUDITH   [*again displeased*] I am afraid you say Yes and No without thinking very deeply.

ESSIE   Yes. At least I mean –

JUDITH   [*severely*] What do you mean?

ESSIE   [*almost crying*] Only – my father was a smuggler; and – [*Someone knocks*].

JUDITH   They are beginning to come. Now remember your aunt's directions, Essie; and be a good girl. [*Christy comes back with the stand of stuffed birds under a glass case, and an inkstand, which he places on the table*]. Good morning, Mr Dudgeon. Will you open the door, please: the people have come.

CHRISTY Good morning. [*He opens the house door*].

The morning is now fairly bright and warm; and Anderson, who is the first to enter, has left his cloak at home. He is accompanied by Lawyer Hawkins, a brisk, middleaged man in brown riding gaiters and yellow breeches, looking as much squire as solicitor. He and Anderson are allowed precedence as representing the learned professions. After them comes the family, headed by the senior uncle, William Dudgeon, a large, shapeless man, bottle-nosed and evidently no ascetic at table. His clothes are not the clothes, nor his anxious wife the wife, of a prosperous man. The junior uncle, Titus Dudgeon, is a wiry little terrier of a man, with an immense and visibly purseproud wife, both free from the cares of the William household.

Hawkins at once goes briskly to the table and takes the chair nearest the sofa, Christy having left the inkstand there. He puts his hat on the floor beside him, and produces the will. Uncle William comes to the fire and stands on the hearth warming his coat tails, leaving Mrs William derelict near the door. Uncle Titus, who is the lady's man of the family, rescues her by giving her his disengaged arm and bringing her to the sofa, where he sits down warmly between his own lady and his brother's.

Anderson hangs up his hat and waits for a word with Judith.

JUDITH She will be here in a moment. Ask them to wait. [*She taps at the bedroom door. Receiving an answer from within, she opens it and passes through*].

ANDERSON [*taking his place at the table at the opposite end to Hawkins*] Our poor afflicted sister will be with us in a moment. Are we all here?

CHRISTY [*at the house door, which he has just shut*] All except Dick.

The callousness with which Christy names the reprobate jars on the moral sense of the family. Uncle William shakes his head slowly and repeatedly. Mrs Titus catches her breath convulsively through her nose. Her husband speaks.

UNCLE TITUS Well, I hope he will have the grace not to come. I hope so.

The Dudgeons all murmur assent, except Christy, who goes to the window and posts himself there, looking out. Hawkins smiles secretively as if he knew something that would change their tune if they knew it. Anderson is uneasy: the love of solemn family councils, especially funereal ones, is not in his nature. Judith appears at the bedroom door.

JUDITH [*with gentle impressiveness*] Friends, Mrs Dudgeon. [*She takes the chair from beside the fireplace; and places it for Mrs Dudgeon, who comes from the bedroom in black, with a clean handkerchief to her eyes. All rise, except Essie. Mrs Titus and Mrs William produce equally clean handkerchiefs and weep. It is an affecting moment*].

UNCLE WILLIAM Would it comfort you, sister, if we were to offer up a prayer?

UNCLE TITUS Or sing a hymn?

ANDERSON [*rather hastily*] I have been with our sister this morning already, friends. In our hearts we ask a blessing.

ALL [*except Essie*] Amen.

They all sit down, except Judith, who stands behind Mrs Dudgeon's chair.

JUDITH [*to Essie*] Essie: did you say Amen?

18

ESSIE [*scaredly*] No.

JUDITH Then say it, like a good girl.

ESSIE Amen.

UNCLE WILLIAM [*encouragingly*] Thats right: thats right. We know who you are; but we are willing to be kind to you if you are a good girl and deserve it. We are all equal before the Throne.

This republican sentiment does not please the women, who are convinced that the Throne is precisely the place where their superiority, often questioned in this world, will be recognized and rewarded.

CHRISTY [*at the window*] Here's Dick.

Anderson and Hawkins look round sociably. Essie, with a gleam of interest breaking through her misery, looks up. Christy grins and gapes expectantly at the door. The rest are petrified with the intensity of their sense of Virtue menaced with outrage by the approach of flaunting Vice. The reprobate appears in the doorway, graced beyond his alleged merits by the morning sunlight. He is certainly the best looking member of the family; but his expression is reckless and sardonic, his manner

defiant and satirical, his dress picturesquely careless. Only, his forehead and mouth betray an extraordinary steadfastness; and his eyes are the eyes of a fanatic.

RICHARD [*on the threshold, taking off his hat*] Ladies and gentlemen: your servant, your very humble servant. [*With this comprehensive insult, he throws his hat to Christy with a suddenness that makes him jump like a negligent wicket keeper, and comes into the middle of the room, where he turns and deliberately surveys the company*]. How happy you all look! how glad to see me! [*He turns towards Mrs Dudgeon's chair; and his lip rolls up horribly from his dog tooth as he meets her look of undisguised hatred*]. Well, mother: keeping up appearances as usual? thats right, thats right. [*Judith pointedly moves away from his neighborhood to the other side of the kitchen, holding her skirt instinctively as if to save it from contamination. Uncle Titus promptly marks his approval of her action by rising from the sofa, and placing a chair for her to sit down upon*]. What! Uncle William! I havnt seen you since you gave up drinking. [*Poor Uncle William, shamed, would protest; but Richard claps him heartily on his shoulder, adding*] you have given it up, havnt you? [*releasing him with a playful push*] of course you have: quite right too: you overdid it. [*He turns away from Uncle William and makes for the sofa*]. And now, where is that upright horsedealer Uncle Titus? Uncle Titus: come forth. [*He comes upon him holding the chair as Judith sits down*]. As usual, looking after the ladies!

UNCLE TITUS [*indignantly*] Be ashamed of yourself, sir –

RICHARD [*interrupting him and shaking his hand in spite of him*] I am: I am; but I am proud of my uncle – proud of all my relatives – [*again surveying them*] who could look at them and not be proud and joyful? [*Uncle Titus, overborne, resumes his seat on the sofa. Richard turns to the table*]. Ah, Mr Anderson, still at the good work, still shepherding them. Keep them up to the mark, minister, keep them up to the mark. Come! [*with a spring he seats himself on the table and takes up the decanter*] clink a glass with me, Pastor, for the sake of old times.

ANDERSON   You know, I think, Mr Dudgeon, that I do not drink before dinner.

RICHARD   You will, some day, Pastor: Uncle William used to drink before breakfast. Come: it will give your sermons unction. [*He smells the wine and makes a wry face*]. But do not begin on my mother's company sherry. I stole some when I was six years old; and I have been a temperate man ever since. [*He puts the decanter down and changes the subject*]. So I hear you are married, Pastor, and that your wife has a most ungodly allowance of good looks.

ANDERSON   [*quietly indicating Judith*] Sir: you are in the presence of my wife. [*Judith rises and stands with stony propriety*].

RICHARD   [*quickly slipping down from the table with instinctive good manners*] Your servant, madam: no offence. [*He looks at her earnestly*]. You deserve your reputation; but I'm sorry to see by your expression that youre a good woman. [*She looks shocked, and sits down amid a murmur of indignant sympathy from his relatives. Anderson, sensible enough to know that these demonstrations can only gratify and encourage a man who is deliberately trying to provoke them, remains perfectly goodhumored*]. All the same, Pastor, I respect you more than I did before. By the way, did I hear, or did I not, that our late lamented Uncle Peter, though unmarried, was a father?

UNCLE TITUS   He had only one irregular child, sir.

RICHARD   *Only* one! He thinks one a mere trifle! I blush for you, Uncle Titus.

ANDERSON   Mr Dudgeon: you are in the presence of your mother and her grief.

RICHARD   It touches me profoundly, Pastor. By the way, what has become of the irregular child?

ANDERSON   [*pointing to Essie*] There, sir, listening to you.

RICHARD   [*shocked into sincerity*] What! Why the devil didnt you tell me that before? Children suffer enough in this house without – [*He hurries remorsefully to Essie*]. Come, little cousin! never mind me: it was not meant to hurt you. [*She looks up gratefully at him. Her tear-stained face affects him violently; and he bursts out, in a*

21

	transport of wrath] Who has been making her cry? Who has been ill-treating her? By God –
MRS DUDGEON	[*rising and confronting him*] Silence your blasphemous tongue. I will bear no more of this. Leave my house.
RICHARD	How do you know it's your house until the will is read? [*They look at one another for a moment with intense hatred; and then she sinks, checkmated, into her chair. Richard goes boldly up past Anderson to the window, where he takes the railed chair in his hand*]. Ladies and gentlemen: as the eldest son of my late father, and the unworthy head of this household, I bid you welcome. By your leave, Minister Anderson: by your leave, Lawyer Hawkins. The head of the table for the head of the family. [*He places the chair at the table between the minister and the attorney; sits down between them; and addresses the assembly with a presidential air*]. We meet on a melancholy occasion: a father dead! an uncle actually hanged, and probably damned. [*He shakes his head deploringly. The relatives freeze with horror*]. *Thats* right: pull your longest faces [*his voice suddenly sweetens gravely as his glance lights on Essie*] provided only there is hope in the eyes of the child. [*Briskly*] Now then, Lawyer Hawkins: business, business. Get on with the will, man.
TITUS	Do not let yourself be ordered or hurried, Mr Hawkins.
HAWKINS	[*very politely and willingly*] Mr Dudgeon means no offence, I feel sure. I will not keep you one second, Mr Dudgeon. Just while I get my glasses – [*he fumbles for them. The Dudgeons look at one another with misgiving*].
RICHARD	Aha! They notice your civility, Mr Hawkins. They are prepared for the worst. A glass of wine to clear your voice before you begin. [*He pours out one for him and hands it; then pours one for himself*].
HAWKINS	Thank you, Mr Dudgeon. Your good health, sir.
RICHARD	Yours, sir. [*With the glass half way to his lips, he checks himself, giving a dubious glance at the wine, and adds, with quaint intensity*] Will anyone oblige me with a glass of water?
	Essie, who has been hanging on his every word and move-

ment, rises stealthily and slips out behind Mrs Dudgeon through the bedroom door, returning presently with a jug and going out of the house as quietly as possible.

HAWKINS   The will is not exactly in proper legal phraseology.

RICHARD   No: my father died without the consolations of the law.

HAWKINS   Good again, Mr Dudgeon, good again. [*Preparing to read*] Are you ready, sir?

RICHARD   Ready, aye ready. For what we are about to receive, may the Lord make us truly thankful. Go ahead.

HAWKINS   [*reading*] "This is the last will and testament of me Timothy Dudgeon on my deathbed at Nevinstown on the road from Springtown to Websterbridge on this twenty-fourth day of September, one thousand seven hundred and seventy seven. I hereby revoke all former wills made by me and declare that I am of sound mind and know well what I am doing and that this is my real will according to my own wish and affections."

RICHARD [*glancing at his mother*] Aha!

HAWKINS [*shaking his head*] Bad phraseology, sir, wrong phraseology. "I give and bequeath a hundred pounds to my younger son Christopher Dudgeon, fifty pounds to be paid to him on the day of his marriage to Sarah Wilkins if she will have him, and ten pounds on the birth of each of his children up to the number of five."

RICHARD How if she wont have him?

CHRISTY She will if I have fifty pounds.

RICHARD Good, my brother. Proceed.

HAWKINS "I give and bequeath to my wife Annie Dudgeon, born Annie Primrose" – you see he did not know the law, Mr Dudgeon: your mother was not born Annie: she was christened so – "an annuity of fifty-two pounds a year for life [*Mrs Dudgeon, with all eyes on her, holds herself convulsively rigid*] to be paid out of the interest on her own money" – *there's* a way to put it, Mr Dudgeon! Her own money!

MRS DUDGEON A very good way to put God's truth. It was every penny my own. Fifty-two pounds a year!

HAWKINS "And I recommend her for her goodness and piety to the forgiving care of her children, having stood between them and her as far as I could to the best of my ability."

MRS DUDGEON And this is my reward! [*Raging inwardly*] You know what I think, Mr Anderson: you know the word I gave to it.

ANDERSON It cannot be helped, Mrs Dudgeon. We must take what comes to us. [*To Hawkins*] Go on, sir.

HAWKINS "I give and bequeath my house at Websterbridge with the land belonging to it and all the rest of my property soever to my eldest son and heir, Richard Dudgeon."

RICHARD Oho! The fatted calf, Minister, the fatted calf.

HAWKINS "On these conditions – "

RICHARD The devil! Are there conditions?

HAWKINS	"To wit: first, that he shall not let my brother Peter's natural child starve or be driven by want to an evil life."
RICHARD	[*emphatically, striking his fist on the table*] Agreed.
	Mrs Dudgeon, turning to look malignantly at Essie, misses her and looks quickly round to see where she has moved to; then, seeing that she has left the room without leave, closes her lips vengefully.
HAWKINS	"Second, that he shall be a good friend to my old horse Jim" – [*again shaking his head*] he should have written James, sir.
RICHARD	James shall live in clover. Go on.
HAWKINS	– "and keep my deaf farm labourer Prodger Feston in his service."
RICHARD	Prodger Feston shall get drunk every Saturday.
HAWKINS	"Third, that he make Christy a present on his marriage out of the ornaments in the best room."
RICHARD	[*holding up the stuffed birds*] Here you are, Christy.
CHRISTY	[*disappointed*] I'd rather have the china peacocks.
RICHARD	You shall have both. [*Christy is greatly pleased*]. Go on.
HAWKINS	"Fourthly and lastly, that he try to live at peace with his mother as far as she will consent to it."
RICHARD	[*dubiously*] Hm! Anything more, Mr Hawkins?
HAWKINS	[*solemnly*] "Finally I give and bequeath my soul into my Maker's hands, humbly asking forgiveness for all my sins and mistakes, and hoping that He will so guide my son that it may not be said that I have done wrong in trusting to him rather than to others in the perplexity of my last hour in this strange place."
ANDERSON	Amen.
THE UNCLES AND AUNTS	Amen.
RICHARD	My mother does not say Amen.
MRS DUDGEON	[*rising, unable to give up her property without a struggle*] Mr Hawkins: is that a proper will? Remember, I have his rightful, legal will, drawn up by yourself, leaving all to me.

25

HAWKINS   This is a very wrongly and irregularly worded will,
              Mrs Dudgeon; though [*turning politely to Richard*] it
              contains in my judgment an excellent disposal of his
              property.

ANDERSON   [*interposing before Mrs Dudgeon can retort*] That is not
              what you are asked, Mr Hawkins. Is it a legal will?

HAWKINS   The courts will sustain it against the other.

ANDERSON   But why, if the other is more lawfully worded?

HAWKINS   Because, sir, the courts will sustain the claim of a
              man – and that man the eldest son – against any
              woman, if they can. I warned you, Mrs Dudgeon,
              when you got me to draw that other will, that it was
              not a wise will, and that though you might make him
              sign it, he would never be easy until he revoked it.
              But you wouldnt take advice; and now Mr Richard
              is cock of the walk. [*He takes his hat from the floor;
              rises; and begins pocketing his papers and spectacles*].

              *This is the signal for the breaking-up of the party.
              Anderson takes his hat from the rack and joins Uncle
              William at the fire. Titus fetches Judith her things from
              the rack. The three on the sofa rise and chat with Haw-
              kins. Mrs Dudgeon, now an intruder in her own house,
              stands inert, crushed by the weight of the law on women,
              accepting it, as she has been trained to accept all mon-
              strous calamities, as proofs of the greatness of the power
              that inflicts them, and of her own wormlike insig-
              nificance. For at this time, remember, Mary Wollstone-
              craft is as yet only a girl of eighteen, and her Vindication
              of the Rights of Women is still fourteen years off.
              Mrs Dudgeon is rescued from her apathy by Essie, who
              comes back with the jug full of water. She is taking it to
              Richard when Mrs Dudgeon stops her.*

MRS DUDGEON   [*threatening her*] Where have you been? [*Essie, ap-
              palled, tries to answer, but cannot*]. How dare you go
              out by yourself after the orders I gave you?

ESSIE   He asked for a drink – [*she stops, her tongue cleaving
              to her palate with terror*].

JUDITH   [*with gentler severity*] *Who* asked for a drink? [*Essie,
              speechless, points to Richard*].

RICHARD   What! I!

JUDITH   [*shocked*] Oh Essie, Essie!

RICHARD   I believe I did. [*He takes a glass and holds it to Essie to be filled. Her hand shakes*]. What! afraid of me?

ESSIE   [*quickly*] No. I – [*She pours out the water*].

RICHARD   [*tasting it*] Ah, youve been up the street to the market gate spring to get that. [*He takes a draught*]. Delicious! Thank you. [*Unfortunately, at this moment he chances to catch sight of Judith's face, which expresses the most prudish disapproval of his evident attraction for Essie, who is devouring him with her grateful eyes. His mocking expression returns instantly. He puts down the glass; deliberately winds his arm round Essie's shoulders; and brings her into the middle of the company. Mrs Dudgeon being in Essie's way as they come past the table, he says*] By your leave, mother [*and compels her to make way for them*]. What do they call you? Bessie?

ESSIE   Essie.

RICHARD   Essie, to be sure. Are you a good girl, Essie?

ESSIE   [*greatly disappointed that he, of all people, should begin at her in this way*] Yes. [*She looks doubtfully at Judith*]. I think so. I mean I – I hope so.

RICHARD   Essie: did you ever hear of a person called the devil?

ANDERSON   [*revolted*] Shame on you, sir, with a mere child –

RICHARD   By your leave, Minister: I do not interfere with your sermons: do not you interrupt mine. [*To Essie*] Do you know what they call me, Essie?

ESSIE   Dick.

RICHARD   [*amused: patting her on the shoulder*] Yes, Dick; but something else too. They call me the Devil's Disciple.

ESSIE   Why do you let them?

RICHARD   [*seriously*] Because it's true. I was brought up in the other service; but I knew from the first that the Devil was my natural master and captain and friend. I saw that he was in the right, and that the world cringed to his conqueror only through fear. I prayed secretly to him; and he comforted me, and saved me from having my spirit broken in this house of children's tears. I promised him my soul, and swore an oath that I would stand up for him in this world and stand by him in the next. [*Solemnly*] That promise and that oath made a man of me. From this day this house is

27

his home; and no child shall cry in it: this hearth is his altar; and no soul shall ever cower over it in the dark evenings and be afraid. Now [*turning forcibly on the rest*] which of you good men will take this child and rescue her from the house of the devil?

JUDITH [*coming to Essie and throwing a protecting arm about her*] I will. You should be burnt alive.

ESSIE But I dont want to. [*She shrinks back, leaving Richard and Judith face to face*].

RICHARD [*to Judith*] Actually doesnt want to, most virtuous lady!

UNCLE TITUS Have a care, Richard Dudgeon. The law –

RICHARD [*turning threateningly on him*] Have a care, you. In an hour from this there will be no law here but martial law. I passed the soldiers within six miles on my way here: before noon Major Swindon's gallows for rebels will be up in the market place.

ANDERSON [*calmly*] What have we to fear from that, sir?

RICHARD More than you think. He hanged the wrong man at Springtown: he thought Uncle Peter was respectable, because the Dudgeons had a good name. But his next example will be the best man in the town to whom he can bring home a rebellious word. Well, we're all rebels; and you know it.

ALL THE MEN [*except Anderson*] No, no, no!

RICHARD Yes, you are. You havnt damned King George up hill and down dale as I have; but youve prayed for his defeat; and you, Anthony Anderson, have conducted the service, and sold your family bible to buy a pair of pistols. They maynt hang me, perhaps; because the moral effect of the Devil's Disciple dancing on nothing wouldnt help them. But a minister! [*Judith, dismayed, clings to Anderson*] or a lawyer! [*Hawkins smiles like a man able to take care of himself*] or an upright horsedealer! [*Uncle Titus snarls at him in rage and terror*] or a reformed drunkard! [*Uncle William, utterly unnerved, moans and wobbles with fear*] eh? Would that shew that King George meant business – ha?

ANDERSON [*perfectly self-possessed*] Come, my dear: he is only trying to frighten you. There is no danger. [*He takes her out of the house. The rest crowd to the door to follow him, except Essie, who remains near Richard*].

RICHARD [*boisterously derisive*] Now then: how many of you will stay with me; run up the American flag on the devil's house; and make a fight for freedom? [*They scramble out, Christy among them, hustling one another in their haste*]. Ha ha! Long live the devil! [*To Mrs Dudgeon, who is following them*] What, mother! Are you off too?

RS DUDGEON [*deadly pale, with her hand on her heart as if she had received a deathblow*] My curse on you! My dying curse! [*She goes out*].

RICHARD [*calling after her*] It will bring me luck. Ha ha ha!

ESSIE [*anxiously*] Maynt I stay?

RICHARD [*turning to her*] What! Have they forgotten to save your soul in their anxiety about their own bodies? Oh yes: you may stay. [*He turns excitedly away again and shakes his fist after them. His left fist, also clenched, hangs down. Essie seizes it and kisses it, her tears falling on it. He starts and looks at it*]. Tears! The devil's baptism! [*She falls on her knees, sobbing. He stoops goodnaturedly to raise her, saying*] Oh yes, you may cry that way, Essie, if you like.

Minister Anderson's house is in the main street of Websterbridge, not far from the town hall. To the eye of the eighteenth century New Englander, it is much grander than the plain farmhouse of the Dudgeons; but it is so plain itself that a modern house agent would let both at about the same rent. The chief dwelling room has the same sort of kitchen fireplace, with boiler, toaster hanging on the bars, movable iron griddle socketed to the hob, hook above for roasting, and broad fender, on which stand a kettle and a plate of buttered toast. The door, between the fireplace and the corner, has neither panels, fingerplates nor handles: it is made of plain boards, and fastens with a latch. The table is a kitchen table, with a treacle colored cover of American cloth, chapped at the corners by draping. The tea service on it consists of two thick cups and saucers of the plainest ware, with milk jug and bowl to match, each large enough to contain nearly a quart, on a black japanned tray, and, in the middle of the table, a wooden trencher with a big loaf upon it, and a square half

30

pound block of butter in a crock. The big oak press facing the fire from the opposite side of the room, is for use and storage, not for ornament; and the minister's house coat hangs on a peg from its door, shewing that he is out; for when he is in, it is his best coat that hangs there. His big riding boots stand beside the press, evidently in their usual place, and rather proud of themselves. In fact, the evolution of the minister's kitchen, dining room and drawing room into three separate apartments has not yet taken place; and so, from the point of view of our pampered period, he is no better off than the Dudgeons.

But there is a difference, for all that. To begin with, Mrs Anderson is a pleasanter person to live with than Mrs Dudgeon. To which Mrs Dudgeon would at once reply, with reason, that Mrs Anderson has no children to look after; no poultry, pigs nor cattle; a steady and sufficient income not directly dependent on harvests and prices at fairs; an affectionate husband who is a tower of strength to her: in short, that life is as easy at the minister's house as it is hard at the farm. This is true; but to explain a fact is not to alter it; and however little credit Mrs Anderson may deserve for making her home happier, she has certainly succeeded in doing it. The outward and visible signs of her superior social pretensions are, a drugget on the floor, a plaster ceiling between the timbers, and chairs which, though not upholstered, are stained and polished. The fine arts are represented by a mezzotint portrait of some Presbyterian divine, a copperplate of Raphael's St Paul preaching at Athens, a rococo presentation clock on the mantelshelf, flanked by a couple of miniatures, a pair of crockery dogs with baskets in their mouths, and, at the corners, two large cowrie shells. A pretty feature of the room is the low wide latticed window, nearly its whole width, with little red curtains running on a rod half way up it to serve as a blind. There is no sofa; but one of the seats, standing near the press, has a railed back and is long enough to accommodate two people easily. On the whole, it is rather the sort of room that the nineteenth century has ended in struggling to get back to under the leadership of Mr Philip Webb and his disciples in domestic architecture, though no genteel clergyman would have tolerated it fifty years ago.

The evening has closed in; and the room is dark except for the cosy firelight and the dim oil lamps seen through the window in the wet street, where there is a quiet, steady, warm, windless downpour of rain. As the town clock strikes the quarter, Judith comes in with a couple of candles in earthenware candlesticks, and sets them on the table. Her self-conscious airs of the morning are gone; she is anxious and frightened. She goes to the window and peers into the street. The first thing she sees there is her husband, hurrying home through the rain. She gives a little gasp of relief, not very far removed from a sob, and turns to the door. Anderson comes in, wrapped in a very wet cloak.

JUDITH [*running to him*] Oh, here you are at last, at last! [*She attempts to embrace him*].

ANDERSON [*keeping her off*] Take care, my love: I'm wet. Wait till I get my cloak off. [*He places a chair with its back to the fire; hangs his cloak on it to dry; shakes the rain from his hat and puts it on the fender; and at last turns with his hands outstretched to Judith*]. Now! [*She flies into his arms*]. I am not late, am I? The town clock struck the quarter as I came in at the front door. And the town clock is always fast.

JUDITH I'm sure it's slow this evening. I'm so glad youre back.

ANDERSON [*taking her more closely in his arms*] Anxious, my dear?

JUDITH A little.

ANDERSON Why, youve been crying.

JUDITH Only a little. Never mind: it's all over now. [*A bugle call is heard in the distance. She starts in terror and retreats to the long seat, listening*]. Whats that?

ANDERSON [*following her tenderly to the seat and making her sit down with him*] Only King George, my dear. He's returning to barracks, or having his roll called, or getting ready for tea, or booting or saddling or something. Soldiers dont ring the bell or call over the banisters when they want anything: they send a boy out with a bugle to disturb the whole town.

JUDITH Do you think there is really any danger?

ANDERSON Not the least in the world.

JUDITH You say that to comfort me, not because you believe it.

ANDERSON My dear: in this world there is always danger for those who are afraid of it. There's a danger that the house will catch fire in the night; but we shant sleep any the less soundly for that.

JUDITH Yes, I know what you always say; and youre quite right. Oh, quite right: I know it. But – I suppose I'm not brave: thats all. My heart shrinks every time I think of the soldiers.

ANDERSON Never mind that, dear: bravery is none the worse for costing a little pain.

JUDITH Yes, I suppose so. [*Embracing him again*] Oh how brave you are, my dear! [*With tears in her eyes*] Well, I'll be brave too: you shant be ashamed of your wife.

ANDERSON Thats right. Now you make me happy. Well. well! [*He rises and goes cheerily to the fire to dry his shoes*]. I called on Richard Dudgeon on my way back; but he wasnt in.

JUDITH [*rising in consternation*] You called on that man!

ANDERSON [*reassuring her*] Oh, nothing happened, dearie. He was out.

JUDITH [*almost in tears, as if the visit were a personal humiliation to her*] But why did you go there?

ANDERSON [*gravely*] Well, it is all the talk that Major Swindon is going to do what he did in Springtown – make an example of some notorious rebel, as he calls us. He pounced on Peter Dudgeon as the worst character there; and it is the general belief that he will pounce on Richard as the worst here.

JUDITH But Richard said –

ANDERSON [*goodhumoredly cutting her short*] Pooh! Richard said! He said what he thought would frighten you and frighten me, my dear. He said what perhaps (God forgive him!) he would like to believe. It's a terrible thing to think of what death must mean for a man like that. I felt that I must warn him. I left a message for him.

JUDITH [*querulously*] What message?

ANDERSON Only that I should be glad to see him for a moment

33

on a matter of importance to himself, and that if he would look in here when he was passing he would be welcome.

JUDITH [*aghast*] You asked that man to come here!

ANDERSON I did.

JUDITH [*sinking on the seat and clasping her hands*] I hope he wont come! Oh, I pray that he may not come!

ANDERSON Why? Dont you want him to be warned?

JUDITH He must know his danger. Oh, Tony, is it wrong to hate a blasphemer and a villain? I do hate him. I cant get him out of my mind: I know he will bring harm with him. He insulted you: he insulted me: he insulted his mother.

ANDERSON [*quaintly*] Well, dear, let's forgive him; and then it wont matter.

JUDITH Oh, I know it's wrong to hate anybody; but –

ANDERSON [*going over to her with humorous tenderness*] Come, dear, youre not so wicked as you think. The worst sin towards our fellow creatures is not to hate them, but to be indifferent to them: thats the essence of inhumanity. After all, my dear, if you watch people carefully, youll be surprised to find how like hate is to love. [*She starts, strangely touched – even appalled. He is amused at her*]. Yes: I'm quite in earnest. Think of how some of our married friends worry one another, tax one another, are jealous of one another, cant bear to let one another out of sight for a day, are more like jailers and slave-owners than lovers. Think of those very same people with their enemies, scrupulous, lofty, self-respecting, determined to be independent of one another, careful of how they speak of one another – pooh! havent you often thought that if they only knew it, they were better friends to their enemies than to their own husbands and wives? Come: depend on it, my dear, you are really fonder of Richard than you are of me, if you only knew it. Eh!

JUDITH Oh, dont say that: dont say that, Tony, even in jest. You dont know what a horrible feeling it gives me.

ANDERSON [*laughing*] Well, well: never mind, pet. He's a bad man; and you hate him as he deserves. And youre going to make the tea, arnt you?

JUDITH [*remorsefully*] Oh yes, I forgot. Ive been keeping you waiting all this time. [*She goes to the fire and puts on the kettle*].

ANDERSON [*going to the press and taking his coat off*] Have you stitched up the shoulder of my old coat?

JUDITH Yes, dear. [*She goes to the table, and sets about putting the tea into the teapot from the caddy*].

ANDERSON [*as he changes his coat for the older one hanging on the press, and replaces it by the one he has just taken off*] Did anyone call when I was out?

JUDITH No, only – [*Someone knocks at the door. With a start which betrays her intense nervousness, she retreats to the further end of the table with the tea caddy and spoon in her hands, exclaiming*] Who's that?

ANDERSON [*going to her and patting her encouragingly on the shoulder*] All right, pet, all right. He wont eat you, whoever he is. [*She tries to smile, and nearly makes herself cry. He goes to the door and opens it. Richard is there, without overcoat or cloak*]. You might have raised the latch and come in, Mr Dudgeon. Nobody stands on much ceremony with us. [*Hospitably*] Come in. [*Richard comes in carelessly and stands at the table, looking round the room with a slight pucker of his nose at the mezzotinted divine on the wall. Judith keeps her eyes on the tea caddy*]. Is it still raining? [*He shuts the door*].

RICHARD Raining like the very [*his eye catches Judith's as she looks quickly and haughtily up*] – I beg your pardon; but [*shewing that his coat is wet*] you see – !

ANDERSON Take it off, sir; and let it hang before the fire a while: my wife will excuse your shirtsleeves. Judith: put in another spoonful of tea for Mr Dudgeon.

RICHARD [*eyeing him cynically*] The magic of property, Pastor! Are even *you* civil to me now that I have succeeded to my father's estate?

Judith throws down the spoon indignantly.

ANDERSON [*quite unruffled, and helping Richard off with his coat*] I think, sir, that since you accept my hospitality, you cannot have so bad an opinion of it. Sit down. [*With the coat in his hand, he points to the railed seat. Richard, in his shirtsleeves, looks at him half quarrelsomely for a*

35

moment; then, with a nod, acknowledges that the minister has got the better of him, and sits down on the seat. Anderson pushes his cloak into a heap on the seat of the chair at the fire, and hangs Richard's coat on the back in its place].

RICHARD   I come, sir, on your own invitation. You left word you had something important to tell me.

ANDERSON   I have a warning which it is my duty to give you.

RICHARD   [*quickly rising*] You want to preach to me. Excuse me: I prefer a walk in the rain [*he makes for his coat*].

ANDERSON   [*stopping him*] Dont be alarmed, sir: I am no great preacher. You are quite safe. [*Richard smiles in spite of himself. His glance softens: he even makes a gesture of excuse. Anderson, seeing that he has tamed him, now addresses him earnestly*]. Mr Dudgeon: you are in danger in this town.

RICHARD   What danger?

ANDERSON   Your uncle's danger. Major Swindon's gallows.

RICHARD   It is you who are in danger. I warned you –

ANDERSON   [*interrupting him goodhumoredly but authoritatively*] Yes, yes, Mr Dudgeon; but they do not think so in the town. And even if I were in danger, I have duties here which I must not forsake. But you are a free man. Why should you run any risk?

RICHARD   Do you think I should be any great loss, Minister?

ANDERSON   I think that a man's life is worth saving, whoever it belongs to. [*Richard makes him an ironical bow. Anderson returns the bow humorously*]. Come: youll have a cup of tea, to prevent you catching cold?

RICHARD I observe that Mrs Anderson is not quite so pressing as you are, Pastor.

JUDITH [*almost stifled with resentment, which she has been expecting her husband to share and express for her at every insult of Richard's*] You are welcome for my husband's sake. [*She brings the teapot to the fireplace and sets it on the hob*].

RICHARD I know I am not welcome for my own, madam. [*He rises*]. But I think I will not break bread here, Minister.

ANDERSON [*cheerily*] Give me a good reason for that.

RICHARD Because there is something in you that I respect, and that makes me desire to have you for my enemy.

ANDERSON Thats well said. On those terms, sir, I will accept your enmity or any man's. Judith: Mr Dudgeon will stay to tea. Sit down: it will take a few minutes to draw by the fire. [*Richard glances at him with a troubled face; then sits down with his head bent, to hide a convulsive swelling of his throat*]. I was just saying to my wife, Mr Dudgeon, that enmity – [*She grasps his hand and looks imploringly at him, doing both with an intensity that checks him at once*]. Well, well, I mustnt tell you, I see; but it was nothing that need leave us worse friend – enemies, I mean. Judith is a great enemy of yours.

RICHARD If all my enemies were like Mrs Anderson, I should be the best Christian in America.

ANDERSON [*gratified, patting her hand*] You hear that, Judith? Mr Dudgeon knows how to turn a compliment.

The latch is lifted from without.

JUDITH [*starting*] Who is that?

Christy comes in.

CHRISTY [*stopping and staring at Richard*] Oh, are *you* here?

RICHARD Yes. Begone, you fool: Mrs Anderson doesnt want the whole family to tea at once.

CHRISTY [*coming further in*] Mother's very ill.

RICHARD Well, does she want to see *me?*

CHRISTY No.

RICHARD I thought not.

CHRISTY   She wants to see the minister – at once.

JUDITH   [*to Anderson*] Oh, not before youve had some tea.

ANDERSON   I shall enjoy it more when I come back, dear. [*He is about to take up his cloak*].

CHRISTY   The rain's over.

ANDERSON   [*dropping the cloak and picking up his hat from the fender*] Where is your mother, Christy?

CHRISTY   At Uncle Titus's.

ANDERSON   Have you fetched the doctor?

CHRISTY   No: she didnt tell me to.

ANDERSON   Go on there at once: I'll overtake you on his doorstep. [*Christy turns to go*]. Wait a moment. Your brother must be anxious to know the particulars.

RICHARD   Psha! not I: he doesnt know; and I dont care. [*Violently*] Be off, you oaf. [*Christy runs out. Richard adds, a little shamefacedly*] We shall know soon enough.

ANDERSON   Well, perhaps you will let me bring you the news myself. Judith: will you give Mr Dudgeon his tea, and keep him here until I return.

JUDITH   [*white and trembling*] Must I –

ANDERSON   [*taking her hands and interrupting her to cover her agitation*] My dear: I can depend on you?

JUDITH   [*with a piteous effort to be worthy of his trust*] Yes.

ANDERSON   [*pressing her hand against his cheek*] You will not mind two old people like us, Mr Dudgeon. [*Going*] I shall not say good evening: you will be here when I come back. [*He goes out*].

         They watch him pass the window, and then look at each other dumbly, quite disconcerted. Richard, noting the quiver of her lips, is the first to pull himself together.

RICHARD   Mrs Anderson: I am perfectly aware of the nature of your sentiments towards me. I shall not intrude on you. Good evening. [*Again he starts for the fireplace to get his coat*].

JUDITH   [*getting between him and the coat*] No, no. Dont go: please dont go.

RICHARD   [*roughly*] Why? You dont want me here.

JUDITH   Yes, I – [*Wringing her hands in despair*] Oh, if I tell you the truth, you will use it to torment me.

RICHARD   [*indignantly*] Torment! What right have you to say that? Do you expect me to stay after that?

JUDITH   I want you to stay; but [*suddenly raging at him like an angry child*] it is not because I like you.

RICHARD   Indeed!

JUDITH   Yes: I had rather you did go than mistake me about that. I hate and dread you; and my husband knows it. If you are not here when he comes back, he will believe that I disobeyed him and drove you away.

RICHARD   [*ironically*] Whereas, of course, you have really been so kind and hospitable and charming to me that I only want to go away out of mere contrariness, eh?

Judith, unable to bear it, sinks on the chair and bursts into tears.

RICHARD   Stop, stop, stop, I tell you. Dont do that. [*Putting his hand to his breast as if to a wound*] He wrung my heart by being a man. Need you tear it by being a woman? Has he not raised you above my insults, like himself? [*She stops crying, and recovers herself somewhat, looking at him with a scared curiosity*]. There: thats right. [*Sympathetically*] Youre better now, arnt you? [*He puts his hand encouragingly on her shoulder. She instantly rises haughtily, and stares at him defiantly. He at once drops into his usual sardonic tone*]. Ah, thats better. You are yourself again: so is Richard. Well, shall we go to tea like a quiet respectable couple, and wait for your husband's return?

JUDITH   [*rather ashamed of herself*] If you please. I – I am sorry to have been so foolish. [*She stoops to take up the plate of toast from the fender*].

RICHARD   I am sorry, for your sake, that I am – what I am. Allow me. [*He takes the plate from her and goes with it to the table*].

JUDITH   [*following with the teapot*] Will you sit down? [*He sits down at the end of the table nearest the press. There is a plate and knife laid there. The other plate is laid near it; but Judith stays at the opposite end of the table, next the fire, and takes her place there, drawing the tray towards her*]. Do you take sugar?

39

RICHARD No; but plenty of milk. Let me give you some toast. [*He puts some on the second plate, and hands it to her, with the knife. The action shews quietly how well he knows that she has avoided her usual place so as to be as far from him as possible*].

JUDITH [*consciously*] Thanks. [*She gives him his tea*]. Wont you help yourself?

RICHARD Thanks. [*He puts a piece of toast on his own plate; and she pours out tea for herself*].

JUDITH [*observing that he tastes nothing*] Dont you like it? You are not eating anything.

RICHARD Neither are you.

JUDITH [*nervously*] I never care much for my tea. Please dont mind me.

RICHARD [*looking dreamily round*] I am thinking. It is all so strange to me. I can see the beauty and peace of this home: I think I have never been more at rest in my life than at this moment; and yet I know quite well I could never live here. It's not in my nature, I suppose, to be domesticated. But it's very beautiful: it's almost holy. [*He muses a moment, and then laughs softly*].

JUDITH [*quickly*] Why do you laugh?

RICHARD I was thinking that if any stranger came in here now, he would take us for man and wife.

JUDITH [*taking offence*] You mean, I suppose, that you are more my age than he is.

RICHARD [*staring at this unexpected turn*] I never thought of such a thing. [*Sardonic again*]. I see there is another side to domestic joy.

JUDITH [*angrily*] I would rather have a husband whom everybody respects than – than –

RICHARD Than the devil's disciple. You are right; but I daresay your love helps him to be a good man, just as your hate helps me to be a bad one.

JUDITH My husband has been very good to you. He has forgiven you for insulting him, and is trying to save you. Can you not forgive him for being so much better than you are? How dare you belittle him by putting yourself in his place?

RICHARD Did I?

JUDITH   Yes, you did. You said that if anybody came in they would take us for man and – [*She stops, terror-stricken, as a squad of soldiers tramps past the window*]. The English soldiers! Oh, what do they –

RICHARD   [*listening*] Sh!

A VOICE   [*outside*] Halt! Four outside: two in with me.

Judith half rises, listening and looking with dilated eyes at Richard, who takes up his cup prosaically, and is drinking his tea when the latch goes up with a sharp click, and an English sergeant walks into the room with two privates, who post themselves at the door. He comes promptly to the table between them.

SERGEANT   Sorry to disturb you, mum. Duty! Anthony Anderson: I arrest you in King George's name as a rebel.

JUDITH   [*pointing at Richard*] But that is not – [*He looks up quickly at her, with a face of iron. She stops her mouth hastily with the hand she has raised to indicate him, and stands staring affrightedly*].

SERGEANT   Come, parson: put your coat on and come along.

RICHARD   Yes: I'll come. [*He rises and takes a step towards his own coat; then recollects himself, and, with his back to the sergeant, moves his gaze slowly round the room without turning his head until he sees Anderson's black coat hanging up on the press. He goes composedly to it; takes it down; and puts it on. The idea of himself as a parson tickles him: he looks down at the black sleeve on his arm, and then smiles slyly at Judith, whose white face shews him that what she is painfully struggling to grasp is not the humor of the situation but its horror. He turns to the sergeant, who is approaching him with a pair of handcuffs hidden behind him, and says lightly*] Did you ever arrest a man of my cloth before, Sergeant?

SERGEANT   [*instinctively respectful, half to the black coat, half to Richard's good breeding*] Well, no sir. At least, only an army chaplain. [*Shewing the handcuffs*] I'm sorry sir; but duty –

RICHARD   Just so, Sergeant. Well, I'm not ashamed of them: thank you kindly for the apology. [*He holds out his hands*].

SERGEANT   [*not availing himself of the offer*] One gentleman to another, sir. Wouldnt you like to say a word to your missis, sir, before you go?

RICHARD   [*smiling*] Oh, we shall meet again before – eh? [*meaning "before you hang me"*].

SERGEANT   [*loudly, with ostentatious cheerfulness*] Oh, of course, of course. No call for the lady to distress herself. Still – [*in a lower voice, intended for Richard alone*] your last chance, sir.

           They look at one another significantly for a moment. Then Richard exhales a deep breath and turns towards Judith.

RICHARD   [*very distinctly*] My love. [*She looks at him, pitiably pale, and tries to answer, but cannot – tries also to come to him, but cannot trust herself to stand without the support of the table*]. This gallant gentleman is good enough to allow us a moment of leavetaking. [*The sergeant retires delicately and joins his men near the door*]. He is trying to spare you the truth; but you had better know it. Are you listening to me? [*She signifies assent*]. Do you understand that I am going to my death? [*She signifies that she understands*]. Remember, you must find our friend who was with us just now. Do you understand? [*She signifies yes*]. See that you get him safely out of harm's way. Dont for your life let him know of my danger; but if he finds it out, tell him that he cannot save me: they would hang him; and they would not spare me. And tell him that I am steadfast in my religion as he is in his, and that he may depend on me to the death. [*He turns to go, and meets the eye of the sergeant, who looks a little suspicious. He considers a moment, and then, turning roguishly to Judith with something of a smile breaking through his earnestness, says*] And now, my dear, I am afraid the sergeant will not believe that you love me like a wife unless you give one kiss before I go.

He approaches her and holds out his arms. She quits the table and almost falls into them.

JUDITH   [*the words choking her*] I ought to – it's murder –

RICHARD   No: only a kiss [*softly to her*] for his sake.

JUDITH   I cant. *You* must –

RICHARD   [*folding her in his arms with an impulse of compassion for her distress*] My poor girl!

Judith, with a sudden effort, throws her arms round him; kisses him; and swoons away, dropping from his arms to the ground as if the kiss had killed her.

RICHARD   [*going quickly to the sergeant*] Now, Sergeant: quick, before she comes to. The handcuffs. [*He puts out his hands*].

SERGEANT   [*pocketing them*] Never mind, sir: I'll trust you. Youre a game one. You ought to a bin a soldier, sir. Between them two, please. [*The soldiers place themselves one before Richard and one behind him. The sergeant opens the door*].

RICHARD   [*taking a last look round him*] Goodbye, wife: goodbye, home. Muffle the drums, and quick march!

The sergeant signs to the leading soldier to march. They file out quickly.

When Anderson returns from Mrs Dudgeon's, he is astonished to find the room apparently empty and almost in darkness except for the glow from the fire; for one of the candles has burnt out, and the other is at its last flicker.

ANDERSON   Why, what on earth – ? [*Calling*] Judith, Judith! [*He listens: there is no answer*]. Hm! [*He goes to the cupboard; takes a candle from the drawer; lights it at the flicker of the expiring one on the table; and looks wonderingly at the untasted meal by its light. Then he sticks it in the candlestick; takes off his hat; and scratches his head, much puzzled. This action causes him to look at the floor for the first time; and there he sees Judith lying motionless with her eyes closed. He runs to her and stoops beside her, lifting her head*]. Judith.

JUDITH   [*waking; for her swoon has passed into the sleep of exhaustion after suffering*] Yes. Did you call? Whats the matter?

ANDERSON   Ive just come in and found you lying here with the candles burnt out and the tea poured out and cold. What has happened?

JUDITH   [*still astray*] I dont know. Have I been asleep? I suppose – [*She stops blankly*]. I dont know.

ANDERSON   [*groaning*] Heaven forgive me, I left you alone with that scoundrel. [*Judith remembers. With an agonized cry, she clutches his shoulders and drags herself to her feet as he rises with her. He clasps her tenderly in his arms*]. My poor pet!

JUDITH   [*frantically clinging to him*] What shall I do? Oh my God, what shall I do?

ANDERSON   Never mind, never mind, my dearest dear: it was my fault. Come: youre safe now; and youre not hurt, are you? [*He takes his arms from her to see whether she can stand*]. There: thats right, thats right. If only you are not hurt, nothing else matters.

JUDITH   No, no, no: I'm not hurt.

ANDERSON   Thank Heaven for that! Come now: [*leading her to the railed seat and making her sit down beside him*] sit down and rest: you can tell me about it to-morrow. Or [*misunderstanding her distress*] you shall not tell me at all if it worries you. There, there! [*Cheerfully*] I'll make you some fresh tea: that will set you up again. [*He goes to the table, and empties the teapot into the slop bowl*].

JUDITH [*in a strained tone*] Tony.

ANDERSON Yes, dear?

JUDITH Do you think we are only in a dream now?

ANDERSON [*glancing round at her for a moment with a pang of anxiety, though he goes on steadily and cheerfully putting fresh tea into the pot*] Perhaps so, pet. But you may as well dream a cup of tea when youre about it.

JUDITH Oh stop, stop. You dont know – [*Distracted, she buries her face in her knotted hands*].

ANDERSON [*breaking down and coming to her*] My dear, what is it? I cant bear it any longer: you must tell me. It was all my fault: I was mad to trust him.

JUDITH No: dont say that. You mustnt say that. He – oh no, no: I cant. Tony: dont speak to me. Take my hands – both my hands. [*He takes them, wondering*]. Make me think of you, not of him. There's danger, frightful danger; but it is your danger; and I cant keep thinking of it: I cant, I cant: my mind goes back to his danger. He must be saved – no: you must be saved: you, you, you. [*She springs up as if to do something or go some-where, exclaiming*] Oh, Heaven help me!

ANDERSON [*keeping his seat and holding her hands with resolute composure*] Calmly, calmly, my pet. Youre quite distracted.

JUDITH I may well be. I dont know what to do. I dont know what to do. [*Tearing her hands away*]. I must save him. [*Anderson rises in alarm as she runs wildly to the door. It is opened in her face by Essie, who hurries in full of anxiety. The surprise is so disagreeable to Judith that it brings her to her senses. Her tone is sharp and angry as she demands*] What do you want?

ESSIE I was to come to you.

ANDERSON Who told you to?

ESSIE [*staring at him, as if his presence astonished her*] Are you here?

JUDITH Of course. Dont be foolish, child.

ANDERSON   Gently, dearest: youll frighten her. [*Going between them*]. Come here, Essie. [*She comes to him*]. Who sent you?

ESSIE   Dick. He sent me word by a soldier. I was to come here at once and do whatever Mrs Anderson told me.

ANDERSON   [*enlightened*] A soldier! Ah, I see it all now! They have arrested Richard. [*Judith makes a gesture of despair*].

ESSIE   No. I asked the soldier. Dick's safe. But the soldier said you had been taken.

ANDERSON   I! [*Bewildered, he turns to Judith for an explanation*].

JUDITH   [*coaxingly*] All right, dear: I understand. [*To Essie*] Thank you, Essie, for coming; but I dont need you now. You may go home.

ESSIE   [*suspicious*] Are you sure Dick has not been touched? Perhaps he told the soldier to say it was the minister. [*Anxiously*] Mrs Anderson: do you think it can have been that?

ANDERSON   Tell her the truth if it is so, Judith. She will learn it from the first neighbor she meets in the street. [*Judith turns away and covers her eyes with her hands*].

ESSIE   [*wailing*] But what will they do to him? Oh, what will they do to him? Will they hang him? [*Judith shudders convulsively, and throws herself into the chair in which Richard sat at the tea table*].

ANDERSON   [*patting Essie's shoulder and trying to comfort her*] I hope not. I hope not. Perhaps if youre very quiet and patient, we may be able to help him in some way.

ESSIE   Yes – help him – yes, yes, yes. I'll be good.

ANDERSON   I must go to him at once, Judith.

JUDITH   [*springing up*] Oh no. You must go away – far away, to some place of safety.

ANDERSON   Pooh!

JUDITH   [*passionately*] Do you want to kill me? Do you think I can bear to live for days and days with every knock at the door – every footstep – giving me a spasm of terror? to lie awake for nights and nights in an agony of dread, listening for them to come and arrest you?

ANDERSON   Do you think it would be better to know that I had run away from my post at the first sign of danger?

JUDITH [*bitterly*] Oh, you wont go. I know it. Youll stay; and
I shall go mad.

ANDERSON My dear, your duty –

JUDITH [*fiercely*] What do I care about my duty?

ANDERSON [*shocked*] Judith!

JUDITH I am doing my duty. I am clinging to my duty. My
duty is to get you away, to save you, to leave him to
his fate [*Essie utters a cry of distress and sinks on the
chair at the fire, sobbing silently*]. My instinct is the
same as hers – to save him above all things, though it
would be so much better for him to die! so much
greater! But I know you will take your own way as he
took it. I have no power. [*She sits down sullenly on the
railed seat*]. I'm only a woman: I can do nothing but
sit here and suffer. Only, tell him I tried to save you –
that I did my best to save you.

ANDERSON My dear, I am afraid he will be thinking more of his
own danger than of mine.

JUDITH Stop; or I shall hate you.

ANDERSON [*remonstrating*] Come, come, come! How am I to leave
you if you talk like this? You are quite out of your
senses. [*He turns to Essie*] Essie.

ESSIE [*eagerly rising and drying her eyes*] Yes?

ANDERSON Just wait outside a moment, like a good girl: Mrs
Anderson is not well. [*Essie looks doubtful*]. Never
fear: I'll come to you presently; and I'll go to Dick.

ESSIE You are sure you will go to him? [*Whispering*] You
wont let *her* prevent you?

ANDERSON [*smiling*] No, no: it's all right. All right. [*She goes*].
Thats a good girl. [*He closes the door, and returns to
Judith*].

JUDITH [*seated – rigid*] You are going to your death.

ANDERSON [*quaintly*] Then I shall go in my best coat, dear. [*He
turns to the press, beginning to take off his coat*].
Where – ? [*He stares at the empty nail for a moment;
then looks quickly round to the fire; strides across to it;
and lifts Richard's coat*]. Why, my dear, it seems that
he has gone in my best coat.

JUDITH [*still motionless*] Yes.

ANDERSON   Did the soldiers make a mistake?

JUDITH   Yes: they made a mistake.

ANDERSON   He might have told them. Poor fellow, he was too upset, I suppose.

JUDITH   Yes: he might have told them. So might I.

ANDERSON   Well, it's all very puzzling – almost funny. It's curious how these little things strike us even in the most – [*He breaks off and begins putting on Richard's coat*]. I'd better take him his own coat. I know what he'll say – [*imitating Richard's sardonic manner*] "Anxious about my soul, Pastor, and also about your best coat." Eh?

JUDITH   Yes, that is just what he will say to you. [*Vacantly*] It doesnt matter: I shall never see either of you again.

ANDERSON   [*rallying her*] Oh pooh, pooh, pooh! [*He sits down beside her*]. Is this how you keep your promise that I shant be ashamed of my brave wife?

JUDITH   No: this is how I break it. I cannot keep my promises to him: why should I keep my promises to you?

ANDERSON   Dont speak so strangely, my love. It sounds insincere to me. [*She looks unutterable reproach at him*]. Yes, dear, nonsense is always insincere; and my dearest is talking nonsense. Just nonsense. [*Her face darkens into dumb obstinacy. She stares straight before her, and does not look at him again, absorbed in Richard's fate. He scans her face; sees that his rallying has produced no effect; and gives it up, making no further effort to conceal his anxiety*]. I wish I knew what has frightened you so. Was there a struggle? Did he fight?

JUDITH   No. He smiled.

ANDERSON   Did he realize his danger, do you think?

JUDITH   He realized yours.

ANDERSON   Mine!

JUDITH   [*monotonously*] He said, "See that you get him safely out of harm's way." I promised: I cant keep my promise. He said, "Dont for your life let him know of my danger." Ive told you of it. He said that if you found it out, you could not save him – that they will hang him and not spare you.

ANDERSON   [*rising in generous indignation*] And you think that I will let a man with that much good in him die like a dog, when a few words might make him die like a Christian. I'm ashamed of you, Judith.

JUDITH   He will be steadfast in his religion as you are in yours; and you may depend on him to the death. He said so.

ANDERSON   God forgive him! What else did he say?

JUDITH   He said goodbye.

ANDERSON   [*fidgeting nervously to and fro in great concern*] Poor fellow, poor fellow! You said goodbye to him in all kindness and charity, Judith, I hope.

JUDITH   I kissed him.

ANDERSON   What! Judith!

JUDITH   Are you angry?

ANDERSON   No, no. You were right: you were right. Poor fellow, poor fellow! [*Greatly distressed*] To be hanged like that at his age! And then did they take him away?

JUDITH   [*wearily*] Then you were here: thats the next thing I remember. I suppose I fainted. Now bid me goodbye, Tony. Perhaps I shall faint again. I wish I could die.

ANDERSON   No, no, my dear: you must pull yourself together and be sensible. I am in no danger – not the least in the world.

JUDITH   [*solemnly*] You are going to your death, Tony – your sure death, if God will let innocent men be murdered. They will not let you see him: they will arrest you the moment you give your name. It was for you the soldiers came.

ANDERSON   [*thunderstruck*] For me!!! [*His fists clinch; his neck thickens; his face reddens; the fleshy purses under his eyes become injected with hot blood; the man of peace vanishes, transfigured into a choleric and formidable man of war. Still, she does not come out of her absorption to look at him: her eyes are steadfast with a mechanical reflection of Richard's steadfastness*].

JUDITH   He took your place: he is dying to save you. That is why he went in your coat. That is why I kissed him.

ANDERSON   [*exploding*] Blood an' owns! [*His voice is rough and dominant, his gesture full of brute energy*]. Here! Essie, Essie!

49

ESSIE [*running in*] Yes.

ANDERSON [*impetuously*] Off with you as hard as you can run, to the inn. Tell them to saddle the fastest and strongest horse they have [*Judith rises breathless, and stares at him incredulously*] – the chestnut mare, if she's fresh – without a moment's delay. Go into the stable yard and tell the black man there that I'll give him a silver dollar if the horse is waiting for me when I come, and that I am close on your heels. Away with you. [*His energy sends Essie flying from the room. He pounces on his riding boots; rushes with them to the chair at the fire; and begins pulling them on*].

JUDITH [*unable to believe such a thing of him*] You are not going to him!

ANDERSON [*busy with the boots*] Going to him! What good would that do? [*Growling to himself as he gets the first boot on with a wrench*] I'll go to them, so I will. [*To Judith peremptorily*] Get me the pistols: I want them. And money, money: I want money – all the money in the house. [*He stoops over the other boot, grumbling*] A great satisfaction it would be to him to have my company on the gallows. [*He pulls on the boot*].

JUDITH You are deserting him, then?

ANDERSON Hold your tongue, woman; and get me the pistols. [*She goes to the press and takes from it a leather belt with two pistols, a powder horn, and a bag of bullets attached to it. She throws it on the table. Then she unlocks a drawer in the press and takes out a purse. Anderson grabs the belt and buckles it on, saying*] If they took him for me in my coat, perhaps they'll take me for him in his. [*Hitching the belt into its place*] Do I look like him?

JUDITH [*turning with the purse in her hand*] Horribly unlike him.

ANDERSON [*snatching the purse from her and emptying it on the table*] Hm! We shall see.

JUDITH [*sitting down helplessly*] Is it of any use to pray, do you think, Tony?

ANDERSON [*counting the money*] Pray! Can we pray Swindon's rope off Richard's neck?

JUDITH God may soften Major Swindon's heart.

ANDERSON [*contemptuously – pocketing a handful of money*] Let him, then. I am not God; and I must go to work another way. [*Judith gasps at the blasphemy. He throws the purse on the table*]. Keep that. Ive taken 25 dollars.

JUDITH Have you forgotten even that you are a minister?

ANDERSON Minister be – faugh! My hat: wheres my hat? [*He snatches up hat and cloak, and puts both on in hot haste*]. Now listen, you. If you can get a word with him by pretending youre his wife, tell him to hold his tongue until morning: that will give me all the start I need.

JUDITH [*solemnly*] You may depend on him to the death.

ANDERSON Youre a fool, a *fool*, Judith. [*For a moment checking the torrent of his haste, and speaking with something of his old quiet and impressive conviction*] You dont know the man youre married to. [*Essie returns. He swoops at her at once*]. Well: is the horse ready?

ESSIE [*breathless*] It will be ready when you come.

ANDERSON Good. [*He makes for the door*].

JUDITH [*rising and stretching out her arms after him involuntarily*] Wont you say goodbye?

ANDERSON And waste another half minute! Psha! [*He rushes out like an avalanche*].

ESSIE [*hurrying to Judith*] He has gone to save Richard, hasnt he?

JUDITH To save Richard! No: Richard has saved him. He has gone to save himself. Richard must die.

Essie screams with terror and falls on her knees, hiding her face. Judith, without heeding her, looks rigidly straight in front of her, at the vision of Richard, dying.

Early next morning the sergeant, at the British head-quarters in the Town Hall, unlocks the door of a little empty panelled waiting room, and invites Judith to enter. She has had a bad night, probably a rather delirious one; for even in the reality of the raw morning, her fixed gaze comes back at moments when her attention is not strongly held.

The sergeant considers that her feelings do her credit, and is sympathetic in an encouraging military way. Being a fine figure of a man, vain of his uniform and of his rank, he feels specially qualified, in a respectful way, to console her.

SERGEANT   You can have a quiet word with him here, mum.

JUDITH   Shall I have long to wait?

SERGEANT   No, mum, not a minute. We kep him in the Bridewell for the night; and he's just been brought over here for the court martial. Dont fret, mum: he slep like a child, and has made a rare good breakfast.

JUDITH   [*incredulously*] He is in good spirits!

SERGEANT   Tip top, mum. The chaplain looked in to see him last night; and he won seventeen shillings off him at spoil five. He spent it among us like the gentleman he is. Duty's duty, mum, of course; but youre among friends here. [*The tramp of a couple of soldiers is heard approaching*]. There: I think he's coming. [*Richard comes in, without a sign of care or captivity in his bearing. The sergeant nods to the two soldiers, and shews them the key of the room in his hand. They withdraw*]. Your good lady, sir.

RICHARD   [*going to her*] What! My wife. My adored one. [*He takes her hand and kisses it with a perverse, raffish gallantry*]. How long do you allow a brokenhearted husband for leave-taking, Sergeant?

SERGEANT   As long as we can, sir. We shall not disturb you till the court sits.

RICHARD   But it has struck the hour.

SERGEANT   So it has, sir; but there's a delay. General Burgoyne's just arrived – Gentlemanly Johnny we call him, sir – and he wont have done finding fault with everything this side of half past. I know him, sir: I served with him in Portugal. You may count on twenty minutes, sir; and by your leave I wont waste any more of them. [*He goes out, locking the door. Richard immediately drops his raffish manner and turns to Judith with considerate sincerity*].

RICHARD   Mrs Anderson: this visit is very kind of you. And how are you after last night? I had to leave you before you recovered; but I sent word to Essie to go and look after you. Did she understand the message?

JUDITH   [*breathless and urgent*] Oh, dont think of me: I havnt come here to talk about myself. Are they going to – to – [*meaning "to hang you"*]?

RICHARD   [*whimsically*] At noon, punctually. At least, that was when they disposed of Uncle Peter. [*She shudders*]. Is your husband safe? Is he on the wing?

JUDITH   He is no longer my husband.

RICHARD   [*opening his eyes wide*] Eh?

JUDITH   I disobeyed you. I told him everything. I expected him to come here and save you. I wanted him to come here and save you. He ran away instead.

53

RICHARD   Well, thats what I meant him to do. What good would his staying have done? Theyd only have hanged us both.

JUDITH   [*with reproachful earnestness*] Richard Dudgeon: on your honour, what would you have done in his place?

RICHARD   Exactly what he has done, of course.

JUDITH   Oh, why will you not be simple with me – honest and straightforward? If you are so selfish as that, why did you let them take you last night?

RICHARD   [*gaily*] Upon my life, Mrs Anderson, I dont know. Ive been asking myself that question ever since; and I can find no manner of reason for acting as I did.

JUDITH   You know you did it for his sake, believing he was a more worthy man than yourself.

RICHARD   [*laughing*] Oho! No: thats a very pretty reason, I must say; but I'm not so modest as that. No: it wasnt for his sake.

JUDITH   [*after a pause, during which she looks shamefacedly at him, blushing painfully*] Was it for my sake?

RICHARD   [*gallantly*] Well, you had a hand in it. It must have been a little for your sake. You let them take me, at all events.

JUDITH   Oh, do you think I have not been telling myself that all night? Your death will be at my door. [*Impulsively, she gives him her hand, and adds, with intense earnestness*] If I could save you as you saved him, I would do it, no matter how cruel the death was.

RICHARD   [*holding her hand and smiling, but keeping her almost at arms length*] I am very sure I shouldnt let you.

JUDITH   Dont you see that I *can* save you?

RICHARD   How? By changing clothes with me, eh?

JUDITH   [*disengaging her hand to touch his lips with it*] Dont [*meaning "Dont jest"*]. No: by telling the Court who you really are.

RICHARD   [*frowning*] No use: they wouldnt spare me; and it would spoil half his chance of escaping. They are determined to cow us by making an example of somebody on that gallows to-day. Well, let us cow them by showing that we can stand by one another to the death. That is the only force that can send Burgoyne back across the Atlantic and make America a nation.

JUDITH [*impatiently*] Oh, what does all that matter?

RICHARD [*laughing*] True: what does it matter? what does anything matter? You see, men have these strange notions, Mrs Anderson; and women see the folly of them.

JUDITH Women have to lose those they love through them.

RICHARD They can easily get fresh lovers.

JUDITH [*revolted*] Oh! [*Vehemently*] Do you realise that you are going to kill yourself?

RICHARD The only man I have any right to kill, Mrs Anderson. Dont be concerned: no woman will lose her lover through my death. [*Smiling*] Bless you, nobody cares for me. Have you heard that my mother is dead?

JUDITH Dead!

RICHARD Of heart disease – in the night. Her last word to me was her curse: I dont think I could have borne her blessing. My other relatives will not grieve much on my account. Essie will cry for a day or two; but I have provided for her: I made my own will last night.

JUDITH [*stonily, after a moment's silence*] And I!

RICHARD [*surprised*] You?

JUDITH Yes, I. Am I not to care at all?

RICHARD [*gaily and bluntly*] Not a scrap. Oh, you expressed your feelings towards me very frankly yesterday. What happened may have softened you for the moment; but believe me, Mrs Anderson, you dont like a bone in my skin or a hair on my head. I shall be as good a riddance at 12 to-day as I should have been at 12 yesterday.

JUDITH [*her voice trembling*] What can I do to shew you that you are mistaken?

RICHARD Dont trouble. I'll give you credit for liking me a little better than you did. All I say is that my death will not break your heart.

JUDITH [*almost in a whisper*] How do you know? [*She puts her hands on his shoulders and looks intently at him*].

RICHARD [*amazed – divining the truth*] Mrs Anderson! [*The bell of the town clock strikes the quarter. He collects himself, and removes her hands, saying rather coldly*] Ex-

55

cuse me: they will be here for me presently. It is too late.

JUDITH   It is not too late. Call me as witness: they will never kill you when they know how heroically you have acted.

RICHARD   [*with some scorn*] Indeed! But if I dont go through with it, where will the heroism be? I shall simply have tricked them; and theyll hang me for that like a dog. Serve me right too!

JUDITH   [*wildly*] Oh, I believe you *want* to die.

RICHARD   [*obstinately*] No I dont.

JUDITH   Then why not try to save yourself? I implore you – listen. You said just now that you saved him for my sake – yes [*clutching him as he recoils with a gesture of denial*] a little for my sake. Well, save yourself for my sake. And I will go with you to the end of the world.

RICHARD   [*taking her by the wrists and holding her a little way from him, looking steadily at her*] Judith.

JUDITH   [*breathless – delighted at the name*] Yes.

RICHARD   If I said – to please you – that I did what I did ever so little for your sake, I lied as men always lie to women. You know how much I have lived with worthless men – aye, and worthless women too. Well, they could all rise to some sort of goodness and kindness when they were in love [*the word love comes from him with true Puritan scorn*]. That has taught me to set very little store by the goodness that only comes out red hot. What I did last night, I did in cold blood, caring not half so much for your husband, or [*ruthlessly*] for you [*she droops, stricken*] as I do for myself. I had no motive and no interest: all I can tell you is that when it came to the point whether I would take my neck out of the noose and put another man's into it, I could not do it. I dont know why not: I see myself as a fool for my pains; but I could not and I cannot. I have been brought up standing by the law of my own nature; and I may not go against it, gallows or no gallows. [*She has slowly raised her head and is now looking full at him*]. I should have done the same for any other man in the town, or any other man's wife. [*Releasing her*] Do you understand that?

JUDITH   Yes: you mean that you do not love me.

RICHARD   [*revolted – with fierce contempt*] Is that all it means to you?

JUDITH   What more – what worse – can it mean to me? [*The sergeant knocks. The blow on the door jars on her heart*]. Oh, one moment more. [*She throws herself on her knees*]. I pray to you –

RICHARD   Hush! [*Calling*] Come in. [*The sergeant unlocks the door and opens it. The guard is with him*].

SERGEANT [*coming in*] Time's up, sir.

RICHARD   Quite ready, Sergeant. Now, my dear. [*He attempts to raise her*].

JUDITH   [*clinging to him*] Only one thing more – I entreat, I implore you. Let me be present in the court. I have seen Major Swindon: he said I should be allowed if you asked it. You will ask it. It is my last request: I shall never ask you anything again. [*She clasps his knee*]. I beg and pray it of you.

RICHARD   If I do, will you be silent?

JUDITH   Yes.

RICHARD   You will keep faith?

JUDITH   I will keep – [*She breaks down, sobbing*].

RICHARD   [*taking her arm to lift her*] Just – her other arm, Sergeant.

They go out, she sobbing convulsively, supported by the two men.

Meanwhile, the Council Chamber is ready for the court martial. It is a large, lofty room, with a chair of state in the middle under a tall canopy with a gilt crown, and maroon curtains with the royal monogram G. R. In front of the chair is a table, also draped in maroon, with a bell, a heavy inkstand, and writing materials on it. Several chairs are set at the table. The door is at the right hand of the occupant of the chair of state when it has an occupant: at present it is empty. Major Swindon, a pale, sandy-haired, very conscientious looking man of about 45, sits at the end of the table with his back to the door, writing. He is alone until the sergeant announces the General in a subdued manner which suggests that Gentlemanly Johnny has been making his presence felt rather heavily.

SERGEANT The General, sir.

Swindon rises hastily. The general comes in: the sergeant goes out. General Burgoyne is 55, and very well preserved. He is a man of fashion, gallant enough to have made a distinguished marriage by an elopement, witty enough to write successful comedies, aristocratically-connected enough to have had opportunities of high military distinction. His eyes, large, brilliant, apprehensive, and intelligent, are his most remarkable feature: without them his fine nose and small mouth would suggest rather more fastidiousness and less force than go to the making of a first rate general. Just now the eyes are angry and tragic, and the mouth and nostrils tense.

BURGOYNE Major Swindon, I presume.

SWINDON Yes. General Burgoyne, if I mistake not. [*They bow to one another ceremoniously*]. I am glad to have the support of your presence this morning. It is not particularly lively business, hanging this poor devil of a minister.

BURGOYNE [*throwing himself into Swindon's chair*] No, sir, it is not. It is making too much of the fellow to execute him: what more could you have done if he had been a member of the Church of England? Martyrdom, sir, is what these people like: it is the only way in which a man can become famous without ability. However, you have committed us to hanging him; and the sooner he is hanged the better.

SWINDON We have arranged it for 12 o'clock. Nothing remains to be done except to try him.

BURGOYNE [*looking at him with suppressed anger*] Nothing – except to save our own necks, perhaps. Have you heard the news from Springtown?

SWINDON Nothing special. The latest reports are satisfactory.

BURGOYNE [*rising in amazement*] Satisfactory, sir! Satisfactory!! [*He stares at him for a moment, and then adds, with grim intensity*] I am glad you take that view of them.

SWINDON [*puzzled*] Do I understand that in your opinion –

BURGOYNE I do not express my opinion. I never stoop to that habit of profane language which unfortunately coarsens our profession. If I did, sir, perhaps I should be able to express my opinion of the news from Springtown – the news which *you* [*severely*] have apparently not heard. How soon do you get news from your supports here? – in the course of a month, eh?

SWINDON [*turning sulky*] I suppose the reports have been taken to you, sir, instead of to me. Is there anything serious?

BURGOYNE [*taking a report from his pocket and holding it up*] Springtown's in the hands of the rebels. [*He throws the report on the table*].

SWINDON [*aghast*] Since yesterday!

BURGOYNE Since two o'clock this morning. Perhaps we shall be in their hands before two o'clock to-morrow morning. Have you thought of that?

SWINDON [*confidently*] As to that, General, the British soldier will give a good account of himself.

BURGOYNE [*bitterly*] And therefore, I suppose, sir, the British officer need not know his business: the British soldier will get him out of all his blunders with the bayonet. In future, sir, I must ask you to be a little less generous with the blood of your men, and a little more generous with your own brains.

SWINDON I am sorry I cannot pretend to your intellectual eminence, sir. I can only do my best, and rely on the devotion of my countrymen.

BURGOYNE [*suddenly becoming suavely sarcastic*] May I ask are you writing a melodrama, Major Swindon?

SWINDON [*flushing*] No, sir.

BURGOYNE What a pity! *What* a pity! [*Dropping his sarcastic tone and facing him suddenly and seriously*] Do you at all realize, sir, that we have nothing standing between us and destruction but our own bluff and the sheepishness of these colonists? They are men of the same English stock as ourselves: six to one of us [*repeating it emphatically*] six to one, sir; and nearly half our troops are Hessians, Brunswickers, German dragoons, and Indians with scalping knives. These are the countrymen on whose devotion you rely! Suppose the colonists find a leader! Suppose the news from Springtown should turn out to mean that they have already found a leader! What shall we do then? Eh?

SWINDON [*sullenly*] Our duty, sir, I presume.

BURGOYNE [*again sarcastic – giving him up as a fool*] Quite so, quite so. Thank you, Major Swindon, thank you. Now youve settled the question, sir – thrown a flood of light on the situation. What a comfort to me to feel that I have at my side so devoted and able an officer to support me in this emergency! I think, sir, it will probably relieve both our feelings if we proceed to hang this dissenter without further delay [*he strikes the bell*] especially as I am debarred by my principles from the customary military vent for my feelings. [*The sergeant appears*]. Bring your man in.

SERGEANT Yes, sir.

BURGOYNE And mention to any officer you may meet that the court cannot wait any longer for him.

SWINDON [*keeping his temper with difficulty*] The staff is perfectly ready, sir. They have been waiting your convenience for fully half an hour. *Perfectly* ready, sir.

BURGOYNE [*blandly*] So am I. [*Several officers come in and take their seats. One of them sits at the end of the table furthest from the door, and acts throughout as clerk to the court, making notes of the proceedings. The uniforms are those of the 9th, 20th, 21st, 24th, 47th, 53rd, and 62nd British Infantry. One officer is a Major General of the Royal Artillery. There are also German officers of the Hessian Rifles, and of German dragoon and Brunswicker regiments].* Oh, good morning, gentlemen. Sorry to disturb you, I am sure. Very good of you to spare us a few moments.

SWINDON Will you preside, sir?

BURGOYNE [*becoming additionally polished, lofty, sarcastic and urbane now that he is in public*] No, sir: I feel my own deficiencies too keenly to presume so far. If you will kindly allow me, I will sit at the feet of Gamaliel. [*He takes the chair at the end of the table next the door, and motions Swindon to the chair of state, waiting for him to be seated before sitting down himself*].

SWINDON [*greatly annoyed*] As you please, sir. I am only trying to do my duty under excessively trying circumstances. [*He takes his place in the chair of state*].

Burgoyne, relaxing his studied demeanor for the moment, sits down and begins to read the report with knitted brows and careworn looks, reflecting on his desperate situation and Swindon's uselessness. Richard is brought in. Judith walks beside him. Two soldiers precede and two follow him, with the sergeant in command. They cross the room to the wall opposite the door; but when Richard has just passed before the chair of state the sergeant stops him with a touch on the arm, and posts himself behind him, at his elbow. Judith stands timidly at the wall. The four soldiers place themselves in a squad near her.

BURGOYNE [*looking up and seeing Judith*] Who is that woman?

SERGEANT Prisoner's wife, sir.

SWINDON [*nervously*] She begged me to allow her to be present; and I thought –

BURGOYNE [*completing the sentence for him ironically*] You thought it would be a pleasure for her. Quite so, quite so. [*Blandly*] Give the lady a chair; and make her thoroughly comfortable.

61

The sergeant fetches a chair and places it near Richard.

JUDITH   *Thank* you, sir. [*She sits down after an awe-stricken curtsy to Burgoyne, which he acknowledges by a dignified bend of his head*].

SWINDON   [*to Richard, sharply*] Your name, sir?

RICHARD   [*affable, but obstinate*] Come: you dont mean to say that youve brought me here without knowing who I am?

SWINDON   As a matter of form, sir, give your name.

RICHARD   As a matter of form then, my name is Anthony Anderson, Presbyterian minister in this town.

BURGOYNE   [*interested*] Indeed! Pray, Mr Anderson, what do you gentlemen believe?

RICHARD   I shall be happy to explain if time is allowed me. I cannot undertake to complete your conversion in less than a fortnight.

SWINDON   [*snubbing him*] We are not here to discuss your views.

BURGOYNE   [*with an elaborate bow to the unfortunate Swindon*] I stand rebuked.

SWINDON   [*embarrassed*] Oh, not you, I as –

BURGOYNE   Dont mention it. [*To Richard, very politely*] Any political views, Mr Anderson?

RICHARD   I understand that that is just what we are here to find out.

SWINDON   [*severely*] Do you mean to deny that you are a rebel?

RICHARD   I am an American, sir.

SWINDON   What do you expect me to think of that speech, Mr Anderson?

RICHARD   I never expect a soldier to think, sir.

Burgoyne is boundlessly delighted by this retort, which almost reconciles him to the loss of America.

SWINDON   [*whitening with anger*] I advise you not to be insolent, prisoner.

RICHARD   You cant help yourself, General. When you make up your mind to hang a man, you put yourself at a disadvantage with him. Why should I be civil to you? I may as well be hanged for a sheep as a lamb.

SWINDON   You have no right to assume that the court has made

62

up its mind without a fair trial. And you will please not address me as General. I am Major Swindon.

RICHARD A thousand pardons. I thought I had the honor of addressing Gentlemanly Johnny.

Sensation among the officers. The sergeant has a narrow escape from a guffaw.

BURGOYNE [*with extreme suavity*] I believe I am Gentlemanly Johnny, sir, at your service. My more intimate friends call me General Burgoyne. [*Richard bows with perfect politeness*]. You will understand, sir, I hope, since you seem to be a gentleman and a man of some spirit in spite of your calling, that if we should have the misfortune to hang you, we shall do so as a mere matter of political necessity and military duty, without any personal ill-feeling.

RICHARD Oh, quite so. That makes all the difference in the world, of course.

They all smile in spite of themselves; and some of the younger officers burst out laughing.

JUDITH [*her dread and horror deepening at every one of these jests and compliments*] How *can* you?

RICHARD You promised to be silent.

BURGOYNE [*to Judith, with studied courtesy*] Believe me, Madam, your husband is placing us under the greatest obligation by taking this very disagreeable business so thoroughly in the spirit of a gentleman. Sergeant: give Mr Anderson a chair. [*The sergeant does so. Richard sits down*]. Now, Major Swindon: we are waiting for you.

SWINDON You are aware, I presume, Mr Anderson, of your obligations as a subject of His Majesty King George the Third.

RICHARD I am aware, sir, that His Majesty King George the Third is about to hang me because I object to Lord North's robbing me.

SWINDON That is a treasonable speech, sir.

RICHARD [*briefly*] Yes. I meant it to be.

BURGOYNE [*strongly deprecating this line of defence, but still polite*] Dont you think, Mr Anderson, that this is rather – if you will excuse the word – a vulgar line to take? Why

63

should you cry out robbery because of a stamp duty and a tea duty and so forth? After all, it is the essence of your position as a gentleman that you pay with a good grace.

RICHARD   It is not the money, General. But to be swindled by a pig-headed lunatic like King George –

SWINDON   [*scandalized*] Chut, sir – silence!

SERGEANT   [*in stentorian tones, greatly shocked*] Silence!

BURGOYNE   [*unruffled*] Ah, that is another point of view. My position does not allow of my going into that, except in private. But [*shrugging his shoulders*] of course, Mr Anderson, if you are determined to be hanged [*Judith flinches*] there's nothing more to be said. An unusual taste! however [*with a final shrug*] – !

SWINDON   [*To Burgoyne*] Shall we call witnesses?

RICHARD   What need is there of witnesses? If the townspeople here had listened to me, you would have found the streets barricaded, the houses loopholed, and the people in arms to hold the town against you to the last man. But you arrived, unfortunately, before we had got out of the talking stage; and then it was too late.

SWINDON   [*severely*] Well, sir, we shall teach you and your townspeople a lesson they will not forget. Have you anything more to say?

RICHARD   I think you might have the decency to treat me as a prisoner of war, and shoot me like a man instead of hanging me like a dog.

BURGOYNE   [*sympathetically*] Now there, Mr Anderson, you talk like a civilian, if you will excuse my saying so. Have you any idea of the average marksmanship of the army of His Majesty King George the Third? If we make you up a firing party, what will happen? Half of them will miss you: the rest will make a mess of the business and leave you to the provo-marshal's pistol. Whereas we can hang you in a perfectly workmanlike and agreeable way. [*Kindly*] Let me persuade you to be hanged, Mr Anderson?

JUDITH   [*sick with horror*] My God!

RICHARD   [*To Judith*] Your promise! [*To Burgoyne*] Thank you, General: that view of the case did not occur to me before. To oblige you, I withdraw my objection to the rope. Hang me, by all means.

BURGOYNE [*smoothly*] Will 12 o'clock suit you, Mr Anderson?

RICHARD I shall be at your disposal then, General.

BURGOYNE [*rising*] Nothing more to be said, gentlemen. [*They all rise*].

JUDITH [*rushing to the table*] Oh, you are not going to murder a man like that, without a proper trial – without thinking of what you are doing – without – [*she cannot find words*].

RICHARD Is this how you keep your promise?

JUDITH If I am not to speak, you must. Defend yourself: save yourself: tell them the truth.

RICHARD [*worriedly*] I have told them truth enough to hang me ten times over. If you say another word you will risk other lives; but you will not save mine.

BURGOYNE My good lady, our only desire is to save unpleasantness. What satisfaction would it give you to have a solemn fuss made, with my friend Swindon in a black cap and so forth? I am sure we are greatly indebted to the admirable tact and gentlemanly feeling shewn by your husband.

JUDITH [*throwing the words in his face*] Oh, you are mad. Is it nothing to you what wicked thing you do if only you do it like a gentleman? Is it nothing to you whether you are a murderer or not, if only you murder in a red coat? [*Desperately*] You shall not hang him: that man is not my husband.

The officers look at one another, and whisper: some of the Germans asking their neighbors to explain what the woman had said. Burgoyne, who has been visibly shaken by Judith's reproach, recovers himself promptly at this new development. Richard meanwhile raises his voice above the buzz.

RICHARD I appeal to you, gentlemen, to put an end to this. She will not believe that she cannot save me. Break up the court.

BURGOYNE [*in a voice so quiet and firm that it restores silence at once*] One moment, Mr Anderson. One moment, gentlemen. [*He resumes his seat. Swindon and the officers follow his example*]. Let me understand you clearly, madam. Do you mean that this gentleman is not your husband, or merely – I wish to put this with all delicacy – that you are not his wife?

JUDITH   I dont know what you mean. I say that he is not my husband – that my husband has escaped. This man took his place to save him. Ask anyone in the town – send out into the street for the first person you find there, and bring him in as a witness. He will tell you that the prisoner is not Anthony Anderson.

BURGOYNE   [*quietly, as before*] Sergeant.

SERGEANT   Yes sir.

BURGOYNE   Go out into the street and bring in the first townsman you see there.

SERGEANT   [*making for the door*] Yes sir.

BURGOYNE   [*as the sergeant passes*] The first clean, sober towns- man you see.

SERGEANT   Yes sir. [*He goes out*].

BURGOYNE   Sit down, Mr Anderson – if I may call you so for the present. [*Richard sits down*]. Sit down, madam, whilst we wait. Give the lady a newspaper.

RICHARD   [*indignantly*] Shame!

BURGOYNE   [*keenly, with a half smile*] If you are not her husband, sir, the case is not a serious one – for *her*. [*Richard bites his lip, silenced*].

JUDITH   [*to Richard, as she returns to her seat*] I couldnt help it. [*He shakes his head. She sits down*].

BURGOYNE   You will understand of course, Mr Anderson, that you must not build on this little incident. We are bound to make an example of somebody.

RICHARD   I quite understand. I suppose there's no use in my explaining.

BURGOYNE   I think we should prefer independent testimony, if you dont mind.

The sergeant, with a packet of papers in his hand, re- turns conducting Christy, who is much scared.

SERGEANT   [*giving Burgoyne the packet*] Dispatches, sir. De- livered by a corporal of the 33rd. Dead beat with hard riding, sir.

66

Burgoyne opens the dispatches, and presently becomes absorbed in them. They are so serious as to take his attention completely from the court martial.

SERGEANT [*to Christy*] Now then. Attention; and take your hat off. [*He posts himself in charge of Christy, who stands on Burgoyne's side of the court*].

RICHARD [*in his usual bullying tone to Christy*] Dont be frightened, you fool: youre only wanted as a witness. Theyre not going to hang *you*.

SWINDON What's your name?

CHRISTY Christy.

RICHARD [*impatiently*] Christopher Dudgeon, you blatant idiot. Give your full name.

SWINDON Be silent, prisoner. You must not prompt the witness.

RICHARD Very well. But I warn you youll get nothing out of him unless you shake it out of him. He has been too well brought up by a pious mother to have any sense or manhood left in him.

BURGOYNE [*springing up and speaking to the sergeant in a startling voice*] Where is the man who brought these?

SERGEANT In the guard-room, sir.

Burgoyne goes out with a haste that sets the officers exchanging looks.

SWINDON [*to Christy*] Do you know Anthony Anderson, the Presbyterian minister?

CHRISTY Of course I do [*implying that Swindon must be an ass not to know it*].

SWINDON Is he here?

CHRISTY [*staring round*] I dont know.

SWINDON Do you see him?

CHRISTY No.

SWINDON You seem to know the prisoner?

CHRISTY Do you mean Dick?

SWINDON Which is Dick?

CHRISTY [*pointing to Richard*] Him.

SWINDON What is his name?

CHRISTY Dick.

RICHARD	Answer properly, you jumping jackass. What do they know about Dick?
CHRISTY	Well, you *are* Dick, aint you? What am I to say?
SWINDON	Address me, sir; and do you, prisoner, be silent. Tell us who the prisoner is.
CHRISTY	He's my brother Dick – Richard – Richard Dudgeon.
SWINDON	Your brother!
CHRISTY	Yes.
SWINDON	You are sure he is not Anderson.
CHRISTY	Who?
RICHARD	[*exasperatedly*] Me, me, me, you –
SWINDON	Silence, sir.
SERGEANT	[*shouting*] Silence.
RICHARD	[*impatiently*] Yah! [*To Christy*] He wants to know am I Minister Anderson. Tell him, and stop grinning like a zany.
CHRISTY	[*grinning more than ever*] *You* Pastor Anderson! [*To Swindon*] Why, Mr Anderson's a minister – a very good man; and Dick's a bad character: the respectable people wont speak to him. He's the bad brother: I'm the good one. [*The officers laugh outright. The soldiers grin*].
SWINDON	Who arrested this man?
SERGEANT	I did, sir. I found him in the minister's house, sitting at tea with the lady with his coat off, quite at home. If he isnt married to her, he ought to be.
SWINDON	Did he answer to the minister's name?
SERGEANT	Yes sir, but not to a minister's nature. You ask the chaplain, sir.
SWINDON	[*to Richard, threateningly*] So, sir, you have attempted to cheat us. And your name is Richard Dudgeon?
RICHARD	Youve found it out at last, have you?
SWINDON	Dudgeon is a name well known to us, eh?
RICHARD	Yes: Peter Dudgeon, whom you murdered, was my uncle.
SWINDON	Hm! [*He compresses his lips, and looks at Richard with vindictive gravity*].

CHRISTY   Are they going to hang you, Dick?

RICHARD   Yes. Get out: theyve done with you.

CHRISTY   And I may keep the china peacocks?

RICHARD   [*jumping up*] Get out. *Get* out, you blithering baboon, you. [*Christy flies, panicstricken*].

SWINDON   [*rising – all rise*] Since you have taken the minister's place, Richard Dudgeon, you shall go through with it. The execution will take place at 12 o'clock as arranged; and unless Anderson surrenders before then, you shall take his place on the gallows. Sergeant: take your man out.

JUDITH   [*distracted*] No, no –

SWINDON   [*fiercely, dreading a renewal of her entreaties*] Take that woman away.

RICHARD   [*springing across the table with a tiger-like bound, and seizing Swindon by the throat*] You infernal scoundrel –

The sergeant rushes to the rescue from one side, the soldiers from the other. They seize Richard and drag him back to his place. Swindon, who has been thrown supine on the table, rises, arranging his stock. He is about to speak, when he is anticipated by Burgoyne, who has just appeared at the door with two papers in his hand: a white letter and a blue dispatch.

BURGOYNE   [*advancing to the table, elaborately cool*] What is this? Whats happening? Mr Anderson: I'm astonished at you.

RICHARD   I am sorry I disturbed you, General. I merely wanted to strangle your understrapper there. [*Breaking out violently at Swindon*] Why do you raise the devil in me by bullying the woman like that? You oatmeal faced dog, I'd twist your cursed head off with the greatest satisfaction. [*He puts out his hands to the sergeant*] Here: handcuff me, will you; or I'll not undertake to keep my fingers off him.

The sergeant takes out a pair of handcuffs and looks to Burgoyne for instructions.

BURGOYNE   Have you addressed profane language to the lady, Major Swindon?

SWINDON   [*very angry*] No, sir, certainly not. That question should not have been put to me. I ordered the woman to be removed, as she was disorderly; and the fellow sprang at me. Put away those handcuffs. I am perfectly able to take care of myself.

RICHARD   Now you talk like a man, I have no quarrel with you.

BURGOYNE   Mr Anderson –

SWINDON   His name is Dudgeon, sir, Richard Dudgeon. He is an impostor.

BURGOYNE   [*brusquely*] Nonsense, sir: you hanged Dudgeon at Springtown.

RICHARD   It was my uncle, General.

BURGOYNE   Oh, your uncle. [*To Swindon, handsomely*] I beg your pardon, Major Swindon. [*Swindon acknowledges the apology stiffly. Burgoyne turns to Richard*]. We are somewhat unfortunate in our relations with your family. Well, Mr Dudgeon, what I wanted to ask you is this. Who is [*reading the name from the letter*] William Maindeck Parshotter?

RICHARD   He is the Mayor of Springtown.

BURGOYNE   Is William – Maindeck and so on – a man of his word?

RICHARD   Is he selling you anything?

BURGOYNE   No.

RICHARD   Then you may depend on him.

BURGOYNE   Thank you, Mr – 'm Dudgeon. By the way, since you are not Mr Anderson, do we still – eh, Major Swindon? [*meaning "do we still hang him?"*]

RICHARD   The arrangements are unaltered, General.

BURGOYNE   Ah, indeed. I am sorry. Good morning, Mr Dudgeon. Good morning, madam.

RICHARD   [*interrupting Judith almost fiercely as she is about to make some wild appeal, and taking her arm resolutely*] Not one word more. Come.

She looks imploringly at him, but is overborne by his determination. They are marched out by the four soldiers: the sergeant, very sulky, walking between Swindon and Richard, whom he watches as if he were a dangerous animal.

BURGOYNE   Gentlemen: we need not detain you. Major Swindon:

a word with you. [*The officers go out. Burgoyne waits with unruffled serenity until the last of them disappears. Then he becomes very grave, and addresses Swindon for the first time without his title*]. Swindon: do you know what this is [*shewing him the letter*]?

SWINDON   What?

BURGOYNE   A demand for a safe-conduct for an officer of their militia to come here and arrange terms with us.

SWINDON   Oh, they are giving in.

BURGOYNE   They add that they are sending the man who raised Springtown last night and drove us out; so that we may know that we are dealing with an officer of importance.

SWINDON   Pooh!

BURGOYNE   He will be fully empowered to arrange the terms of – guess what.

SWINDON   Their surrender, I hope.

BURGOYNE   No: our evacuation of the town. They offer us just six hours to clear out.

SWINDON   What monstrous impudence!

BURGOYNE   What shall we do, eh?

SWINDON   March on Springtown and strike a decisive blow at once.

BURGOYNE   [*quietly*] Hm! [*Turning to the door*] Come to the adjutant's office.

SWINDON   What for?

BURGOYNE   To write out that safe-conduct. [*He puts his hand to the door knob to open it*].

SWINDON   [*who has not budged*] General Burgoyne.

BURGOYNE   [*returning*] Sir?

SWINDON   It is my duty to tell you, sir, that I do not consider the threats of a mob of rebellious tradesmen a sufficient reason for our giving way.

BURGOYNE   [*imperturbable*] Suppose I resign my command to you, what will you do?

SWINDON   I will undertake to do what we have marched south from Quebec to do, and what General Howe has marched north from New York to do: effect a junction at Albany and wipe out the rebel army with our united forces.

BURGOYNE [*enigmatically*] And will you wipe out our enemies in London, too?

SWINDON In London! What enemies?

BURGOYNE [*forcibly*] Jobbery and snobbery, incompetence and Red Tape. [*He holds up the dispatch and adds, with despair in his face and voice*] I have just learnt, sir, that General Howe is still in New York.

SWINDON [*thunderstruck*] Good God! He has disobeyed orders!

BURGOYNE [*with sardonic calm*] He has received no orders, sir. Some gentleman in London forgot to dispatch them: he was leaving town for his holiday, I believe. To avoid upsetting his arrangements, England will lose her American colonies; and in a few days you and I will be at Saratoga with 5,000 men to face 18,000 rebels in an impregnable position.

SWINDON [*appalled*] Impossible?

BURGOYNE [*coldly*] I beg your pardon!

SWINDON I cant believe it! What will History say?

BURGOYNE History, sir, will tell lies, as usual. Come: we must send the safe-conduct. [*He goes out*].

SWINDON [*following distractedly*] My God, my God! We shall be wiped out.

As noon approaches there is excitement in the market place. The gallows which hangs there permanently for the terror of evildoers, with such minor advertizers and examples of crime as the pillory, the whipping post, and the stocks, has a new rope attached, with the noose hitched up to one of the uprights, out of reach of the boys. Its ladder, too, has been brought out and placed in position by the town beadle, who stands by to guard it from unauthorized climbing. The Websterbridge townsfolk are present in force, and in high spirits; for the news has spread that it is the devil's disciple and not the minister that King George and his terrible general are about to hang: consequently the execution can be enjoyed without any misgivings as to its righteousness, or to the cowardice of allowing it to take place without a struggle. There is even some fear of a disappointment as midday approaches and the arrival of the beadle with the ladder remains the only sign of preparation. But at last reassuring shouts of Here they come: Here they are, are heard; and a company of soldiers with fixed bayonets, half British infantry, half Hessians, tramp quickly into the middle of the market place, driving the crowd to the sides.

SERGEANT   Halt. Front. Dress. [*The soldiers change their column into a square enclosing the gallows, their petty officers, energetically led by the sergeant, hustling the persons who find themselves inside the square out at the corners*]. Now then! Out of it with you: out of it. Some o youll

73

get strung up yourselves presently. Form that square there, will you, you damned Hoosians. No use talkin German to them: talk to their toes with the butt ends of your muskets: theyll understand that. *Get* out of it, will you. [*He comes upon Judith, standing near the gallows*]. Now then: *youve* no call here.

JUDITH May I not stay? What harm am I doing?

SERGEANT I want none of your argufying. You ought to be ashamed of yourself, running to see a man hanged thats not your husband. And he's no better than yourself. I told my major he was a gentleman; and then he goes and tries to strangle him, and calls his blessed Majesty a lunatic. So out of it with you, double quick.

JUDITH Will you take these two silver dollars and let me stay?

The sergeant, without an instant's hesitation, looks quickly and furtively round as he shoots the money dexterously into his pocket. Then he raises his voice in virtuous indignation.

THE SERGEANT *Me* take money in the execution of my duty! Certainly not. Now I'll tell you what I'll do, to teach you to corrupt the King's officer. I'll put you under arrest until the execution's over. You just stand there; and dont let me see you as much as move from that spot until youre let. [*With a swift wink at her he points to the corner of the square behind the gallows on his right, and turns noisily away, shouting*] Now then, dress up and keep em back, will you.

Cries of Hush and Silence are heard among the towns-

folk; and the sound of a military band, playing the Dead March from Saul, is heard. The crowd becomes quiet at once; and the sergeant and petty officers, hurrying to the back of the square, with a few whispered orders and some stealthy hustling cause it to open and admit the funeral procession, which is protected from the crowd by a double file of soldiers. First come Burgoyne and Swindon, who, on entering the square, glance with distaste at the gallows, and avoid passing under it by wheeling a little to the right and stationing themselves on that side. Then Mr Brudenell, the chaplain, in his surplice, with his prayer book open in his hand, walking beside Richard, who is moody and disorderly. He walks doggedly through the gallows framework, and posts himself a little in front of it. Behind him comes the executioner, a stalwart soldier in his shirtsleeves. Following him, two soldiers haul a light military waggon. Finally comes the band, which posts itself at the back of the square, and finishes the Dead March. Judith, watching Richard painfully, steals down to the gallows, and stands leaning against its right post. During the conversation which follows, the two soldiers place the cart under the gallows, and stand by the shafts, which point backwards. The executioner takes a set of steps from the cart and places it ready for the prisoner to mount. Then he climbs the tall ladder which stands against the gallows, and cuts the string by which the rope is hitched up; so that the noose drops dangling over the cart, into which he steps as he descends.

RICHARD [*with suppressed impatience, to Brudenell*] Look here,

sir: this is no place for a man of your profession. Hadnt you better go away?

SWINDON I appeal to you, prisoner, if you have any sense of decency left, to listen to the ministrations of the chaplain, and pay due heed to the solemnity of the occasion.

THE CHAPLAIN [*gently reproving Richard*] Try to control yourself, and submit to the divine will. [*He lifts his book to proceed with the service*].

RICHARD Answer for your own will, sir, and those of your accomplices here [*indicating Burgoyne and Swindon*]: I see little divinity about them or you. You talk to me of Christianity when you are in the act of hanging your enemies. Was there ever such blasphemous nonsense! [*To Swindon, more rudely*] Youve got up the solemnity of the occasion, as you call it, to impress the people with your own dignity – Handel's music and a clergyman to make murder look like piety! Do you suppose *I* am going to help you? Youve asked me to choose the rope because you dont know your own trade well enough to shoot me properly. Well, hang away and have done with it.

SWINDON [*to the chaplain*] Can you do nothing with him, Mr Brudenell?

CHAPLAIN I will try, sir. [*Beginning to read*] Man that is born of woman hath –

RICHARD [*fixing his eyes on him*] "Thou shalt not kill."

The book drops in Brudenell's hands.

CHAPLAIN [*confessing his embarrassment*] What *am* I to say, Mr Dudgeon?

RICHARD Let me alone, man, cant you?

BURGOYNE [*with extreme urbanity*] I think, Mr Brudenell, that as the usual professional observations seem to strike Mr Dudgeon as incongruous under the circumstances, you had better omit them until – er – until Mr Dudgeon can no longer be inconvenienced by them. [*Brudenell, with a shrug, shuts his book and retires behind the gallows*]. You seem in a hurry, Mr Dudgeon.

RICHARD [*with the horror of death upon him*] Do you think this is a pleasant sort of thing to be kept waiting for? Youve made up your mind to commit murder: well, do it and have done with it.

BURGOYNE Mr Dudgeon: we are only doing this –

RICHARD Because youre paid to do it.

SWINDON You insolent – [*he swallows his rage*].

BURGOYNE [*with much charm of manner*] Ah, I am really sorry that you should think that, Mr Dudgeon. If you knew what my commission cost me, and what my pay is, you would think better of me. I should be glad to part from you on friendly terms.

RICHARD Hark ye, General Burgoyne. If you think that I like being hanged, youre mistaken. I dont like it; and I dont mean to pretend that I do. And if you think I'm obliged to you for hanging me in a gentlemanly way, youre wrong there too. I take the whole business in devilish bad part; and the only satisfaction I have in it is that youll feel a good deal meaner than I'll look when it's over. [*He turns away, and is striding to the cart when Judith advances and interposes with her arms stretched out to him. Richard, feeling that a very little will upset his self-possession, shrinks from her, crying*] What are you doing here? This is no place for you. [*She makes a gesture as if to touch him. He recoils impatiently*] No: go away, go away: youll unnerve me. Take her away, will you.

JUDITH Wont you bid me good-bye?

RICHARD [*allowing her to take his hand*] Oh good-bye, good-bye. Now go – go – quickly. [*She clings to his hand – will not be put off with so cold a last farewell – at last, as he tries to disengage himself, throws herself on his breast in agony*].

SWINDON [*angrily to the sergeant, who, alarmed at Judith's movement, has come from the back of the square to pull her back, and stopped irresolutely on finding that he is too late*] How is this? Why is she inside the lines?

SERGEANT [*guiltily*] I dunno, sir. She's that artful – cant keep her away.

BURGOYNE You were bribed.

SERGEANT [*protesting*] No, sir –

SWINDON [*severely*] Fall back. [*He obeys*].

RICHARD [*imploringly to those around him, and finally to Burgoyne, as the least stolid of them*] Take her away. Do you think I want a woman near me now?

BURGOYNE [*going to Judith and taking her hand*] Here, madam: you had better keep inside the lines; but stand here behind us; and dont look.

Richard, with a great sobbing sigh of relief as she releases him and turns to Burgoyne, flies for refuge to the cart and mounts into it. The executioner takes off his coat and pinions him.

JUDITH [*resisting Burgoyne quietly and drawing her hand away*] No: I must stay. I wont look. [*She goes to the right of the gallows. She tries to look at Richard, but turns away with a frightful shudder, and falls on her knees in prayer. Brudenell comes towards her from the back of the square*].

BURGOYNE [*nodding approvingly as she kneels*] Ah, quite so. Do not disturb her, Mr Brudenell: that will do very nicely. [*Brudenell nods also, and withdraws a little, watching her sympathetically. Burgoyne resumes his former position, and takes out a handsome gold chronometer*]. Now then, are those preparations made? We must not detain Mr Dudgeon.

By this time Richard's hands are bound behind him; and the noose is round his neck. The two soldiers take the shaft of the waggon, ready to pull it away. The executioner, standing in the cart behind Richard, makes a sign to the sergeant.

SERGEANT [*to Burgoyne*] Ready, sir.

BURGOYNE Have you anything more to say, Mr Dudgeon? It wants two minutes of twelve still.

RICHARD [*in the strong voice of a man who has conquered the bitterness of death*] Your watch is two minutes slow by the town clock, which I can see from here, General. [*The town clock strikes the first stroke of twelve. Involuntarily the people flinch at the sound, and a subdued groan breaks from them*]. Amen! my life for the world's future!

ANDERSON [*shouting as he rushes into the market place*] Amen; and stop the execution. [*He bursts through the line of sol-

diers opposite Burgoyne, and rushes, panting, to the gallows]. I am Anthony Anderson, the man you want.

The crowd, intensely excited, listens with all its ears. Judith, half rising, stares at him; then lifts her hands like one whose dearest prayer has been granted.

SWINDON   Indeed. Then you are just in time to take your place on the gallows. Arrest him.

At a sign from the sergeant, two soldiers come forward to seize Anderson.

ANDERSON   [*thrusting a paper under Swindon's nose*] There's my safe-conduct, sir.

SWINDON   [*taken aback*] Safe-conduct! Are you – !

ANDERSON   [*emphatically*] I am. [*The two soldiers take him by the elbows*]. Tell these men to take their hands off me.

SWINDON   [*to the men*] Let him go.

SERGEANT   Fall back.

The two men return to their places. The townsfolk raise a cheer; and begin to exchange exultant looks, with a presentiment of triumph as they see their Pastor speaking with their enemies in the gate.

ANDERSON   [*exhaling a deep breath of relief, and dabbing his perspiring brow with his handkerchief*] Thank God, I was in time!

BURGOYNE   [*calm as ever, and still watch in hand*] Ample time, sir.

79

Plenty of time. I should never dream of hanging any gentleman by an American clock. [*He puts up his watch*].

ANDERSON   Yes: we are some minutes ahead of you already, General. Now tell them to take the rope from the neck of that American citizen.

BURGOYNE   [*to the executioner in the cart – very politely*] Kindly undo Mr Dudgeon.

The executioner takes the rope from Richard's neck, unties his hands, and helps him on with his coat.

JUDITH   [*stealing timidly to Anderson*] Tony.

ANDERSON   [*putting his arm round her shoulders and bantering her affectionately*] Well, what do you think of your husband *now*, eh? – eh?? – eh???

JUDITH   I am ashamed – [*she hides her face against his breast*].

BURGOYNE   [*to Swindon*] You look disappointed, Major Swindon.

SWINDON   You look defeated, General Burgoyne.

BURGOYNE   I am, sir; and I am humane enough to be glad of it. [*Richard jumps down from the cart, Brudenell offering his hand to help him, and runs to Anderson, whose left hand he shakes heartily, the right being occupied by Judith*]. By the way, Mr Anderson, I do not quite understand. The safe-conduct was for a commander of the militia. I understand you are a – [*He looks as pointedly as his good manners permit at the riding boots, the pistols, and Richard's coat, and adds*] – a clergyman.

ANDERSON   [*between Judith and Richard*] Sir: it is in the hour of trial that a man finds his true profession. This foolish young man [*placing his hand on Richard's shoulder*] boasted himself the Devil's Disciple; but when the hour of trial came to him, he found that it was his destiny to suffer and be faithful to the death. I thought myself a decent minister of the gospel of peace; but when the hour of trial came to me, I found that it was my destiny to be a man of action, and that my place was amid the thunder of the captains and the shouting. So I am starting life at fifty as Captain Anthony Anderson of the Springtown militia; and the Devil's Disciple here will start presently as the Reverend Richard Dudgeon, and wag his pow in my old pulpit, and give good advice to this silly senti-mental little wife of mine [*putting his other hand on her shoulder. She steals a glance at Richard to see how the prospect pleases him*]. Your mother told me, Rich-ard, that I should never have chosen Judith if I'd been born for the ministry. I am afraid she was right; so, by your leave, you may keep my coat and I'll keep yours.

RICHARD Minister – I should say Captain. I have behaved like a fool.

JUDITH Like a hero.

RICHARD Much the same thing, perhaps. [*With some bitterness towards himself*] But no: if I had been any good, I should have done for you what you did for me, in-stead of making a vain sacrifice.

ANDERSON Not vain, my boy. It takes all sorts to make a world – saints as well as soldiers. [*Turning to Burgoyne*] And now, General, time presses; and America is in a hurry. Have you realized that though you may occupy towns and win battles, you cannot conquer a nation?

BURGOYNE My good sir, without a Conquest you cannot have an aristocracy. Come and settle the matter at my quarters.

ANDERSON At your service, sir. [*To Richard*] See Judith home for me, will you, my boy. [*He hands her over to him*]. Now, General. [*He goes busily up the market place towards the Town Hall, leaving Judith and Richard to-gether. Burgoyne follows him a step or two; then checks himself and turns to Richard*].

BURGOYNE Oh, by the way, Mr Dudgeon, I shall be glad to see you at lunch at half-past one. [*He pauses a moment, and adds, with politely veiled slyness*] Bring Mrs Anderson, if she will be so good. [*To Swindon, who is fuming*] Take it quietly, Major Swindon: your friend the British soldier can stand up to anything except the British War Office. [*He follows Anderson*].

SERGEANT [*to Swindon*] What orders, sir?

SWINDON [*savagely*] Orders! What use are orders now? There's no army. Back to quarters; and be d—— [*He turns on his heel and goes*].

SERGEANT [*pugnacious and patriotic, repudiating the idea of defeat*] 'Tention. Now then: cock up your chins, and shew em you dont care a damn for em. Slope arms! Fours! Wheel! Quick march!

The drum marks time with a tremendous bang; the band strikes up British Grenadiers; and the sergeant, Brudenell, and the English troops march off defiantly to their quarters. The townsfolk press in behind, and follow them up the market, jeering at them; and the town band, a very primitive affair, brings up the rear, playing Yankee Doodle. Essie, who comes in with them, runs to Richard.

ESSIE Oh, Dick!

RICHARD [*good-humoredly, but wilfully*] Now, now: come, come! I dont mind being hanged; but I will not be cried over.

ESSIE No, I promise. I'll be good. [*She tries to restrain her tears, but cannot*]. I – I want to see where the soldiers are going to. [*She goes a little way up the market, pretending to look after the crowd*].

JUDITH Promise me you will never tell him.

RICHARD Dont be afraid.

They shake hands on it.

ESSIE [*calling to them*] Theyre coming back. They want you.

Jubilation in the market. The townsfolk surge back again in wild enthusiasm with their band, and hoist Richard on their shoulders, cheering him.

CÆSAR AND CLEOPATRA

ACT 1

An October night on the Syrian border of Egypt towards the end of the XXXIII Dynasty, in the year 706 by Roman computation, afterwards reckoned by Christian computation as 48 B.C. A great radiance of silver fire, the dawn of a moonlit night, is rising in the east. The stars and the cloudless sky are our own contemporaries, nineteen and a half centuries younger than we know them; but you would not guess that from their appearance. Below them are two notable drawbacks of civilization: a palace, and soldiers. The palace, an old, low, Syrian building of whitened mud, is not so ugly as Buckingham Palace; and the officers in the courtyard are more highly civilized than modern English officers: for example, they do not dig up the corpses of their dead enemies and mutilate them, as we dug up Cromwell and the Mahdi. They are in two groups: one intent on the gambling of their captain Belzanor, a warrior of fifty, who, with his spear on the ground beside his knee, is stooping to throw dice with a sly-looking young Persian recruit; the other gathered about a guardsman who has just finished telling a naughty story (still current in English barracks) at which they are laughing uproariously. They are about a dozen in number, all highly aristocratic young Egyptian guardsmen, handsomely equipped with weapons and armor, very unEnglish in

point of not being ashamed of and uncomfortable in their professional dress; on the contrary, rather ostentatiously and arrogantly warlike, as valuing themselves on their military caste.

Belzanor is a typical veteran, tough and wilful; prompt, capable and crafty where brute force will serve; helpless and boyish when it will not: an effective sergeant, an incompetent general, a deplorable dictator. Would, if influentially connected, be employed in the two last capacities by a modern European State on the strength of his success in the first. Is rather to be pitied just now in view of the fact that Julius Cæsar is invading his country. Not knowing this, is intent on his game with the Persian, whom, as a foreigner, he considers quite capable of cheating him.

His subalterns are mostly handsome young fellows whose interest in the game and the story symbolize with tolerable completeness the main interests in life of which they are conscious. Their spears are leaning against the walls, or lying on the ground ready to their hands. The corner of the courtyard forms a triangle of which one side is the front of the palace, with a doorway, the other a wall with a gateway. The storytellers are on the palace side: the gamblers, on the gateway side. Close to the gateway, against the wall, is a stone block high enough to enable a Nubian sentinel, standing on it, to look over the wall. The yard is lighted by a torch stuck in the wall. As the laughter from the group round the storyteller dies away, the kneeling Persian, winning the throw, snatches up the stake from the ground.

BELZANOR By Apis, Persian, thy gods are good to thee.

THE PERSIAN Try yet again, O captain. Double or quits!

BELZANOR No more. I am not in the vein.

THE SENTINEL [*poising his javelin as he peers over the wall*] Stand. Who goes there?

They all start, listening. A strange voice replies from without.

VOICE The bearer of evil tidings.

BELZANOR [*calling to the sentry*] Pass him.

THE SENTINEL [*grounding his javelin*] Draw near, O bearer of evil tidings.

88

BELZANOR [*pocketing the dice and picking up his spear*] Let us receive this man with honor. He bears evil tidings.

*The guardsmen seize their spears and gather about the
gate, leaving a way through for the new comer.*

PERSIAN [*rising from his knee*] Are evil tidings, then, so hon-
orable?

BELZANOR O barbarous Persian, hear my instruction. In Egypt
the bearer of good tidings is sacrificed to the gods as
a thank offering; but no god will accept the blood of
the messenger of evil. When we have good tidings, we
are careful to send them in the mouth of the cheapest
slave we can find. Evil tidings are borne by young
noblemen who desire to bring themselves into notice.
[*They join the rest at the gate*].

SENTINEL Pass, O young captain; and bow the head in the House
of the Queen.

VOICE Go anoint thy javelin with fat of swine, O Blacka-
moor; for before morning the Romans will make thee
eat it to the very butt.

*The owner of the voice, a fairhaired dandy, dressed in a
different fashion from that affected by the guardsmen,
but no less extravagantly, comes through the gateway
laughing. He is somewhat battlestained; and his left
forearm, bandaged, comes through a torn sleeve. In his
right hand he carries a Roman sword in its sheath. He
swaggers down the courtyard, the Persian on his right,
Belzanor on his left, and the guardsmen crowding down
behind him.*

BELZANOR Who art thou that laughest in the House of Cleopatra
the Queen, and in the teeth of Belzanor, the captain
of her guard?

NEW COMER I am Bel Affris, descended from the gods.

BELZANOR [*ceremoniously*] Hail, cousin!

ALL [*except the Persian*] Hail, cousin!

PERSIAN All the Queen's guards are descended from the gods,
O stranger, save myself. I am Persian, and descended
from many kings.

BEL AFFRIS [*to the guardsmen*] Hail, cousins! [*To the Persian, con-
descendingly*] Hail, mortal!

BELZANOR You have been in battle, Bel Affris; and you are a soldier among soldiers. You will not let the Queen's women have the first of your tidings.

BEL AFFRIS I have no tidings, except that we shall have our throats cut presently, women, soldiers, and all.

PERSIAN [*to Belzanor*] I told you so.

THE SENTINEL [*who has been listening*] Woe, alas!

BEL AFFRIS [*calling to him*] Peace, peace, poor Ethiop: destiny is with the gods who painted thee black. [*To Belzanor*] What has this mortal [*indicating the Persian*] told you?

BELZANOR He says that the Roman Julius Cæsar, who has landed on our shores with a handful of followers, will make himself master of Egypt. He is afraid of the Roman soldiers. [*The guardsmen laugh with boisterous scorn*]. Peasants, brought up to scare crows and follow the plough! Sons of smiths and millers and tanners! And we nobles, consecrated to arms, descended from the gods!

PERSIAN Belzanor: the gods are not always good to their poor relations.

BELZANOR [*hotly, to the Persian*] Man to man, are we worse than the slaves of Cæsar?

BEL AFFRIS [*stepping between them*] Listen, cousin. Man to man, we Egyptians are as gods above the Romans.

GUARDSMEN [*exultantly*] Aha!

BEL AFFRIS But this Cæsar does not pit man against man: he throws a legion at you where you are weakest as he throws a stone from a catapult; and that legion is as a man with one head, a thousand arms, and no religion. I have fought against them; and I know.

BELZANOR [*derisively*] Were you frightened, cousin?

The guardsmen roar with laughter, their eyes sparkling at the wit of their captain.

BEL AFFRIS No, cousin; but I was beaten. They were frightened (perhaps); but they scattered us like chaff.

The guardsmen, much damped, utter a growl of contemptuous disgust.

BELZANOR Could you not die?

BEL AFFRIS No: that was too easy to be worthy of a descendant of the gods. Besides, there was no time: all was over in a moment. The attack came just where we least expected it.

BELZANOR That shews that the Romans are cowards.

BEL AFFRIS They care nothing about cowardice, these Romans: they fight to win. The pride and honor of war are nothing to them.

PERSIAN Tell us the tale of the battle. What befell?

GUARDSMEN [*gathering eagerly round Bel Affris*] Ay: the tale of the battle.

BEL AFFRIS Know then, that I am a novice in the guard of the temple of Ra in Memphis, serving neither Cleopatra nor her brother Ptolemy, but only the high gods. We went a journey to inquire of Ptolemy why he had driven Cleopatra into Syria, and how we of Egypt should deal with the Roman Pompey, newly come to our shores after his defeat by Cæsar at Pharsalia. What, think ye, did we learn? Even that Cæsar is coming also in hot pursuit of his foe, and that Ptolemy has slain Pompey, whose severed head he holds in readiness to present to the conqueror. [*Sensation among the guardsmen*]. Nay, more: we found that Cæsar is already come; for we had not made half a day's journey on our way back when we came upon a city rabble flying from his legions, whose landing they had gone out to withstand.

BELZANOR And ye, the temple guard! did ye not withstand these legions?

BEL AFFRIS What man could, that we did. But there came the sound of a trumpet whose voice was as the cursing of a black mountain. Then saw we a moving wall of shields coming towards us. You know how the heart burns when you charge a fortified wall; but how if the fortified wall were to charge *you*?

THE PERSIAN [*exulting in having told them so*] Did I not say it?

BEL AFFRIS When the wall came nigh, it changed into a line of men – common fellows enough, with helmets, leather tunics, and breastplates. Every man of them flung his javelin: the one that came my way drove through my shield as through a papyrus – lo there! [*he points to the bandage on his left arm*] and would have gone through my neck had I not stooped. They were

91

charging at the double then, and were upon us with short swords almost as soon as their javelins. When a man is close to you with such a sword, you can do nothing with our weapons: they are all too long.

THE PERSIAN   What did you do?

BEL AFFRIS   Doubled my fist and smote my Roman on the sharpness of his jaw. He was but mortal after all: he lay down in a stupor; and I took his sword and laid it on. [*Drawing the sword*] Lo! a Roman sword with Roman blood on it!

GUARDSMEN   [*approvingly*] Good! [*They take the sword and hand it round, examining it curiously*].

THE PERSIAN   And your men?

BEL AFFRIS   Fled. Scattered like sheep.

BELZANOR   [*furiously*] The cowardly slaves! Leaving the descendants of the gods to be butchered!

BEL AFFRIS   [*with acid coolness*] The descendants of the gods did not stay to be butchered, cousin. The battle was not to the strong; but the race was to the swift. The Romans, who have no chariots, sent a cloud of horsemen in pursuit, and slew multitudes. Then our high priest's captain rallied a dozen descendants of the gods and exhorted us to die fighting. I said to myself: surely it is safer to stand than to lose my breath and be stabbed in the back; so I joined our captain and stood. Then the Romans treated us with respect; for no man attacks a lion when the field is full of sheep, except for the pride and honor of war, of which these Romans know nothing. So we escaped with our lives; and I am come to warn you that you must open your gates to Cæsar; for his advance guard is scarce an hour behind me; and not an Egyptian warrior is left standing between you and his legions.

THE SENTINEL   Woe, alas! [*He throws down his javelin and flies into the palace*].

BELZANOR   Nail him to the door, quick! [*The guardsmen rush for him with their spears; but he is too quick for them*]. Now this news will run through the palace like fire through stubble.

BEL AFFRIS   What shall we do to save the women from the Romans?

92

BELZANOR	Why not kill them?
PERSIAN	Because we should have to pay blood money for some of them. Better let the Romans kill them: it is cheaper.
BELZANOR	[*awestruck at his brain power*] O subtle one! O serpent!
BEL AFFRIS	But your Queen?
BELZANOR	True: we must carry off Cleopatra.
BEL AFFRIS	Will ye not await her command?
BELZANOR	Command! a girl of sixteen! Not we. At Memphis ye deem her a Queen: here we know better. I will take her on the crupper of my horse. When we soldiers have carried her out of Cæsar's reach, then the priests and the nurses and the rest of them can pretend she is a queen again, and put their commands into her mouth.
PERSIAN	Listen to me, Belzanor.
BELZANOR	Speak, O subtle beyond thy years.
THE PERSIAN	Cleopatra's brother Ptolemy is at war with her. Let us sell her to him.
GUARDSMEN	O subtle one! O serpent!
BELZANOR	We dare not. We are descended from the gods; but Cleopatra is descended from the river Nile; and the lands of our fathers will grow no grain if the Nile rises not to water them. Without our father's gifts we should live the lives of dogs.
PERSIAN	It is true: the Queen's guard cannot live on its pay. But hear me further, O ye kinsmen of Osiris.
GUARDSMEN	Speak, O subtle one. Hear the serpent begotten!
PERSIAN	Have I heretofore spoken truly to you of Cæsar, when you thought I mocked you?
GUARDSMEN	Truly, truly.
BELZANOR	[*reluctantly admitting it*] So Bel Affris says.
PERSIAN	Hear more of him, then. This Cæsar is a great lover of women: he makes them his friends and counsellors.
BELZANOR	Faugh! This rule of women will be the ruin of Egypt.
THE PERSIAN	Let it rather be the ruin of Rome! Cæsar grows old now: he is past fifty and full of labors and battles. He is too old for the young women; and the old women are too wise to worship him.

93

BEL AFFRIS	Take heed, Persian. Cæsar is by this time almost within earshot.
PERSIAN	Cleopatra is not yet a woman: neither is she wise. But she already troubles men's wisdom.
BELZANOR	Ay: that is because she is descended from the river Nile and a black kitten of the sacred White Cat. What then?
PERSIAN	Why, sell her secretly to Ptolemy, and then offer ourselves to Cæsar as volunteers to fight for the overthrow of her brother and the rescue of our Queen, the Great Granddaughter of the Nile.
GUARDSMEN	O serpent!
PERSIAN	He will listen to us if we come with her picture in our mouths. He will conquer and kill her brother, and reign in Egypt with Cleopatra for his Queen. And we shall be her guard.
GUARDSMEN	O subtlest of all the serpents! O admiration! O wisdom!
BEL AFFRIS	He will also have arrived before you have done talking, O word spinner.
BELZANOR	That is true. [*An affrighted uproar in the palace interrupts him*]. Quick: the flight has begun: guard the door. [*They rush to the door and form a cordon before it with their spears. A mob of women-servants and nurses surges out. Those in front recoil from the spears, screaming to those behind to keep back. Belzanor's voice dominates the disturbance as he shouts*] Back there. In again, unprofitable cattle.
GUARDSMEN	Back, unprofitable cattle.
BELZANOR	Send us out Ftatateeta, the Queen's chief nurse.
THE WOMEN	[*calling into the palace*] Ftatateeta, Ftatateeta. Come, come. Speak to Belzanor.
A WOMAN	Oh, keep back. You are thrusting me on the spearheads.

A huge grim woman, her face covered with a network of tiny wrinkles, and her eyes old, large, and wise; sinewy handed, very tall, very strong; with the mouth of a bloodhound and the jaws of a bulldog, appears on the threshold. She is dressed like a person of consequence in the palace, and confronts the guardsmen insolently.

FTATATEETA   Make way for the Queen's chief nurse.

BELZANOR   [*with solemn arrogance*] Ftatateeta: I am Belzanor, the captain of the Queen's guard, descended from the gods.

FTATATEETA   [*retorting his arrogance with interest*] Belzanor: I am Ftatateeta, the Queen's chief nurse; and your divine ancestors were proud to be painted on the wall in the pyramids of the kings whom my fathers served.

The women laugh triumphantly.

BELZANOR   [*with grim humor*] Ftatateeta: daughter of a long-tongued, swivel-eyed chameleon, the Romans are at hand. [*A cry of terror from the women: they would fly but for the spears*]. Not even the descendants of the gods can resist them; for they have each man seven arms, each carrying seven spears. The blood in their veins is boiling quicksilver; and their wives become mothers in three hours, and are slain and eaten the next day.

A shudder of horror from the women. Ftatateeta, despising them and scorning the soldiers, pushes her way through the crowd and confronts the spear points undismayed.

FTATATEETA   Then fly and save yourselves, O cowardly sons of the cheap clay gods that are sold to fish porters; and leave us to shift for ourselves.

BELZANOR   Not until you have first done our bidding, O terror of manhood. Bring out Cleopatra the Queen to us; and then go whither you will.

FTATATEETA   [*with a derisive laugh*] Now I know why the gods have taken her out of our hands. [*The guardsmen start and look at one another*]. Know, thou foolish soldier, that the Queen has been missing since an hour past sundown.

BELZANOR   [*furiously*] Hag: you have hidden her to sell to Cæsar or her brother. [*He grasps her by the left wrist, and drags her, helped by a few of the guard, to the middle of the courtyard, where, as they fling her on her knees, he draws a murderous looking knife*]. Where is she? Where is she? or – [*he threatens to cut her throat*].

FTATATEETA   [*savagely*] Touch me, dog; and the Nile will not rise on your fields for seven times seven years of famine.

BELZANOR   [*frightened, but desperate*] I will sacrifice: I will pay. Or stay. [*To the Persian*] You, O subtle one: your father's lands lie far from the Nile. Slay her.

PERSIAN   [*threatening her with his knife*] Persia has but one god; yet he loves the blood of old women. Where is Cleopatra?

FTATATEETA   Persian: as Osiris lives, I do not know. I chid her for bringing evil days upon us by talking to the sacred cats of the priests, and carrying them in her arms. I told her she would be left alone here when the Romans came as a punishment for her disobedience. And now she is gone – run away – hidden. I speak the truth. I call Osiris to witness –

THE WOMEN   [*protesting officiously*] She speaks the truth, Belzanor.

BELZANOR   You have frightened the child: she is hiding. Search – quick – into the palace – search every corner.

The guards, led by Belzanor, shoulder their way into the palace through the flying crowd of women, who escape through the courtyard gate.

FTATATEETA   [*screaming*] Sacrilege! Men in the Queen's chambers! Sa – [*her voice dies away as the Persian puts his knife to her throat*].

BEL AFFRIS   [*laying a hand on Ftatateeta's left shoulder*] Forbear her yet a moment, Persian. [*To Ftatateeta, very sig-*

96

	nificantly] Mother: your gods are asleep or away hunting; and the sword is at your throat. Bring us to where the Queen is hid, and you shall live.
FTATATEETA	[*contemptuously*] Who shall stay the sword in the hand of a fool, if the high gods put it there? Listen to me, ye young men without understanding. Cleopatra fears me; but she fears the Romans more. There is but one power greater in her eyes than the wrath of the Queen's nurse and the cruelty of Cæsar; and that is the power of the Sphinx that sits in the desert watching the way to the sea. What she would have it know, she tells into the ears of the sacred cats; and on her birthday she sacrifices to it and decks it with poppies. Go ye therefore into the desert and seek Cleopatra in the shadow of the Sphinx; and on your heads see to it that no harm comes to her.
BEL AFFRIS	[*to the Persian*] May we believe this, O subtle one?
PERSIAN	Which way come the Romans?
BEL AFFRIS	Over the desert, from the sea, by this very Sphinx.
PERSIAN	[*to Ftatateeta*] O mother of guile! O aspic's tongue! You have made up this tale so that we two may go into the desert and perish on the spears of the Romans. [*Lifting his knife*] Taste death.
FTATATEETA	Not from thee, baby. [*She snatches his ankle from under him and flies stooping along the palace wall, vanishing in the darkness within its precinct. Bel Affris roars with laughter as the Persian tumbles. The guardsmen rush out of the palace with Belzanor and a mob of fugitives, mostly carrying bundles*].

PERSIAN   Have you found Cleopatra?

BELZANOR   She is gone. We have searched every corner.

THE NUBIAN   [*appearing at the door of the palace*] Woe! Alas! Fly,
SENTINEL   fly!

BELZANOR   What is the matter now?

SENTINEL   The sacred white cat has been stolen.

ALL   Woe! woe! [*General panic. They all fly with cries of
consternation. The torch is thrown down and extin-
guished in the rush. Darkness. The noise of the fugitives
dies away. Dead silence. Suspense. Then the blackness
and stillness break softly into silver mist and strange
airs as the windswept harp of Memnon plays at the
dawning of the moon. It rises full over the desert; and a
vast horizon comes into relief, broken by a huge shape
which soon reveals itself in the spreading radiance as a
Sphinx pedestalled on the sands. The light still clears,
until the upraised eyes of the image are distinguished
looking straight forward and upward in infinite fearless
vigil, and a mass of color between its great paws defines
itself as a heap of red poppies on which a girl lies motionless, her silken vest heaving gently and regularly with
the breathing of a dreamless sleeper, and her braided
hair glittering in a shaft of moonlight like a bird's wing.*

*Suddenly there comes from afar a vaguely fearful sound
(it might be the bellow of a Minotaur softened by great
distance) and Memnon's music stops. Silence: then a
few faint high-ringing trumpet notes. Then silence again.
Then a man comes from the south with stealing steps,
ravished by the mystery of the night, all wonder, and
halts, lost in contemplation, opposite the left flank of the
Sphinx, whose bosom, with its burden, is hidden from
him by its massive shoulder.*

THE MAN   Hail, Sphinx: salutation from Julius Cæsar! I have
wandered in many lands, seeking the lost regions from
which my birth into this world exiled me, and the
company of creatures such as I myself. I have found
flocks and pastures, men and cities, but no other
Cæsar, no air native to me, no man kindred to me,
none who can do my day's deed, and think my
night's thought. In the little world yonder, Sphinx,
my place is as high as yours in this great desert; only I
wander, and you sit still; I conquer, and you endure;

I work and wonder, you watch and wait; I look up
and am dazzled, look down and am darkened, look
round and am puzzled, whilst your eyes never turn
from looking out – out of the world – to the lost
region – the home from which we have strayed.
Sphinx, you and I, strangers to the race of men, are
no strangers to one another: have I not been conscious of you and of this place since I was born? Rome
is a madman's dream: this is my Reality. These
starry lamps of yours I have seen from afar in Gaul,
in Britain, in Spain, in Thessaly, signalling great
secrets to some eternal sentinel below, whose post I
never could find. And here at last is their sentinel –
an image of the constant and immortal part of my life,
silent, full of thoughts, alone in the silver desert.
Sphinx, Sphinx: I have climbed mountains at night
to hear in the distance the stealthy footfall of the
winds that chase your sands in forbidden play – our
invisible children, O Sphinx, laughing in whispers.
My way hither was the way of destiny; for I am he of
whose genius you are the symbol: part brute, part
woman, and part god – nothing of man in me at all.
Have I read your riddle, Sphinx?

THE GIRL [who has wakened, and peeped cautiously from her nest
to see who is speaking] Old gentleman.

CÆSAR [starting violently, and clutching his sword] Immortal
gods!

THE GIRL Old gentleman: dont run away.

CÆSAR [stupefied] "Old gentleman: dont run away"! ! ! This!
to Julius Cæsar!

THE GIRL [urgently] Old gentleman.

CÆSAR Sphinx: you presume on your centuries. I am
younger than you, though your voice is but a girl's
voice as yet.

THE GIRL Climb up here, quickly; or the Romans will come and
eat you.

CÆSAR [running forward past the Sphinx's shoulder, and seeing
her] A child at its breast! a divine child!

THE GIRL Come up quickly. You must get up at its side and
creep round.

99

CÆSAR [*amazed*] Who are you?

THE GIRL Cleopatra, Queen of Egypt.

CÆSAR Queen of the Gypsies, you mean.

CLEOPATRA You must not be disrespectful to me, or the Sphinx will let the Romans eat you. Come up. It is quite cosy here.

CÆSAR [*to himself*] What a dream! What a magnificent dream! Only let me not wake, and I will conquer ten continents to pay for dreaming it out to the end. [*He climbs to the Sphinx's flank, and presently reappears to her on the pedestal, stepping round its right shoulder*].

CLEOPATRA Take care. That's right. Now sit down: you may have its other paw. [*She seats herself comfortably on its left paw*]. It is very powerful and will protect us; but [*shivering, and with plaintive loneliness*] it would not take any notice of me or keep me company. I am glad you have come: I was very lonely. Did you happen to see a white cat anywhere?

CÆSAR [*sitting slowly down on the right paw in extreme wonderment*] Have you lost one?

CLEOPATRA Yes: the sacred white cat: is it not dreadful? I brought him here to sacrifice him to the Sphinx; but when we got a little way from the city a black cat called him, and he jumped out of my arms and ran away to it. Do you think that the black cat can have been my great-great-great-grandmother?

CÆSAR [*staring at her*] Your great-great-great-grandmother! Well, why not? Nothing would surprise me on this night of nights.

CLEOPATRA I think it must have been. My great-grandmother's great-grandmother was a black kitten of the sacred white cat; and the river Nile made her his seventh wife. That is why my hair is so wavy. And I always want to be let do as I like, no matter whether it is the will of the gods or not: that is because my blood is made with Nile water.

CÆSAR What are you doing here at this time of night? Do you live here?

CLEOPATRA Of course not: I am the Queen: and I shall live in the palace at Alexandria when I have killed my brother, who drove me out of it. When I am old enough I shall do just what I like. I shall be able to poison the slaves and see them wriggle, and pretend to Ftatateeta that she is going to be put into the fiery furnace.

CÆSAR Hm! Meanwhile why are you not at home and in bed?

CLEOPATRA Because the Romans are coming to eat us all. *You* are not at home and in bed either.

CÆSAR [*with conviction*] Yes I am. I live in a tent; and I am now in that tent, fast asleep and dreaming. Do you suppose that I believe you are real, you impossible little dream witch?

CLEOPATRA [*giggling and leaning trustfully towards him*] You are a funny old gentleman. I like you.

CÆSAR Ah, that spoils the dream. Why dont you dream that I am young?

CLEOPATRA I wish you were; only I think I should be more afraid of you. I like men, especially young men with round strong arms; but I am afraid of them. You are old and rather thin and stringy; but you have a nice voice; and I like to have somebody to talk to, though I think you are a little mad. It is the moon that makes you talk to yourself in that silly way.

CÆSAR What! you heard that, did you? I was saying my prayers to the great Sphinx.

CLEOPATRA But this isnt the great Sphinx.

CÆSAR [*much disappointed, looking up at the statue*] What!

CLEOPATRA This is only a dear little kitten of a Sphinx. Why, the great Sphinx is so big that it has a temple between its paws. This is my pet Sphinx. Tell me: do you think the Romans have any sorcerers who could take us away from the Sphinx by magic?

CÆSAR Why? Are you afraid of the Romans?

CLEOPATRA [*very seriously*] Oh, they would eat us if they caught us. They are barbarians. Their chief is called Julius Cæsar. His father was a tiger and his mother a burning mountain; and his nose is like an elephant's trunk. [*Cæsar involuntarily rubs his nose*]. They all have long noses, and ivory tusks, and little tails, and seven arms with a hundred arrows in each; and they live on human flesh.

101

CÆSAR Would you like me to shew you a real Roman?

CLEOPATRA [terrified] No. You are frightening me.

CÆSAR No matter: this is only a dream –

CLEOPATRA [excitedly] It is not a dream: it is not a dream. See, see. [She plucks a pin from her hair and jabs it repeatedly into his arm].

CÆSAR Ffff – Stop. [Wrathfully] How dare you?

CLEOPATRA [abashed] You said you were dreaming. [Whimpering] I only wanted to shew you –

CÆSAR [gently] Come, come: dont cry. A queen mustnt cry. [He rubs his arm, wondering at the reality of the smart]. Am I awake? [He strikes his hand against the Sphinx to test its solidity. It feels so real that he begins to be alarmed, and says perplexedly] Yes, I – [quite panic-stricken] no: impossible: madness, madness! [Desperately] Back to camp – to camp [He rises to spring down from the pedestal].

CLEOPATRA [flinging her arms in terror round him] No: you shant leave me. No, no, no: dont go. I'm afraid – afraid of the Romans.

CÆSAR [as the conviction that he is really awake forces itself on him] Cleopatra: can you see my face well?

CLEOPATRA Yes. It is so white in the moonlight.

CÆSAR Are you sure it is the moonlight that makes me look whiter than an Egyptian? [Grimly] Do you notice that I have a rather long nose?

CLEOPATRA [recoiling, paralyzed by a terrible suspicion] Oh!

CÆSAR It is a Roman nose, Cleopatra.

CLEOPATRA Ah! [With a piercing scream she springs up; darts round the left shoulder of the Sphinx; scrambles down to the sand; and falls on her knees in frantic supplication, shrieking] Bite him in two, Sphinx: bite him in two. I meant to sacrifice the white cat – I did indeed – I [Cæsar, who has slipped down from the pedestal, touches her on the shoulder]. Ah! [She buries her head in her arms].

CÆSAR Cleopatra: shall I teach you a way to prevent Cæsar from eating you?

CLEOPATRA [clinging to him piteously] Oh, do, do, do. I will steal

	Ftatateeta's jewels and give them to you. I will make the river Nile water your lands twice a year.
CÆSAR	Peace, peace, my child. Your gods are afraid of the Romans: you see the Sphinx dare not bite me, nor prevent me carrying you off to Julius Cæsar.
CLEOPATRA	[*in pleading murmurings*] You wont, you wont. You said you wouldnt.
CÆSAR	Cæsar never eats women.
CLEOPATRA	[*springing up full of hope*] What!
CÆSAR	[*impressively*] But he eats girls [*she relapses*] and cats. Now you are a silly little girl; and you are descended from the black kitten. You are both a girl and a cat.
CLEOPATRA	[*trembling*] And will he eat *me?*
CÆSAR	Yes; unless you make him believe that you are a woman.
CLEOPATRA	Oh, you must get a sorcerer to make a woman of me. Are you a sorcerer?
CÆSAR	Perhaps. But it will take a long time; and this very night you must stand face to face with Cæsar in the palace of your fathers.
CLEOPATRA	No, no. I darent.
CÆSAR	Whatever dread may be in your soul – however terrible Cæsar may be to you – you must confront him as a brave woman and a great queen; and you must feel no fear. If your hand shakes: if your voice quavers; then – night and death! [*She moans*]. But if he thinks you worthy to rule, he will set you on the throne by his side and make you the real ruler of Egypt.
CLEOPATRA	[*despairingly*] No: he will find me out: he will find me out.
CÆSAR	[*rather mournfully*] He is easily deceived by women. Their eyes dazzle him; and he sees them not as they are, but as he wishes them to appear to him.
CLEOPATRA	[*hopefully*] Then we will cheat him. I will put on Ftatateeta's head-dress; and he will think me quite an old woman.
CÆSAR	If you do that he will eat you at one mouthful.
CLEOPATRA	But I will give him a cake with my magic opal

	and seven hairs of the white cat baked in it; and –
CÆSAR	[*abruptly*] Pah! you are a little fool. He will eat your cake and you too. [*He turns contemptuously from her*].
CLEOPATRA	[*running after him and clinging to him*] Oh please, *please!* I will do whatever you tell me. I will be good. I will be your slave. [*Again the terrible bellowing note sounds across the desert, now closer at hand. It is the bucina, the Roman war trumpet*].
CÆSAR	Hark!
CLEOPATRA	[*trembling*] What was that?
CÆSAR	Cæsar's voice.
CLEOPATRA	[*pulling at his hand*] Let us run away. Come. Oh come.
CÆSAR	You are safe with me until you stand on your throne to receive Cæsar. Now lead me thither.
CLEOPATRA	[*only too glad to get away*] I will, I will. [*Again the bucina*]. Oh come, come, come: the gods are angry. Do you feel the earth shaking?
CÆSAR	It is the tread of Cæsar's legions.
CLEOPATRA	[*drawing him away*] This way, quickly. And let us look for the white cat as we go. It is he that has turned you into a Roman.
CÆSAR	Incorrigible, oh, incorrigible! Away! [*He follows her, the bucina sounding louder as they steal across the desert. The moonlight wanes: the horizon again shows black against the sky, broken only by the fantastic silhouette of the Sphinx. The sky itself vanishes in darkness, from which there is no relief until the gleam of a distant torch falls on great Egyptian pillars supporting the roof of a majestic corridor. At the further end of this corridor a Nubian slave appears carrying the torch. Cæsar, still led by Cleopatra, follows him. They come down the corridor, Cæsar peering keenly about at the strange architecture, and at the pillar shadows between which, as the passing torch makes them hurry noiselessly backwards, figures of men with wings and hawks' heads, and vast black marble cats, seem to flit in and out of ambush. Further along, the wall turns a corner and makes a spacious transept in which Cæsar sees, on his right, a throne, and behind the throne a door. On each side of the throne is a slender pillar with a lamp on it.*]

CÆSAR   What place is this?

CLEOPATRA   This is where I sit on the throne when I am allowed to wear my crown and robes. [*The slave holds his torch to shew the throne*].

CÆSAR   Order the slave to light the lamps.

CLEOPATRA   [*shyly*] Do you think I may?

CÆSAR   Of course. You are the Queen. [*She hesitates*]. Go on.

CLEOPATRA   [*timidly, to the slave*] Light all the lamps.

FTATATEETA   [*suddenly coming from behind the throne*] Stop. [*The slave stops. She turns sternly to Cleopatra, who quails like a naughty child*]. Who is this you have with you; and how dare you order the lamps to be lighted without my permission? [*Cleopatra is dumb with apprehension*].

CÆSAR   Who is she?

CLEOPATRA   Ftatateeta.

FTATATEETA   [*arrogantly*] Chief nurse to –

CÆSAR   [*cutting her short*] I speak to the Queen. Be silent. [*To Cleopatra*] Is this how your servants know their places? Send her away; and do you [*to the slave*] do as the Queen has bidden. [*The slave lights the lamps. Meanwhile Cleopatra stands hesitating, afraid of Ftatateeta*]. You are the Queen: send her away.

CLEOPATRA   [*cajoling*] Ftatateeta, dear: you must go away – just for a little.

CÆSAR   You are not commanding her to go away: you are begging her. You are no Queen. You will be eaten. Farewell. [*He turns to go*].

CLEOPATRA   [*clutching him*] No, no, no. Dont leave me.

CÆSAR   A Roman does not stay with queens who are afraid of their slaves.

CLEOPATRA   I am not afraid. Indeed I am not afraid.

FTATATEETA   We shall see who is afraid here. [*Menacingly*] Cleopatra –

CÆSAR   On your knees, woman: am I also a child that you dare trifle with me? [*He points to the floor at Cleopatra's feet. Ftatateeta, half cowed, half savage, hesitates. Cæsar calls to the Nubian*] Slave. [*The Nubian comes to him*]. Can you cut off a head? [*The Nubian*

105

nods and grins ecstatically, showing all his teeth. Cæsar takes his sword by the scabbard, ready to offer the hilt to the Nubian, and turns again to Ftatateeta, repeating his gesture]. Have you remembered yourself, mistress?

Ftatateeta, crushed, kneels before Cleopatra, who can hardly believe her eyes.

FTATATEETA   [*hoarsely*] O Queen, forget not thy servant in the days of thy greatness.

CLEOPATRA   [*blazing with excitement*] Go. Begone. Go away. [*Ftatateeta rises with stooped head, and moves backwards towards the door. Cleopatra watches her submission eagerly, almost clapping her hands, which are trembling. Suddenly she cries*] Give me something to beat her with. [*She snatches a snake-skin from the throne and dashes after Ftatateeta, whirling it like a scourge in the air. Cæsar makes a bound and manages to catch her and hold her while Ftatateeta escapes*].

CÆSAR   You scratch, kitten, do you?

CLEOPATRA   [*breaking from him*] I *will* beat somebody. I will beat him. [*She attacks the slave*]. There, there, there! [*The slave flies for his life up the corridor and vanishes. She throws the snake-skin away and jumps on the step of the throne with her arms waving, crying*] I am a real Queen at last – a real, real Queen! Cleopatra the Queen! [*Cæsar shakes his head dubiously, the advantage of the change seeming open to question from the point of view of the general welfare of Egypt. She turns and looks at him exultantly. Then she jumps down from the step, runs to him, and flings her arms round him rapturously, crying*] Oh, I love you for making me a Queen.

CÆSAR   But queens love only kings.

CLEOPATRA   I will make all the men I love kings. I will make you a king. I will have many young kings, with round, strong arms; and when I am tired of them I will whip them to death; but you shall always be my king: my nice, kind, wise, good old king.

CÆSAR   Oh, my wrinkles, my wrinkles! And my child's heart! You will be the most dangerous of all Cæsar's conquests.

CLEOPATRA   [*appalled*] Cæsar! I forgot Cæsar. [*Anxiously*] You will tell him that I am a Queen, will you not? – a real

106

Queen. Listen! [*stealthily coaxing him*]: let us run away and hide until Cæsar is gone.

CÆSAR   If you fear Cæsar, you are no true queen; and though you were to hide beneath a pyramid, he would go straight to it and lift it with one hand. And then – ! [*he chops his teeth together*].

CLEOPATRA   [*trembling*] Oh!

CÆSAR   Be afraid if you dare. [*The note of the bucina resounds again in the distance. She moans with fear. Cæsar exults in it, exclaiming*] Aha! Cæsar approaches the throne of Cleopatra. Come: take your place. [*He takes her hand and leads her to the throne. She is too downcast to speak*]. Ho, there, Teetatota. How do you call your slaves?

CLEOPATRA   [*spiritlessly, as she sinks on the throne and cowers there, shaking*]. Clap your hands.

He claps his hands. Ftatateeta returns.

CÆSAR   Bring the Queen's robes, and her crown, and her women; and prepare her.

CLEOPATRA   [*eagerly – recovering herself a little*] Yes, the crown, Ftatateeta: I shall wear the crown.

FTATATEETA   For whom must the Queen put on her state?

107

CÆSAR   For a citizen of Rome. A king of kings, Totateeta.

CLEOPATRA   [*stamping at her*] How dare you ask questions? Go and do as you are told. [*Ftatateeta goes out with a grim smile. Cleopatra goes on eagerly, to Cæsar*] Cæsar will know that I am a Queen when he sees my crown and robes, will he not?

CÆSAR   No. How shall he know that you are not a slave dressed up in the Queen's ornaments?

CLEOPATRA   You must tell him.

CÆSAR   He will not ask me. He will know Cleopatra by her pride, her courage, her majesty, and her beauty. [*She looks very doubtful*]. Are you trembling?

CLEOPATRA   [*shivering with dread*] No, I – I – [*in a very sickly voice*] No.

Ftatateeta and three women come in with the regalia.

FTATATEETA   Of all the Queen's women, these three alone are left. The rest are fled. [*They begin to deck Cleopatra, who submits, pale and motionless*].

CÆSAR   Good, good. Three are enough. Poor Cæsar generally has to dress himself.

FTATATEETA   [*contemptuously*] The queen of Egypt is not a Roman barbarian. [*To Cleopatra*] Be brave, my nursling. Hold up your head before this stranger.

CÆSAR   [*admiring Cleopatra, and placing the crown on her head*] Is it sweet or bitter to be a Queen, Cleopatra?

CLEOPATRA   Bitter.

CÆSAR   Cast out fear; and you will conquer Cæsar. Tota: are the Romans at hand?

FTATATEETA   They are at hand; and the guard has fled.

THE WOMEN   [*wailing subduedly*] Woe to us!

The Nubian comes running down the hall.

NUBIAN   The Romans are in the courtyard. [*He bolts through the door. With a shriek, the women fly after him. Ftatateeta's jaw expresses savage resolution: she does not budge. Cleopatra can hardly restrain herself from following them. Cæsar grips her wrist, and looks stead-fastly at her. She stands like a martyr*].

CÆSAR   The Queen must face Cæsar alone. Answer "So be it."

CLEOPATRA [*white*] So be it.

CÆSAR [*releasing her*] Good.

A tramp and tumult of armed men is heard. Cleopatra's terror increases. The bucina sounds close at hand, followed by a formidable clangor of trumpets. This is too much for Cleopatra: she utters a cry and darts towards the door. Ftatateeta stops her ruthlessly.

FTATATEETA You are my nursling. You have said "So be it"; and if you die for it, you must make the Queen's word good. [*She hands Cleopatra to Cæsar, who takes her back, almost beside herself with apprehension, to the throne*].

CÆSAR Now, if you quail –! [*He seats himself on the throne*].

She stands on the step, all but unconscious, waiting for death. The Roman soldiers troop in tumultuously through the corridor, headed by their ensign with his eagle, and their bucinator, a burly fellow with his instrument coiled round his body, its brazen bell shaped like the head of a howling wolf. When they reach the transept, they stare in amazement at the throne; dress into ordered rank opposite it; draw their swords and lift them in the air with a shout of Hail, Cæsar. *Cleopatra turns and stares wildly at Cæsar; grasps the situation; and, with a great sob of relief, falls into his arms.*

ACT 2

*Alexandria. A hall on the first floor of the Palace,
ending in a loggia approached by two steps. Through
the arches of the loggia the Mediterranean can be seen,
bright in the morning sun. The clean lofty walls, painted
with a procession of the Egyptian theocracy, presented
in profile as flat ornament, and the absence of mirrors,
sham perspectives, stuffy upholstery and textiles, make
the place handsome, wholesome, simple and cool, or, as
a rich English manufacturer would express it, poor,
bare, ridiculous and unhomely. For Tottenham Court
Road civilization is to this Egyptian civilization as
glass bead and tattoo civilization is to Tottenham Court
Road.*

*The young king Ptolemy Dionysus (aged ten) is at the
top of the steps, on his way in through the loggia, led by
his guardian Pothinus, who has him by the hand. The*

111

court is assembled to receive him. It is made up of men and women (some of the women being officials) of various complexions and races, mostly Egyptian; some of them, comparatively fair, from lower Egypt; some, much darker, from upper Egypt; with a few Greeks and Jews. Prominent in a group on Ptolemy's right hand is Theodotus, Ptolemy's tutor. Another group, on Ptolemy's left, is headed by Achillas, the general of Ptolemy's troops. Theodotus is a little old man, whose features are as cramped and wizened as his limbs, except his tall straight forehead, which occupies more space than all the rest of his face. He maintains an air of magpie keenness and profundity, listening to what the others say with the sarcastic vigilance of a philosopher listening to the exercises of his disciples. Achillas is a tall handsome man of thirty-five, with a fine black beard curled like the coat of a poodle. Apparently not a clever man, but distinguished and dignified. Pothinus is a vigorous man of fifty, a eunuch, passionate, energetic and quick witted, but of common mind and character; impatient and unable to control his temper. He has fine tawny hair, like fur. Ptolemy, the King, looks much older than an English boy of ten; but he has the childish air, the habit of being in leading strings, the mixture of impotence and petulance, the appearance of being excessively washed, combed and dressed by other hands, which is exhibited by court-bred princes of all ages.

All receive the King with reverences. He comes down the steps to a chair of state which stands a little to his right, the only seat in the hall. Taking his place before it, he looks nervously for instructions to Pothinus, who places himself at his left hand.

POTHINUS The king of Egypt has a word to speak.

THEODOTUS [*in a squeak which he makes impressive by sheer self-opinionativeness*] Peace for the King's word!

PTOLEMY [*without any vocal inflexions: he is evidently repeating a lesson*] Take notice of this all of you. I am the first-born son of Auletes the Flute Blower who was your King. My sister Berenice drove him from his throne and reigned in his stead but – but – [*he hesitates*] –

POTHINUS [*stealthily prompting*] – but the gods would not suffer –

112

PTOLEMY Yes – the gods would not suffer – not suffer – [*He stops; then, crestfallen*] I forget what the gods would not suffer.

THEODOTUS Let Pothinus, the King's guardian, speak for the King.

POTHINUS [*suppressing his impatience with difficulty*] The King wished to say that the gods would not suffer the impiety of his sister to go unpunished.

PTOLEMY [*hastily*] Yes: I remember the rest of it. [*He resumes his monotone*]. Therefore the gods sent a stranger one Mark Antony a Roman captain of horsemen across the sands of the desert and he set my father again upon the throne. And my father took Berenice my sister and struck her head off. And now that my father is dead yet another of his daughters my sister Cleopatra would snatch the kingdom from me and reign in my place. But the gods would not suffer – [*Pothinus coughs admonitorily*] – the gods – the gods would not suffer –

POTHINUS [*prompting*] – will not maintain –

PTOLEMY Oh yes – will not maintain such iniquity they will give her head to the axe even as her sister's. But with the help of the witch Ftatateeta she hath cast a spell on the Roman Julius Cæsar to make him uphold her false pretence to rule in Egypt. Take notice then that I will not suffer – that I will not suffer – [*pettishly, to Pothinus*] What is it that I will not suffer?

POTHINUS [*suddenly exploding with all the force and emphasis of political passion*] The King will not suffer a foreigner to take from him the throne of our Egypt. [*A shout of applause*]. Tell the King, Achillas, how many soldiers and horsemen follow the Roman?

THEODOTUS Let the King's general speak!

ACHILLAS But two Roman legions, O King. Three thousand soldiers and scarce a thousand horsemen.

The court breaks into derisive laughter; and a great chattering begins, amid which Rufio, a Roman officer, appears in the loggia. He is a burly, black-bearded man of middle age, very blunt, prompt and rough, with small clear eyes and plump nose and cheeks, which, however, like the rest of his flesh, are in ironhard condition.

RUFIO [*from the steps*] Peace, ho! [*The laughter and chatter cease abruptly*]. Cæsar approaches.

THEODOTUS [*with much presence of mind*] The King permits the Roman commander to enter!

Cæsar, plainly dressed, but wearing an oak wreath to conceal his baldness, enters from the loggia, attended by Britannus, his secretary, a Briton, about forty, tall, solemn, and already slightly bald, with a heavy, drooping, hazel-colored moustache trained so as to lose its ends in a pair of trim whiskers. He is carefully dressed in blue, with portfolio, inkhorn, and reed pen at his girdle. His serious air and sense of the importance of the business in hand is in marked contrast to the kindly interest of Cæsar, who looks at the scene, which is new to him, with the frank curiosity of a child, and then turns to the king's chair: Britannus and Rufio posting themselves near the steps at the other side.

CÆSAR [*looking at Pothinus and Ptolemy*] Which is the King? the man or the boy?

POTHINUS I am Pothinus, the guardian of my lord the King.

CÆSAR [*patting Ptolemy kindly on the shoulder*] So you are the King. Dull work at your age, eh? [*To Pothinus*] Your servant, Pothinus. [*He turns away unconcernedly and comes slowly along the middle of the hall, looking from side to side at the courtiers until he reaches Achillas*]. And this gentleman?

THEODOTUS Achillas, the King's general.

CÆSAR [*to Achillas, very friendly*] A general, eh? I am a general myself. But I began too old, too old. Health and many victories, Achillas!

ACHILLAS As the gods will, Cæsar.

CÆSAR [*turning to Theodotus*] And you, sir, are – ?

THEODOTUS Theodotus, the King's tutor.

CÆSAR You teach men how to be kings, Theodotus. That is very clever of you. [*Looking at the gods on the walls as he turns away from Theodotus and goes up again to Pothinus*] And this place?

POTHINUS The council chamber of the chancellors of the King's treasury, Cæsar.

CÆSAR Ah! that reminds me. I want some money.

114

POTHINUS   The King's treasury is poor, Cæsar.

CÆSAR   Yes: I notice that there is but one chair in it.

RUFIO   [*shouting gruffly*] Bring a chair there, some of you, for Cæsar.

PTOLEMY   [*rising shyly to offer his chair*] Cæsar –

CÆSAR   [*kindly*] No, no, my boy: that is your chair of state. Sit down.

He makes Ptolemy sit down again. Meanwhile Rufio, looking about him, sees in the nearest corner an image of the god Ra, represented as a seated man with the head of a hawk. Before the image is a bronze tripod, about as large as a three-legged stool, with a stick of incense burning on it. Rufio, with Roman resourcefulness and indifference to foreign superstitions, promptly seizes the tripod; shakes off the incense; blows away the ash; and dumps it down behind Cæsar, nearly in the middle of the hall.

RUFIO   Sit on that, Cæsar.

A shiver runs through the court, followed by a hissing whisper of Sacrilege!

CÆSAR   [*seating himself*] Now, Pothinus, to business. I am badly in want of money.

BRITANNUS   [*disapproving of these informal expressions*] My master would say that there is a lawful debt due to Rome by Egypt, contracted by the King's deceased father to the Triumvirate; and that it is Cæsar's duty to his country to require immediate payment.

CÆSAR   [*blandly*] Ah, I forgot. I have not made my companions known here. Pothinus: this is Britannus, my secretary. He is an islander from the western end of the world, a day's voyage from Gaul. [*Britannus bows stiffly*]. This gentleman is Rufio, my comrade in arms. [*Rufio nods*]. Pothinus: I want 1,600 talents.

The courtiers, appalled, murmur loudly, and Theodotus and Achillas appeal mutely to one another against so monstrous a demand.

POTHINUS   [*aghast*] Forty million sesterces! Impossible. There is not so much money in the King's treasury.

CÆSAR   [*encouragingly*] *Only* sixteen hundred talents, Pothinus. Why count it in sesterces? A sestertius is only worth a loaf of bread.

POTHINUS And a talent is worth a racehorse. I say it is impossible. We have been at strife here, because the King's sister Cleopatra falsely claims his throne. The King's taxes have not been collected for a whole year.

CÆSAR Yes they have, Pothinus. My officers have been collecting them all the morning. [*Renewed whisper and sensation, not without some stifled laughter, among the courtiers*].

RUFIO [*bluntly*] You must pay, Pothinus. Why waste words? You are getting off cheaply enough.

POTHINUS [*bitterly*] Is it possible that Cæsar, the conqueror of the world, has time to occupy himself with such a trifle as our taxes?

CÆSAR My friend: taxes are the chief business of a conqueror of the world.

POTHINUS Then take warning, Cæsar. This day, the treasures of the temples and the gold of the King's treasury shall be sent to the mint to be melted down for our ransom in the sight of the people. They shall see us sitting under bare walls and drinking from wooden cups. And their wrath be on your head, Cæsar, if you force us to this sacrilege!

CÆSAR Do not fear, Pothinus: the people know how well wine tastes in wooden cups. In return for your bounty, I will settle this dispute about the throne for you, if you will. What say you?

POTHINUS If I say no, will that hinder you?

RUFIO [*defiantly*] No.

CÆSAR You say the matter has been at issue for a year, Pothinus. May I have ten minutes at it?

POTHINUS You will do your pleasure, doubtless.

CÆSAR Good! But first, let us have Cleopatra here.

THEODOTUS She is not in Alexandria: she is fled into Syria.

CÆSAR I think not. [*To Rufio*] Call Totateeta.

RUFIO [*Calling*] Ho there, Teetatota.

Ftatateeta enters the loggia, and stands arrogantly at the top of the steps.

116

FTATATEETA   Who pronounces the name of Ftatateeta, the Queen's chief nurse?

CÆSAR   Nobody can pronounce it, Tota, except yourself. Where is your mistress?

Cleopatra, who is hiding behind Ftatateeta, peeps out at them, laughing. Cæsar rises.

CÆSAR   Will the Queen favor us with her presence for a moment?

CLEOPATRA   [*pushing Ftatateeta aside and standing haughtily on the brink of the steps*] Am I to behave like a Queen?

CÆSAR   Yes.

Cleopatra immediately comes down to the chair of state; seizes Ptolemy; drags him out of his seat; then takes his place in the chair. Ftatateeta seats herself on the step of the loggia, and sits there, watching the scene with sibylline intensity.

PTOLEMY   [*mortified, and struggling with his tears*] Cæsar: this is how she treats me always. If I am a king why is she allowed to take everything from me?

CLEOPATRA   You are not to be King, you little cry-baby. You are to be eaten by the Romans.

CÆSAR   [*touched by Ptolemy's distress*] Come here, my boy, and stand by me.

Ptolemy goes over to Cæsar, who, resuming his seat on the tripod, takes the boy's hand to encourage him. Cleopatra, furiously jealous, rises and glares at them.

CLEOPATRA   [*with flaming cheeks*] Take your throne: I dont want it. [*She flings away from the chair, and approaches Ptolemy, who shrinks from her*]. Go this instant and sit down in your place.

CÆSAR   Go, Ptolemy. Always take a throne when it is offered to you.

RUFIO   I hope you will have the good sense to follow your own advice when we return to Rome, Cæsar.

Ptolemy slowly goes back to the throne, giving Cleopatra a wide berth, in evident fear of her hands. She takes his place beside Cæsar.

CÆSAR   Pothinus –

CLEOPATRA   [*interrupting him*] Are you not going to speak to me?

117

CÆSAR   Be quiet. Open your mouth again before I give you leave; and you shall be eaten.

CLEOPATRA   I am not afraid. A queen must not be afraid. Eat my husband there, if you like: *he* is afraid.

CÆSAR   [*starting*] Your husband! What do you mean?

CLEOPATRA   [*pointing to Ptolemy*] That little thing.

The two Romans and the Briton stare at one another in amazement.

THEODOTUS   Cæsar: you are a stranger here, and not conversant with our laws. The kings and queens of Egypt may not marry except with their own royal blood. Ptolemy and Cleopatra are born king and consort just as they are born brother and sister.

BRITANNUS   [*shocked*] Cæsar: this is not proper.

THEODOTUS   [*outraged*] How!

CÆSAR   [*recovering his self-possession*] Pardon him, Theodotus: he is a barbarian, and thinks that the customs of his tribe and island are the laws of nature.

BRITANNUS   On the contrary, Cæsar, it is these Egyptians who are barbarians; and you do wrong to encourage them. I say it is a scandal.

CÆSAR   Scandal or not, my friend, it opens the gate of peace. [*He addresses Pothinus seriously*]. Pothinus: hear what I propose.

RUFIO   Hear Cæsar there.

CÆSAR   Ptolemy and Cleopatra shall reign jointly in Egypt.

ACHILLAS   What of the King's younger brother and Cleopatra's younger sister?

RUFIO   [*explaining*] There is another little Ptolemy, Cæsar: so they tell me.

CÆSAR   Well, the little Ptolemy can marry the other sister; and we will make them both a present of Cyprus.

POTHINUS   [*impatiently*] Cyprus is of no use to anybody.

CÆSAR   No matter: you shall have it for the sake of peace.

BRITANNUS   [*unconsciously anticipating a later statesman*] Peace with honor, Pothinus.

POTHINUS   [*mutinously*] Cæsar: be honest. The money you demand is the price of our freedom. Take it; and leave us to settle our own affairs.

THE BOLDER COURTIERS [*encouraged by Pothinus's tone and Cæsar's quietness*] Yes, yes. Egypt for the Egyptians!

The conference now becomes an altercation, the Egyptians becoming more and more heated. Cæsar remains unruffled; but Rufio grows fiercer and doggeder, and Britannus haughtily indignant.

RUFIO [*contemptuously*] Egypt for the Egyptians! Do you forget that there is a Roman army of occupation here, left by Aulus Gabinius when he set up your toy king for you?

ACHILLAS [*suddenly asserting himself*] And now under *my* command. I am the Roman general here, Cæsar.

CÆSAR [*tickled by the humor of the situation*] And also the Egyptian general, eh?

POTHINUS [*triumphantly*] That is so, Cæsar.

CÆSAR [*to Achillas*] So you can make war on the Egyptians in the name of Rome, and on the Romans – on *me*, if necessary – in the name of Egypt?

ACHILLAS That is so, Cæsar.

CÆSAR And which side are you on at present, if I may presume to ask, general?

ACHILLAS On the side of the right and of the gods.

CÆSAR Hm! How many men have you?

ACHILLAS That will appear when I take the field.

RUFIO [*truculently*] Are your men Romans? If not, it matters not how many there are, provided you are no stronger than 500 to ten.

POTHINUS It is useless to try to bluff us, Rufio. Cæsar has been defeated before and may be defeated again. A few weeks ago Cæsar was flying for his life before Pompey: a few months hence he may be flying for his life before Cato and Juba of Numidia, the African King.

ACHILLAS [*following up Pothinus's speech menacingly*] What can you do with 4,000 men?

THEODOTUS [*following up Achillas's speech with a raucous squeak*] And without money? Away with you.

ALL THE COURTIERS [*shouting fiercely and crowding towards Cæsar*] Away with you. Egypt for the Egyptians! Begone.

Rufio bites his beard, too angry to speak. Cæsar sits as

comfortably as if he were at breakfast, and the cat were clamoring for a piece of Finnan-haddie.

CLEOPATRA Why do you let them talk to you like that, Cæsar? Are you afraid?

CÆSAR Why, my dear, what they say is quite true.

CLEOPATRA But if you go away, I shall not be Queen.

CÆSAR I shall not go away until you are Queen.

POTHINUS Achillas: if you are not a fool, you will take that girl whilst she is under your hand.

RUFIO [*daring them*] Why not take Cæsar as well, Achillas?

POTHINUS [*retorting the defiance with interest*] Well said, Rufio. Why not?

RUFIO Try, Achillas. [*Calling*] Guard there.

The loggia immediately fills with Cæsar's soldiers, who stand, sword in hand, at the top of the steps, waiting the word to charge from their centurion, who carries a cudgel. For a moment the Egyptians face them proudly: then they retire sullenly to their former places.

BRITANNUS You are Cæsar's prisoners, all of you.

CÆSAR [*benevolently*] Oh no, no, no. By no means. Cæsar's guests, gentlemen.

CLEOPATRA Wont you cut their heads off?

CÆSAR What! Cut off your brother's head?

CLEOPATRA Why not? He would cut off mine, if he got the chance. Wouldnt you, Ptolemy?

PTOLEMY [*pale and obstinate*] I would. I will, too, when I grow up.

Cleopatra is rent by a struggle between her newly-acquired dignity as a queen, and a strong impulse to put out her tongue at him. She takes no part in the scene which follows, but watches it with curiosity and wonder, fidgeting with the restlessness of a child, and sitting down on Cæsar's tripod when he rises.

POTHINUS Cæsar: if you attempt to detain us –

RUFIO He will succeed, Egyptian: make up your mind to that. We hold the palace, the beach, and the eastern harbor. The road to Rome is open; and you shall travel it if Cæsar chooses.

CÆSAR [*courteously*] I could do no less, Pothinus, to secure the retreat of my own soldiers. I am accountable for every life among them. But you are free to go. So are all here, and in the palace.

RUFIO [*aghast at this clemency*] What! Renegades and all?

CÆSAR [*softening the expression*] Roman army of occupation and all, Rufio.

POTHINUS [*desperately*] Then I make a last appeal to Cæsar's justice. I shall call a witness to prove that but for us, the Roman army of occupation, led by the greatest soldier in the world, would now have Cæsar at its mercy. [*Calling through the loggia*] Ho, there, Lucius Septimius [*Cæsar starts, deeply moved*]: if my voice can reach you, come forth and testify before Cæsar.

CÆSAR [*shrinking*] No, no.

THEODOTUS Yes, I say. Let the military tribune bear witness.

Lucius Septimius, a clean shaven, trim athlete of about 40, with symmetrical features, resolute mouth, and handsome, thin Roman nose, in the dress of a Roman officer, comes in through the loggia and confronts Cæsar, who hides his face with his robe for a moment; then, mastering himself, drops it, and confronts the tribune with dignity.

POTHINUS Bear witness, Lucius Septimius. Cæsar came hither in pursuit of his foe. Did we shelter his foe?

LUCIUS As Pompey's foot touched the Egyptian shore, his head fell by the stroke of my sword.

THEODOTUS [*with viperish relish*] Under the eyes of his wife and child! Remember that, Cæsar! They saw it from the ship he had just left. We have given you a full and sweet measure of vengeance.

CÆSAR [*with horror*] Vengeance!

POTHINUS Our first gift to you, as your galley came into the roadstead, was the head of your rival for the empire of the world. Bear witness, Lucius Septimius: is it not so?

LUCIUS It is so. With this hand, that slew Pompey, I placed his head at the feet of Cæsar.

CÆSAR Murderer! So would you have slain Cæsar, had Pompey been victorious at Pharsalia.

LUCIUS Woe to the vanquished, Cæsar! When I served Pompey, I slew as good men as he, only because he conquered them. His turn came at last.

THEODOTUS [*flatteringly*] The deed was not yours, Cæsar, but ours – nay, mine; for it was done by my counsel. Thanks to us, you keep your reputation for clemency, and have your vengeance too.

CÆSAR Vengeance! Vengeance!! Oh, if I could stoop to vengeance, what would I not exact from you as the price of this murdered man's blood? [*They shrink back, appalled and disconcerted*]. Was he not my son-in-law, my ancient friend, for 20 years the master of great Rome, for 30 years the compeller of victory? Did not I, as a Roman, share his glory? Was the Fate that forced us to fight for the mastery of the world, of our making? Am I Julius Cæsar, or am I a wolf, that you fling to me the grey head of the old soldier, the laurelled conqueror, the mighty Roman, treacherously struck down by this callous ruffian, and then claim my gratitude for it! [*To Lucius Septimius*] Begone: you fill me with horror.

LUCIUS [*cold and undaunted*] Pshaw! You have seen severed heads before, Cæsar, and severed right hands too, I think; some thousands of them, in Gaul, after you vanquished Vercingetorix. Did you spare him, with all your clemency? Was that vengeance?

CÆSAR No, by the gods! would that it had been! Vengeance at least is human. No, I say: those severed right hands, and the brave Vercingetorix basely strangled in a vault beneath the Capitol, were [*with shuddering satire*] a wise severity, a necessary protection to the commonwealth, a duty of statesmanship – follies and fictions ten times bloodier than honest vengeance! What a fool was I then! to think that men's lives should be at the mercy of such fools! [*Humbly*] Lucius Septimius, pardon me: why should the slayer of Vercingetorix rebuke the slayer of Pompey? You are free to go with the rest. Or stay if you will: I will find a place for you in my service.

LUCIUS The odds are against you, Cæsar. I go. [*He turns to go out through the loggia*].

RUFIO [*full of wrath at seeing his prey escaping*] That means that he is a Republican.

LUCIUS [*turning defiantly on the loggia steps*] And what are you?

RUFIO A Cæsarian, like all Cæsar's soldiers.

CÆSAR [*courteously*] Lucius: believe me, Cæsar is no Cæsarian. Were Rome a true republic, then were Cæsar the first of Republicans. But you have made your choice. Farewell.

LUCIUS Farewell. Come, Achillas, whilst there is yet time.

Cæsar, seeing that Rufio's temper threatens to get the worse of him, puts his hand on his shoulder and brings him down the hall out of harm's way, Britannus accompanying them and posting himself on Cæsar's right hand. This movement brings the three in a little group to the place occupied by Achillas, who moves haughtily

away and joins Theodotus on the other side. Lucius Septimius goes out through the soldiers in the loggia. Pothinus, Theodotus and Achillas follow him with the courtiers, very mistrustful of the soldiers, who close up in their rear and go out after them, keeping them moving without much ceremony. The King is left in his chair, piteous, obstinate, with twitching face and fingers. During these movements Rufio maintains an energetic grumbling, as follows:

RUFIO [*as Lucius departs*] Do you suppose he would let us go if he had our heads in his hands?

CÆSAR I have no right to suppose that his ways are any baser than mine.

RUFIO Psha!

CÆSAR Rufio: if I take Lucius Septimius for my model, and become exactly like him, ceasing to be Cæsar, will you serve me still?

BRITANNUS Cæsar: this is not good sense. Your duty to Rome demands that her enemies should be prevented from doing further mischief. [*Cæsar, whose delight in the moral eye-to-business of his British secretary is inexhaustible, smiles indulgently*].

RUFIO It is no use talking to him, Britannus: you may save your breath to cool your porridge. But mark this, Cæsar. Clemency is very well for you; but what is it for your soldiers, who have to fight to-morrow the men you spared yesterday? You may give what orders you please; but I tell you that your next victory will be a massacre, thanks to your clemency. *I*, for one, will take no prisoners. I will kill my enemies in the field: and then you can preach as much clemency as you please: I shall never have to fight them again. And now, with your leave, I will see these gentry off the premises. [*He turns to go*].

CÆSAR [*turning also and seeing Ptolemy*] What! have they left the boy alone! Oh shame, shame!

RUFIO [*taking Ptolemy's hand and making him rise*] Come, your majesty!

PTOLEMY [*to Cæsar, drawing away his hand from Rufio*] Is he turning me out of my palace?

RUFIO [*grimly*] You are welcome to stay if you wish.

CÆSAR [*kindly*] Go, my boy. I will not harm you; but you will be safer away, among your friends. Here you are in the lion's mouth.

PTOLEMY [*turning to go*] It is not the lion I fear, but [*looking at Rufio*] the jackal. [*He goes out through the loggia*].

CÆSAR [*laughing approvingly*] Brave boy!

CLEOPATRA [*jealous of Cæsar's approbation, calling after Ptolemy*] Little silly. You think that very clever.

CÆSAR Britannus: attend the King. Give him in charge to that Pothinus fellow. [*Britannus goes out after Ptolemy*].

RUFIO [*pointing to Cleopatra*] And this piece of goods? What is to be done with *her?* However, I suppose I may leave that to you. [*He goes out through the loggia*].

CLEOPATRA [*flushing suddenly and turning on Cæsar*] Did you mean me to go with the rest?

CÆSAR [*a little preoccupied, goes with a sigh to Ptolemy's chair, whilst she waits for his answer with red cheeks and clenched fists*] You are free to do just as you please, Cleopatra.

CLEOPATRA Then you do not care whether I stay or not?

CÆSAR [*smiling*] Of course I had rather you stayed.

CLEOPATRA Much, *much* rather?

CÆSAR [*nodding*] Much, much rather.

CLEOPATRA Then I consent to stay, because I am asked. But I do not want to, mind.

CÆSAR That is quite understood. [*Calling*] Totateeta.

Ftatateeta, still seated, turns her eyes on him with a sinister expression, but does not move.

CLEOPATRA [*with a splutter of laughter*] Her name is not Totateeta: it is Ftatateeta. [*Calling*] Ftatateeta. [*Ftatateeta instantly rises and comes to Cleopatra*].

CÆSAR [*stumbling over the name*] Tfatafeeta will forgive the erring tongue of a Roman. Tota: the Queen will hold her state here in Alexandria. Engage women to attend upon her; and do all that is needful.

FTATATEETA Am I then the mistress of the Queen's household?

CLEOPATRA [*sharply*] No: *I* am the mistress of the Queen's household. Go and do as you are told, or I will have you

125

thrown into the Nile this very afternoon, to poison the poor crocodiles.

CÆSAR [*shocked*] Oh no, no.

CLEOPATRA Oh yes, yes. You are very sentimental, Cæsar; but you are clever; and if you do as I tell you, you will soon learn to govern.

Cæsar, quite dumbfounded by this impertinence, turns in his chair and stares at her.

Ftatateeta, smiling grimly, and showing a splendid set of teeth, goes, leaving them alone together.

CÆSAR Cleopatra: I really think I must eat you, after all.

CLEOPATRA [*kneeling beside him and looking at him with eager interest, half real, half affected to shew how intelligent she is*] You must not talk to me now as if I were a child.

CÆSAR You have been growing up since the sphinx introduced us the other night; and you think you know more than I do already.

CLEOPATRA [*taken down, and anxious to justify herself*] No: that would be very silly of me: of course I know that. But – [*suddenly*] are you angry with me?

CÆSAR No.

CLEOPATRA [*only half believing him*] Then why are you so thoughtful?

CÆSAR [*rising*] I have work to do, Cleopatra.

CLEOPATRA [*drawing back*] Work! [*Offended*] You are tired of talking to me; and that is your excuse to get away from me.

CÆSAR [*sitting down again to appease her*] Well, well: another minute. But then – work!

CLEOPATRA Work! what nonsense! You must remember that you are a king now: I have made you one. Kings dont work.

CÆSAR Oh! Who told you that, little kitten? Eh?

CLEOPATRA My father was King of Egypt; and he never worked. But he was a great king, and cut off my sister's head because she rebelled against him and took the throne from him.

CÆSAR Well; and how did he get his throne back again?

126

CLEOPATRA [*eagerly, her eyes lighting up*] I will tell you. A beautiful young man, with strong round arms, came over the desert with many horsemen, and slew my sister's husband and gave my father back his throne. [*Wistfully*] I was only twelve then. Oh, I wish he would come again, now that I am a queen. I would make him my husband.

CÆSAR It might be managed, perhaps; for it was I who sent that beautiful young man to help your father.

CLEOPATRA [*enraptured*] You know him!

CÆSAR [*nodding*] I do.

CLEOPATRA Has he come with you? [*Cæsar shakes his head: she is cruelly disappointed*]. Oh, I wish he had, I wish he had. If only I were a little older; so that he might not think me a mere kitten, as you do! But perhaps that is because *you* are old. He is many *many* years younger than you, is he not?

CÆSAR [*as if swallowing a pill*] He is somewhat younger.

CLEOPATRA Would he be my husband, do you think, if I asked him?

CÆSAR Very likely.

CLEOPATRA But I should not like to ask him. Could you not persuade him to ask me – without knowing that I wanted him to?

CÆSAR [*touched by her innocence of the beautiful young man's character*] My poor child!

CLEOPATRA Why do you say that as if you were sorry for me? Does he love anyone else?

CÆSAR I am afraid so.

CLEOPATRA [*tearfully*] Then I shall not be his first love.

CÆSAR Not quite the first. He is greatly admired by women.

CLEOPATRA I wish I could be the first. But if he loves me, I will make him kill all the rest. Tell me: is he still beautiful? Do his strong round arms shine in the sun like marble?

CÆSAR He is in excellent condition – considering how much he eats and drinks.

CLEOPATRA Oh, you must not say common, earthly things about him; for I love him. He is a god.

127

CÆSAR He is a great captain of horsemen, and swifter of foot than any other Roman.

CLEOPATRA What is his real name?

CÆSAR [*puzzled*] His *real* name?

CLEOPATRA Yes. I always call him Horus, because Horus is the most beautiful of our gods. But I want to know his real name.

CÆSAR His name is Mark Antony.

CLEOPATRA [*musically*] Mark Antony, Mark Antony, Mark Antony! What a beautiful name! [*She throws her arms round Cæsar's neck*]. Oh, how I love you for sending him to help my father! Did you love my father very much?

CÆSAR No, my child; but your father, as you say, never worked. I always work. So when he lost his crown he had to promise me 16,000 talents to get it back for him.

CLEOPATRA Did he ever pay you?

CÆSAR Not in full.

CLEOPATRA He was quite right: it was too dear. The whole world is not worth 16,000 talents.

CÆSAR That is perhaps true, Cleopatra. Those Egyptians who work paid as much of it as he could drag from them. The rest is still due. But as I most likely shall not get it, I must go back to my work. So you must run away for a little and send my secretary to me.

CLEOPATRA [*coaxing*] No: I want to stay and hear you talk about Mark Antony.

CÆSAR But if I do not get to work, Pothinus and the rest of them will cut us off from the harbor; and then the way from Rome will be blocked.

CLEOPATRA No matter: I dont want you to go back to Rome.

CÆSAR But you want Mark Antony to come from it.

CLEOPATRA [*springing up*] Oh, yes, yes, yes: I forgot. Go quickly and work, Cæsar; and keep the way over the sea open for my Mark Antony. [*She runs out through the loggia, kissing her hand to Mark Antony across the sea*].

CÆSAR [*going briskly up the middle of the hall to the loggia steps*] Ho, Britannus. [*He is startled by the entry of a wounded Roman soldier, who confronts him from the upper step*]. What now?

SOLDIER [*pointing to his bandaged head*] This, Cæsar; and two of my comrades killed in the market place.

CÆSAR [*quiet, but attending*] Ay. Why?

SOLDIER There is an army come to Alexandria, calling itself the Roman army.

CÆSAR The Roman army of occupation. Ay?

SOLDIER Commanded by one Achillas.

CÆSAR Well?

SOLDIER The citizens rose against us when the army entered the gates. I was with two others in the market place when the news came. They set upon us. I cut my way out; and here I am.

CÆSAR Good. I am glad to see you alive. [*Rufio enters the loggia hastily, passing behind the soldier to look out through one of the arches at the quay beneath*]. Rufio: we are besieged.

RUFIO What! Already?

CÆSAR Now or to-morrow: what does it matter? We *shall* be besieged.

Britannus runs in.

BRITANNUS Cæsar –

CÆSAR [*anticipating him*] Yes: I know. [*Rufio and Britannus come down the hall from the loggia at opposite sides, past Cæsar, who waits for a moment near the step to say to the soldier*] Comrade: give the word to turn out on the beach and stand by the boats. Get your wound attended to. Go. [*The soldier hurries out. Cæsar comes down the hall between Rufio and Britannus*] Rufio: we have some ships in the west harbor. Burn them.

RUFIO [*staring*] Burn them!!

CÆSAR Take every boat we have in the east harbor, and seize the Pharos – that island with the lighthouse. Leave half our men behind to hold the beach and the quay outside this palace: that is the way home.

RUFIO [*disapproving strongly*] Are we to give up the city?

CÆSAR We have not got it, Rufio. This palace we have; and – what is that building next door?

RUFIO The theatre.

CÆSAR We will have that too: it commands the strand. For the rest, Egypt for the Egyptians!

RUFIO Well, you know best, I suppose. Is that all?

CÆSAR That is all. Are those ships burnt yet?

RUFIO Be easy: I shall waste no more time. [*He runs out*].

BRITANNUS Cæsar: Pothinus demands speech of you. In my opinion he needs a lesson. His manner is most insolent.

CÆSAR Where is he?

BRITANNUS He waits without.

CÆSAR Ho there! admit Pothinus.

Pothinus appears in the loggia, and comes down the hall very haughtily to Cæsar's left hand.

CÆSAR Well, Pothinus?

POTHINUS I have brought you our ultimatum, Cæsar.

CÆSAR Ultimatum! The door was open: you should have gone out through it before you declared war. You are my prisoner now. [*He goes to the chair and loosens his toga*].

POTHINUS [*scornfully*] I *your* prisoner! Do you know that you are in Alexandria, and that King Ptolemy, with an army outnumbering your little troop a hundred to one, is in possession of Alexandria?

CÆSAR [*unconcernedly taking off his toga and throwing it on the chair*] Well, my friend, get out if you can. And tell your friends not to kill any more Romans in the market place. Otherwise my soldiers, who do not share my celebrated clemency, will probably kill you. Britannus: pass the word to the guard; and fetch my armor. [*Britannus runs out. Rufio returns*]. Well?

RUFIO [*pointing from the loggia to a cloud of smoke drifting over the harbor*] See there! [*Pothinus runs eagerly up the steps to look out*].

CÆSAR What, ablaze already! Impossible!

RUFIO Yes, five good ships, and a barge laden with oil grappled to each. But it is not my doing: the Egyptians have saved me the trouble. They have captured the west harbor.

CÆSAR [*anxiously*] And the east harbor? The lighthouse, Rufio?

RUFIO [*with a sudden splutter of raging ill usage, coming down to Cæsar and scolding him*] Can I embark a legion in five minutes? The first cohort is already on the beach. We can do no more. If you want faster work, come and do it yourself.

CÆSAR [*soothing him*] Good, good. Patience, Rufio, patience.

RUFIO Patience! Who is impatient here, you or I? Would I be here, if I could not oversee them from that balcony?

CÆSAR Forgive me, Rufio; and [*anxiously*] hurry them as much as –

He is interrupted by an outcry as of an old man in the extremity of misfortune. It draws near rapidly; and Theodotus rushes in, tearing his hair, and speaking the most lamentable exclamations. Rufio steps back to stare at him, amazed at his frantic condition. Pothinus turns to listen.

THEODOTUS [*on the steps, with uplifted arms*] Horror unspeakable! Woe, alas! Help!

RUFIO What now?

CÆSAR [*frowning*] Who is slain?

THEODOTUS Slain! Oh, worse than the death of ten thousand men! Loss irreparable to mankind!

RUFIO What has happened, man?

THEODOTUS [*rushing down the hall between them*] The fire has spread from your ships. The first of the seven wonders of the world perishes. The library of Alexandria is in flames.

RUFIO Psha! [*Quite relieved, he goes up to the loggia and watches the preparations of the troops on the beach*].

CÆSAR Is that all?

THEODOTUS [*unable to believe his senses*] All! Cæsar: will you go down to posterity as a barbarous soldier too ignorant to know the value of books?

CÆSAR Theodotus: I am an author myself; and I tell you it is better that the Egyptians should live their lives than dream them away with the help of books.

131

THEODOTUS [*kneeling, with genuine literary emotion: the passion of the pedant*] Cæsar: once in ten generations of men, the world gains an immortal book.

CÆSAR [*inflexible*] If it did not flatter mankind, the common executioner would burn it.

THEODOTUS Without history, death will lay you beside your meanest soldier.

CÆSAR Death will do that in any case. I ask no better grave.

THEODOTUS What is burning there is the memory of mankind.

CÆSAR A shameful memory. Let it burn.

THEODOTUS [*wildly*] Will you destroy the past?

CÆSAR Ay, and build the future with its ruins. [*Theodotus, in despair, strikes himself on the temples with his fists*]. But harken, Theodotus, teacher of kings: you who valued Pompey's head no more than a shepherd values an onion, and who now kneel to me, with tears in your old eyes, to plead for a few sheepskins scrawled with errors. I cannot spare you a man or a bucket of water just now; but you shall pass freely out of the palace. Now, away with you to Achillas; and borrow his legions to put out the fire. [*He hurries him to the steps*].

POTHINUS [*significantly*] You understand, Theodotus: I remain a prisoner.

THEODOTUS A prisoner!

CÆSAR Will you stay to talk whilst the memory of mankind is burning? [*Calling through the loggia*] Ho there! Pass Theodotus out. [*To Theodotus*] Away with you.

THEODOTUS [*To Pothinus*] I must go to save the library. [*He hurries out*].

CÆSAR Follow him to the gate, Pothinus. Bid him urge your people to kill no more of my soldiers, for your sake.

POTHINUS My life will cost you dear if you take it, Cæsar. [*He goes out after Theodotus*].

Rufio, absorbed in watching the embarkation, does not notice the departure of the two Egyptians.

RUFIO [*shouting from the loggia to the beach*] All ready, there?

A CENTURION [*from below*] All ready. We wait for Cæsar.

CÆSAR   Tell them Cæsar is coming – the rogues! [*Calling*]
        Britannicus. [*This magniloquent version of his secre-
        tary's name is one of Cæsar's jokes. In later years it
        would have meant, quite seriously and officially, Con-
        queror of Britain*].

RUFIO   [*calling down*] Push off, all except the longboat. Stand
        by it to embark, Cæsar's guard there. [*He leaves the
        balcony and comes down into the hall*]. Where are those
        Egyptians? Is this more clemency? Have you let them
        go?

CÆSAR   [*chuckling*] I have let Theodotus go to save the library.
        We must respect literature, Rufio.

RUFIO   [*raging*] Folly on folly's head! I believe if you could
        bring back all the dead of Spain, Gaul and Thessaly
        to life, you would do it that we might have the
        trouble of fighting them over again.

CÆSAR   Might not the gods destroy the world if their only
        thought were to be at peace next year? [*Rufio, out of
        all patience, turns away in anger. Cæsar suddenly grips
        his sleeve, and adds slyly in his ear*] Besides, my friend:
        every Egyptian we imprison means imprisoning two
        Roman soldiers to guard him. Eh?

RUFIO   Agh! I might have known there was some fox's trick
        behind your fine talking. [*He gets away from Cæsar
        with an ill-humored shrug, and goes to the balcony for
        another look at the preparations; finally goes out*].

CÆSAR   Is Britannus asleep? I sent him for my armor an hour
        ago. [*Calling*] Britannicus, thou British islander.
        Britannicus!

        *Cleopatra runs in through the loggia with Cæsar's hel-
        met and sword, snatched from Britannus, who follows
        her with a cuirass and greaves. They come down to
        Cæsar, she to his left hand, Britannus to his right.*

CLEOPATRA   I am going to dress you, Cæsar. Sit down. [*He obeys*].
        These Roman helmets are so becoming! [*She takes off
        his wreath*]. Oh! [*She bursts out laughing at him*].

CÆSAR   What are you laughing at?

CLEOPATRA   Youre bald [*beginning with a big B, and ending with a
        splutter*].

CÆSAR   [*almost annoyed*] Cleopatra! [*He rises, for the con-

venience of Britannus, who puts the cuirass on him].

CLEOPATRA So that is why you wear the wreath – to hide it.

BRITANNUS Peace, Egyptian: they are the bays of the conqueror. [*He buckles the cuirass*].

CLEOPATRA Peace, thou: islander! [*To Cæsar*] You should rub your head with strong spirits of sugar, Cæsar. That will make it grow.

CÆSAR [*with a wry face*] Cleopatra: do you like to be reminded that you are very young?

CLEOPATRA [*pouting*] No.

CÆSAR [*sitting down again, and setting out his leg for Britannus, who kneels to put on his greaves*] Neither do I like to be reminded that I am – middle aged. Let me give you ten of my superfluous years. That will make you 26, and leave me only – no matter. Is it a bargain?

CLEOPATRA Agreed. 26, mind. [*She puts the helmet on him*]. Oh! How nice! You look only about 50 in it!

BRITANNUS [*looking up severely at Cleopatra*] You must not speak in this manner to Cæsar.

CLEOPATRA Is it true that when Cæsar caught you on that island, you were painted all over blue?

BRITANNUS Blue is the color worn by all Britons of good standing. In war we stain our bodies blue; so that though our enemies may strip us of our clothes and our lives, they cannot strip us of our respectability. [*He rises*].

CLEOPATRA [*with Cæsar's sword*] Let me hang this on. Now you look splendid. Have they made any statues of you in Rome?

CÆSAR Yes, many statues.

CLEOPATRA You must send for one and give it to me.

RUFIO [*coming back into the loggia, more impatient than ever*] Now Cæsar: have you done talking? The moment your foot is aboard there will be no holding our men back: the boats will race one another for the lighthouse.

CÆSAR [*drawing his sword and trying the edge*] Is this well set to-day, Britannicus? At Pharsalia it was as blunt as a barrel-hoop.

BRITANNUS It will split one of the Egyptian's hairs to-day, Cæsar. I have set it myself.

134

CLEOPATRA [*suddenly throwing her arms in terror round Cæsar*] Oh, you are not really going into battle to be killed?

CÆSAR No, Cleopatra. No man goes to battle to be killed.

CLEOPATRA But they do get killed. My sister's husband was killed in battle. You must not go. Let *him* go [*pointing to Rufio. They all laugh at her*]. Oh please, *please* dont go. What will happen to *me* if you never come back?

CÆSAR [*gravely*] Are you afraid?

CLEOPATRA [*shrinking*] No.

CÆSAR [*with quiet authority*] Go to the balcony; and you shall see us take the Pharos. You must learn to look on battles. Go. [*She goes, downcast, and looks out from the balcony*]. That is well. Now, Rufio. March.

CLEOPATRA [*suddenly clapping her hands*] Oh, you will not be able to go!

CÆSAR Why? What now?

CLEOPATRA They are drying up the harbor with buckets – a multitude of soldiers – over there [*pointing out across the sea to her left*] – they are dipping up the water.

RUFIO [*hastening to look*] It is true. The Egyptian army! Crawling over the edge of the west harbor like locusts. [*With sudden anger he strides down to Cæsar*]. This is your accursed clemency, Cæsar. Theodotus has brought them.

CÆSAR [*delighted at his own cleverness*] I meant him to, Rufio. They have come to put out the fire. The library will keep them busy whilst we seize the lighthouse. Eh? [*He rushes out buoyantly through the loggia, followed by Britannus*].

RUFIO [*disgustedly*] More foxing! Agh! [*He rushes off. A shout from the soldiers announces the appearance of Cæsar below*].

CENTURION [*below*] All aboard. Give way there. [*Another shout*].

CLEOPATRA [*waving her scarf through the loggia arch*] Goodbye, goodbye, dear Cæsar. Come back safe. Goodbye!

ACT 3

The edge of the quay in front of the palace, looking out west over the east harbor of Alexandria to Pharos island, just off the end of which, and connected with it by a narrow mole, is the famous lighthouse, a gigantic square tower of white marble diminishing in size storey by storey to the top, on which stands a cresset beacon. The island is joined to the main land by the Heptastadium, a great mole or causeway five miles long bounding the harbor on the south.

In the middle of the quay a Roman sentinel stands on guard, pilum in hand, looking out to the lighthouse with strained attention, his left hand shading his eyes. The pilum is a stout wooden shaft 4½ feet long, with an iron spit about three feet long fixed in it. The sentinel is so absorbed that he does not notice the approach from the north end of the quay of four Egyptian market porters carrying rolls of carpet, preceded by Ftatateeta and Apollodorus the Sicilian. Apollodorus is a dashing young man of about 24, handsome and debonair, dressed with deliberate æstheticism in the most delicate purples and dove greys, with ornaments of bronze, oxydized silver, and stones of jade and agate. His sword, designed as carefully as a medieval cross, has a blued blade showing through an openwork scabbard of purple leather and

137

filagree. The porters, conducted by Ftatateeta, pass along the quay behind the sentinel to the steps of the palace, where they put down their bales and squat on the ground. Apollodorus does not pass along with them: he halts, amused by the preoccupation of the sentinel.

APOLLODORUS [*calling to the sentinel*] Who goes there, eh?

SENTINEL [*starting violently and turning with his pilum at the charge, revealing himself as a small, wiry, sandy-haired, conscientious young man with an elderly face*] Whats this? Stand. Who are you?

APOLLODORUS I am Apollodorus the Sicilian. Why, man, what are you dreaming of? Since I came through the lines beyond the theatre there, I have brought my caravan past three sentinels, all so busy staring at the light-house that not one of them challenged me. Is this Roman discipline?

SENTINEL We are not here to watch the land but the sea. Cæsar has just landed on the Pharos. [*Looking at Ftatateeta*] What have you here? Who is this piece of Egyptian crockery?

FTATATEETA Apollodorus: rebuke this Roman dog; and bid him bridle his tongue in the presence of Ftatateeta, the mistress of the Queen's household.

APOLLODORUS My friend: this is a great lady, who stands high with Cæsar.

SENTINEL [*not at all impressed, pointing to the carpets*] And what is all this truck?

APOLLODORUS Carpets for the furnishing of the Queen's apartments in the palace. I have picked them from the best carpets in the world; and the Queen shall choose the best of my choosing.

SENTINEL So you are the carpet merchant?

APOLLODORUS [*hurt*] My friend: I am a patrician.

SENTINEL A patrician! A patrician keeping a shop instead of following arms!

APOLLODORUS I do not keep a shop. Mine is a temple of the arts. I am a worshipper of beauty. My calling is to choose beautiful things for beautiful queens. My motto is Art for Art's sake.

138

SENTINEL   That is not the password.

APOLLODORUS   It is a universal password.

SENTINEL   I know nothing about universal passwords. Either give me the password for the day or get back to your shop.

Ftatateeta, roused by his hostile tone, steals towards the edge of the quay with the step of a panther, and gets behind him.

APOLLODORUS   How if I do neither?

SENTINEL   Then I will drive this pilum through you.

APOLLODORUS   At your service, my friend. [*He draws his sword, and springs to his guard with unruffled grace*].

FTATATEETA   [*suddenly seizing the sentinel's arms from behind*] Thrust your knife into the dog's throat, Apollodorus. [*The chivalrous Apollodorus laughingly shakes his head; breaks ground away from the sentinel towards the palace; and lowers his point*].

SENTINEL   [*struggling vainly*] Curse on you! Let me go. Help ho!

FTATATEETA   [*lifting him from the ground*] Stab the little Roman reptile. Spit him on your sword.

A couple of Roman soldiers, with a centurion, come running along the edge of the quay from the north end. They rescue their comrade, and throw off Ftatateeta, who is sent reeling away on the left hand of the sentinel.

CENTURION   [*an unattractive man of fifty, short in his speech and manners, with a vinewood cudgel in his hand*] How now? What is all this?

FTATATEETA   [*to Apollodorus*] Why did you not stab him? There was time!

APOLLODORUS   Centurion: I am here by order of the Queen to –

CENTURION   [*interrupting him*] The Queen! Yes, yes: [*to the sentinel*] pass him in. Pass all these bazaar people in to the Queen, with their goods. But mind you pass no one out that you have not passed in – not even the Queen herself.

SENTINEL   This old woman is dangerous: she is as strong as three men. She wanted the merchant to stab me.

APOLLODORUS   Centurion: I am not a merchant. I am a patrician and a votary of art.

139

CENTURION   Is the woman your wife?

APOLLODORUS   [*horrified*] No, no! [*Correcting himself politely*] Not that the lady is not a striking figure in her own way. But [*emphatically*] she is *not* my wife.

FTATATEETA   [*to the centurion*] Roman: I am Ftatateeta, the mistress of the Queen's household.

CENTURION   Keep your hands off our men, mistress; or I will have you pitched into the harbor, though you were as strong as ten men. [*To his men*] To your posts: march! [*He returns with his men the way they came*].

FTATATEETA   [*looking malignantly after him*] We shall see whom Isis loves best: her servant Ftatateeta or a dog of a Roman.

SENTINEL   [*to Apollodorus, with a wave of his pilum towards the palace*] Pass in there; and keep your distance. [*Turning to Ftatateeta*] Come within a yard of me, you old crocodile; and I will give you this [*the pilum*] in your jaws.

CLEOPATRA   [*calling from the palace*] Ftatateeta, Ftatateeta.

FTATATEETA   [*looking up, scandalized*] Go from the window, go from the window. There are men here.

CLEOPATRA   I am coming down.

FTATATEETA   [*distracted*] No, no. What are you dreaming of? O ye gods, ye gods! Apollodorus: bid your men pick up your bales; and in with me quickly.

APOLLODORUS   Obey the mistress of the Queen's household.

FTATATEETA   [*impatiently, as the porters stoop to lift the bales*] Quick, quick: she will be out upon us. [*Cleopatra comes from the palace and runs across the quay to Ftatateeta*]. Oh that ever I was born!

CLEOPATRA   [*eagerly*] Ftatateeta: I have thought of something. I want a boat – at once.

FTATATEETA A boat! No, no: you cannot. Apollodorus: speak to the Queen.

APOLLODORUS [*gallantly*] Beautiful queen: I am Apollodorus the Sicilian, your servant, from the bazaar. I have brought you the three most beautiful Persian carpets in the world to choose from.

CLEOPATRA I have no time for carpets to-day. Get me a boat.

FTATATEETA What whim is this? You cannot go on the water except in the royal barge.

APOLLODORUS Royalty, Ftatateeta, lies not in the barge but in the Queen. [*To Cleopatra*] The touch of your majesty's foot on the gunwale of the meanest boat in the harbor will make it royal. [*He turns to the harbor and calls seaward*] Ho there, boatman! Pull in to the steps.

CLEOPATRA Apollodorus: you are my perfect knight; and I will always buy my carpets through you. [*Apollodorus bows joyously. An oar appears above the quay; and the boatman, a bullet-headed, vivacious, grinning fellow, burnt almost black by the sun, comes up a flight of steps from the water on the sentinel's right, oar in hand, and waits at the top*]. Can you row, Apollodorus?

APOLLODORUS My oars shall be your majesty's wings. Whither shall I row my Queen?

CLEOPATRA To the lighthouse. Come. [*She makes for the steps*].

SENTINEL [*opposing her with his pilum at the charge*] Stand. You cannot pass.

CLEOPATRA [*flushing angrily*] How dare you? Do you know that I am the Queen?

SENTINEL I have my orders. You cannot pass.

CLEOPATRA I will make Cæsar have you killed if you do not obey me.

SENTINEL He will do worse to me if I disobey my officer. Stand back.

CLEOPATRA Ftatateeta: strangle him.

SENTINEL [*alarmed – looking apprehensively at Ftatateeta, and brandishing his pilum*] Keep off, there.

CLEOPATRA [*running to Apollodorus*] Apollodorus: make your slaves help us.

POLLODORUS I shall not need their help, lady. [*He draws his sword*].

141

Now, soldier: choose which weapon you will defend yourself with. Shall it be sword against pilum, or sword against sword?

SENTINEL Roman against Sicilian, curse you. Take that. [*He hurls his pilum at Apollodorus, who drops expertly on one knee. The pilum passes whizzing over his head and falls harmless. Apollodorus, with a cry of triumph, springs up and attacks the sentinel, who draws his sword and defends himself, crying*] Ho there, guard. Help!

Cleopatra, half frightened, half delighted, takes refuge near the palace, where the porters are squatting among the bales. The boatman, alarmed, hurries down the steps out of harm's way, but stops, with his head just visible above the edge of the quay, to watch the fight. The sentinel is handicapped by his fear of an attack in the rear from Ftatateeta. His swordsmanship, which is of a rough and ready sort, is heavily taxed, as he has occasionally to strike at her to keep her off between a blow and a guard with Apollodorus. The centurion returns with several soldiers. Apollodorus springs back towards Cleopatra as this reinforcement confronts him.

CENTURION [*coming to the sentinel's right hand*] What is this? What now?

SENTINEL [*panting*] I could do well enough by myself if it werent for the old woman. Keep her off me: that is all the help I need.

CENTURION Make your report, soldier. What has happened?

FTATATEETA Centurion: he would have slain the Queen.

SENTINEL [*bluntly*] I would, sooner than let her pass. She wanted to take boat, and go – so she said – to the lighthouse. I stopped her, as I was ordered to; and she set this fellow on me. [*He goes to pick up his pilum and returns to his place with it*].

CENTURION [*turning to Cleopatra*] Cleopatra: I am loth to offend you; but without Cæsar's express order we dare not let you pass beyond the Roman lines.

APOLLODORUS Well, Centurion; and has not the lighthouse been within the Roman lines since Cæsar landed there?

CLEOPATRA Yes, yes. Answer that, if you can.

142

CENTURION [to Apollodorus] As for you, Apollodorus, you may thank the gods that you are not nailed to the palace door with a pilum for your meddling.

APOLLODORUS [urbanely] My military friend, I was not born to be slain by so ugly a weapon. When I fall, it will be [holding up his sword] by this white queen of arms, the only weapon fit for an artist. And now that you are convinced that we do not want to go beyond the lines, let me finish killing your sentinel and depart with the Queen.

CENTURION [as the sentinel makes an angry demonstration] Peace there. Cleopatra: I must abide by my orders, and not by the subtleties of this Sicilian. You must withdraw into the palace and examine your carpets there.

CLEOPATRA [pouting] I will not: I am the Queen. Cæsar does not speak to me as you do. Have Cæsar's centurions changed manners with his scullions?

CENTURION [sulkily] I do my duty. That is enough for me.

APOLLODORUS Majesty: when a stupid man is doing something he is ashamed of, he always declares that it is his duty.

CENTURION [angry] Apollodorus –

APOLLODORUS [interrupting him with defiant elegance] I will make amends for that insult with my sword at fitting time and place. Who says artist, says duellist. [To Cleopatra] Hear my counsel, star of the east. Until word comes to these soldiers from Cæsar himself, you are a prisoner. Let me go to him with a message from you, and a present; and before the sun has stooped half way to the arms of the sea, I will bring you back Cæsar's order of release.

CENTURION [sneering at him] And you will sell the Queen the present, no doubt.

APOLLODORUS Centurion: the Queen shall have from me, without payment, as the unforced tribute of Sicilian taste to Egyptian beauty, the richest of these carpets for her present to Cæsar.

CLEOPATRA [exultantly, to the centurion] Now you see what an ignorant common creature you are!

CENTURION [curtly] Well, a fool and his wares are soon parted. [He turns to his men]. Two more men to this post here; and see that no one leaves the palace but this man and

143

his merchandize. If he draws his sword again inside the lines, kill him. To your posts. March.

He goes out, leaving two auxiliary sentinels with the other.

APOLLODORUS [*with polite goodfellowship*] My friends: will you not enter the palace and bury our quarrel in a bowl of wine? [*He takes out his purse, jingling the coins in it*]. The Queen has presents for you all.

SENTINEL [*very sulky*] You heard our orders. Get about your business.

1ST AUXILIARY Yes: you ought to know better. Off with you.

2ND AUXILIARY [*looking longingly at the purse – this sentinel is a hook-nosed man, unlike his comrade, who is squab faced*] Do not tantalize a poor man.

APOLLODORUS [*to Cleopatra*] Pearl of Queens: the centurion is at hand; and the Roman soldier is incorruptible when his officer is looking. I must carry your word to Cæsar.

CLEOPATRA [*who has been meditating among the carpets*] Are these carpets very heavy?

APOLLODORUS It matters not how heavy. There are plenty of porters.

CLEOPATRA How do they put the carpets into boats? Do they throw them down?

APOLLODORUS Not into small boats, majesty. It would sink them.

CLEOPATRA Not into that man's boat, for instance? [*pointing to the boatman*].

APOLLODORUS No. Too small.

CLEOPATRA But you can take a carpet to Cæsar in it if I send one?

APOLLODORUS Assuredly.

CLEOPATRA And you will have it carried gently down the steps and take great care of it?

APOLLODORUS Depend on me.

CLEOPATRA Great, *great* care?

APOLLODORUS More than of my own body.

CLEOPATRA You will promise me not to let the porters drop it or throw it about?

APOLLODORUS Place the most delicate glass goblet in the palace in

144

	the heart of the roll, Queen; and if it be broken, my head shall pay for it.
CLEOPATRA	Good. Come, Ftatateeta. [*Ftatateeta comes to her. Apollodorus offers to squire them into the palace*]. No, Apollodorus, you must not come. I will choose a carpet for myself. You must wait here. [*She runs into the palace*].
POLLODORUS	[*to the porters*] Follow this lady [*indicating Ftatateeta*]; and obey her.
	The porters rise and take up their bales.
FTATATEETA	[*addressing the porters as if they were vermin*] This way. And take your shoes off before you put your feet on those stairs.
	She goes in, followed by the porters with the carpets. Meanwhile Apollodorus goes to the edge of the quay and looks out over the harbor. The sentinels keep their eyes on him malignantly.
POLLODORUS	[*addressing the sentinel*] My friend –
SENTINEL	[*rudely*] Silence there.
1T AUXILIARY	Shut your muzzle, you.
D AUXILIARY	[*in a half whisper, glancing apprehensively towards the north end of the quay*] Cant you wait a bit?
POLLODORUS	Patience, worthy three-headed donkey. [*They mutter ferociously; but he is not at all intimidated*]. Listen: were you set here to watch me, or to watch the Egyptians?
SENTINEL	We know our duty.
POLLODORUS	Then why dont you do it? There is something going on over there [*pointing southwestward to the mole*].
SENTINEL	[*sulkily*] I do not need to be told what to do by the like of you.
POLLODORUS	Blockhead. [*He begins shouting*] Ho there, Centurion. Hoiho!
SENTINEL	Curse your meddling. [*Shouting*] Hoiho! Alarm! Alarm!
1ST AND 2ND AUXILIARIES	Alarm! alarm! Hoiho! [*The Centurion comes running in with his guard.*]
CENTURION	What now? Has the old woman attacked you again? [*Seeing Apollodorus*] Are *you* here still?

APOLLODORUS [*pointing as before*] See there. The Egyptians are moving. They are going to recapture the Pharos. They will attack by sea and land: by land along the great mole; by sea from the west harbor. Stir yourselves, my military friends: the hunt is up. [*A clangor of trumpets from several points along the quay*]. Aha! I told you so.

CENTURION [*quickly*] The two extra men pass the alarm to the south posts. One man keep guard here. The rest with me – quick.

The two auxiliary sentinels run off to the south. Tne centurion and his guard run off northward; and immediately afterwards the bucina sounds. The four porters come from the palace carrying a carpet, followed by Ftatateeta.

SENTINEL [*handling his pilum apprehensively*] You again! [*The porters stop*].

FTATATEETA Peace, Roman fellow: you are now singlehanded. Apollodorus: this carpet is Cleopatra's present to Cæsar. It has rolled up in it ten precious goblets of the thinnest Iberian crystal, and a hundred eggs of the sacred blue pigeon. On your honor, let not one of them be broken.

APOLLODORUS On my head be it! [*To the porters*] Into the boat with them carefully.

The porters carry the carpet to the steps.

1ST PORTER [*looking down at the boat*] Beware what you do, sir. Those eggs of which the lady speaks must weigh more than a pound apiece. This boat is too small for such a load.

BOATMAN [*excitedly rushing up the steps*] Oh thou injurious porter! Oh thou unnatural son of a she-camel! [*To Apollodorus*] My boat, sir, hath often carried five men. Shall it not carry your lordship and a bale of pigeons' eggs? [*To the porter*] Thou mangey dromedary, the gods shall punish thee for this envious wickedness.

1ST PORTER [*stolidly*] I cannot quit this bale now to beat thee; but another day I will lie in wait for thee.

APOLLODORUS [*going between them*] Peace there. If the boat were but a single plank, I would get to Cæsar on it.

146

FTATATEETA [*anxiously*] In the name of the gods, Apollodorus, run no risks with that bale.

APOLLODORUS Fear not, thou venerable grotesque: I guess its great worth. [*To the porters*] Down with it, I say; and gently; or ye shall eat nothing but stick for ten days.

The boatman goes down the steps, followed by the porters with the bale: Ftatateeta and Apollodorus watching from the edge.

APOLLODORUS Gently, my sons, my children – [*with sudden alarm*] gently, ye dogs. Lay it level in the stern – so – tis well.

FTATATEETA [*screaming down at one of the porters*] Do not step on it, do not step on it. Oh thou brute beast!

FIRST PORTER [*ascending*] Be not excited, mistress: all is well.

FTATATEETA [*panting*] All well! Oh, thou hast given my heart a turn! [*She clutches her side, gasping*].

The four porters have now come up and are waiting at the stairhead to be paid.

APOLLODORUS Here, ye hungry ones. [*He gives money to the first porter, who holds it in his hand to shew to the others. They crowd greedily to see how much it is, quite prepared, after the Eastern fashion, to protest to heaven against their patron's stinginess. But his liberality overpowers them*].

1ST PORTER O bounteous prince!

2ND PORTER O lord of the bazaar!

3RD PORTER O favored of the gods!

4TH PORTER O father to all the porters of the market!

SENTINEL [*enviously, threatening them fiercely with his pilum*] Hence, dogs: off. Out of this. [*They fly before him northward along the quay*].

APOLLODORUS Farewell, Ftatateeta. I shall be at the lighthouse before the Egyptians. [*He descends the steps*].

FTATATEETA The gods speed thee and protect my nursling!

The sentry returns from chasing the porters and looks down at the boat, standing near the stairhead lest Ftatateeta should attempt to escape.

APOLLODORUS [*from beneath, as the boat moves off*] Farewell, valiant pilum pitcher.

SENTINEL Farewell, shopkeeper.

APOLLODORUS Ha, ha! Pull, thou brave boatman, pull. Soho-o-o-o-o! [*He begins to sing in barcarolle measure to the rhythm of the oars*]

> My heart, my heart, spread out thy wings:
> Shake off thy heavy load of love –

Give me the oars, O son of a snail.

SENTINEL [*threatening Ftatateeta*] Now mistress: back to your henhouse. In with you.

FTATATEETA [*falling on her knees and stretching her hands over the waters*] Gods of the seas, bear her safely to the shore!

SENTINEL Bear *who* safely? What do you mean?

FTATATEETA [*looking darkly at him*] Gods of Egypt and of Vengeance, let this Roman fool be beaten like a dog by his captain for suffering her to be taken over the waters.

SENTINEL Accursed one: is she then in the boat? [*He calls over the sea*] Hoiho, there, boatman! Hoiho!

APOLLODORUS [*singing in the distance*]

> My heart, my heart, be whole and free:
> Love is thine only enemy.

Meanwhile Rufio, the morning's fighting done, sits munching dates on a faggot of brushwood outside the door of the lighthouse, which towers gigantic to the clouds on his left. His helmet, full of dates, is between his knees; and a leathern bottle of wine is by his side. Behind him the great stone pedestal of the lighthouse is

shut in from the open sea by a low stone parapet, with a couple of steps in the middle to the broad coping. A huge chain with a hook hangs down from the lighthouse crane above his head. Faggots like the one he sits on lie beneath it ready to be drawn up to feed the beacon.

Cæsar is standing on the step at the parapet looking out anxiously, evidently ill at ease. Britannus comes out of the lighthouse door.

RUFIO Well, my British islander. Have you been up to the top?

BRITANNUS I have. I reckon it at 200 feet high.

RUFIO Anybody up there?

BRITANNUS One elderly Tyrian to work the crane; and his son, a well conducted youth of 14.

RUFIO [*looking at the chain*] What! An old man and a boy work that! Twenty men, you mean.

BRITANNUS Two only, I assure you. They have counterweights, and a machine with boiling water in it which I do not understand: it is not of British design. They use it to haul up barrels of oil and faggots to burn in the brazier on the roof.

RUFIO But –

BRITANNUS Excuse me: I came down because there are messengers coming along the mole to us from the island. I must see what their business is. [*He hurries out past the lighthouse*].

CÆSAR [*coming away from the parapet, shivering and out of sorts*] Rufio: this has been a mad expedition. We shall be beaten. I wish I knew how our men are getting on with that barricade across the great mole.

RUFIO [*angrily*] Must I leave my food and go starving to bring you a report?

CÆSAR [*soothing him nervously*] No, Rufio, no. Eat, my son, eat. [*He takes another turn, Rufio chewing dates meanwhile*]. The Egyptians cannot be such fools as not to storm the barricade and swoop down on us here before it is finished. It is the first time I have ever run an avoidable risk. I should not have come to Egypt.

RUFIO An hour ago you were all for victory.

CÆSAR [*apologetically*] Yes: I was a fool – rash, Rufio – boyish.

RUFIO Boyish! Not a bit of it. Here [*offering him a handful of dates*].

CÆSAR What are these for?

RUFIO To eat. Thats whats the matter with you. When a man comes to your age, he runs down before his mid-day meal. Eat and drink; and then have another look at our chances.

CÆSAR [*taking the dates*] My age! [*He shakes his head and bites a date*]. Yes, Rufio: I am an old man – worn out now – true, quite true. [*He gives way to melancholy contemplation, and eats another date*]. Achillas is still in his prime: Ptolemy is a boy. [*He eats another date, and plucks up a little*]. Well, every dog has his day; and I have had mine: I cannot complain. [*With sudden cheerfulness*] These dates are not bad, Rufio. [*Britannus returns, greatly excited, with a leathern bag. Cæsar is himself again in a moment*]. What now?

BRITANNUS [*triumphantly*] Our brave Rhodian mariners have captured a treasure. There! [*He throws the bag down at Cæsar's feet*]. Our enemies are delivered into our hands.

CÆSAR In that bag?

BRITANNUS Wait till you hear, Cæsar. This bag contains all the letters which have passed between Pompey's party and the army of occupation here.

CÆSAR Well?

BRITANNUS [*impatient of Cæsar's slowness to grasp the situation*] Well, we shall now know who your foes are. The name of every man who has plotted against you since you crossed the Rubicon may be in these papers, for all we know.

CÆSAR Put them in the fire.

BRITANNUS Put them – [*he gasps*]!!!!

CÆSAR In the fire. Would you have me waste the next three years of my life in proscribing and condemning men who will be my friends when I have proved that my friendship is worth more than Pompey's was – than Cato's is. O incorrigible British islander: am I a bull dog, to seek quarrels merely to shew how stubborn my jaws are?

BRITANNUS   But your honor – the honor of Rome –

CÆSAR   I do not make human sacrifices to my honor, as your Druids do. Since you will not burn these, at least I can drown them. [*He picks up the bag and throws it over the parapet into the sea*].

BRITANNUS   Cæsar: this is mere eccentricity. Are traitors to be allowed to go free for the sake of a paradox?

RUFIO   [*rising*] Cæsar: when the islander has finished preaching, call me again. I am going to have a look at the boiling water machine. [*He goes into the lighthouse*].

BRITANNUS   [*with genuine feeling*] O Cæsar, my great master, if I could but persuade you to regard life seriously, as men do in my country!

CÆSAR   Do they truly do so, Britannus?

BRITANNUS   Have you not been there? Have you not seen them? What Briton speaks as you do in your moments of levity? What Briton neglects to attend the services at the sacred grove? What Briton wears clothes of many colors as you do, instead of plain blue, as all solid, well esteemed men should? These are moral questions with us.

CÆSAR   Well, well, my friend: some day I shall settle down and have a blue toga, perhaps. Meanwhile, I must get on as best I can in my flippant Roman way. [*Apollodorus comes past the lighthouse*]. What now?

BRITANNUS   [*turning quickly, and challenging the stranger with official haughtiness*] What is this? Who are you? How did you come here?

APOLLODORUS   Calm yourself, my friend: I am not going to eat you. I have come by boat, from Alexandria, with precious gifts for Cæsar.

CÆSAR   From Alexandria!

BRITANNUS   [*severely*] That is Cæsar, sir.

RUFIO   [*appearing at the lighthouse door*] Whats the matter now?

APOLLODORUS   Hail, great Cæsar! I am Apollodorus the Sicilian, an artist.

BRITANNUS   An artist! Why have they admitted this vagabond?

CÆSAR   Peace, man. Apollodorus is a famous patrician amateur.

151

BRITANNUS [*disconcerted*] I crave the gentleman's pardon. [*To Cæsar*] I understood him to say that he was a professional. [*Somewhat out of countenance, he allows Apollodorus to approach Cæsar, changing places with him. Rufio, after looking Apollodorus up and down with marked disparagement, goes to the other side of the platform*].

CÆSAR You are welcome, Apollodorus. What is your business?

APOLLODORUS First, to deliver to you a present from the Queen of Queens.

CÆSAR Who is that?

APOLLODORUS Cleopatra of Egypt.

CÆSAR [*taking him into his confidence in his most winning manner*] Apollodorus: this is no time for playing with presents. Pray you, go back to the Queen, and tell her that if all goes well I shall return to the palace this evening.

APOLLODORUS Cæsar: I cannot return. As I approached the lighthouse, some fool threw a great leathern bag into the sea. It broke the nose of my boat; and I had hardly time to get myself and my charge to the shore before the poor little cockleshell sank.

CÆSAR I am sorry, Apollodorus. The fool shall be rebuked. Well, well: what have you brought me? The Queen will be hurt if I do not look at it.

RUFIO Have we time to waste on this trumpery? The Queen is only a child.

CÆSAR Just so: that is why we must not disappoint her. What is the present, Apollodorus?

APOLLODORUS Cæsar: it is a Persian carpet – a beauty! And in it are – so I am told – pigeons' eggs and crystal goblets and fragile precious things. I dare not for my head have it carried up that narrow ladder from the causeway.

RUFIO Swing it up by the crane, then. We will send the eggs to the cook; drink our wine from the goblets; and the carpet will make a bed for Cæsar.

APOLLODORUS The crane! Cæsar: I have sworn to tender this bale of carpet as I tender my own life.

CÆSAR [*cheerfully*] Then let them swing you up at the same time; and if the chain breaks, you and the pigeons' eggs will perish together. [*He goes to the chain and looks up along it, examining it curiously*].

APOLLODORUS [*to Britannus*] Is Cæsar serious?

BRITANNUS His manner is frivolous because he is an Italian; but he means what he says.

APOLLODORUS Serious or not, he spake well. Give me a squad of soldiers to work the crane.

BRITANNUS Leave the crane to me. Go and await the descent of the chain.

APOLLODORUS Good. You will presently see me there [*turning to them all and pointing with an eloquent gesture to the sky above the parapet*] rising like the sun with my treasure.

He goes back the way he came. Britannus goes into the lighthouse.

RUFIO [*ill-humoredly*] Are you really going to wait here for this foolery, Cæsar?

CÆSAR [*backing away from the crane as it gives signs of working*] Why not?

RUFIO The Egyptians will let you know why not if they have the sense to make a rush from the shore end of the mole before our barricade is finished. And here we are waiting like children to see a carpet full of pigeons' eggs.

The chain rattles, and is drawn up high enough to clear the parapet. It then swings round out of sight behind the lighthouse.

CÆSAR Fear not, my son Rufio. When the first Egyptian takes his first step along the mole, the alarm will sound; and we two will reach the barricade from our end before the Egyptians reach it from their end – we two, Rufio: I, the old man, and you, his biggest boy. And the old man will be there first. So peace; and give me some more dates.

APOLLODORUS [*from the causeway below*] Soho, haul away. So-ho-o-o-o! [*The chain is drawn up and comes round again from behind the lighthouse. Apollodorus is swinging in the air with his bale of carpet at the end of it. He breaks into song as he soars above the parapet*]

153

<blockquote>
Aloft, aloft, behold the blue
That never shone in woman's eyes –
</blockquote>

Easy there: stop her. [*He ceases to rise*] Further round! [*The chain comes forward above the platform*].

RUFIO [*calling up*] Lower away there. [*The chain and its load begin to descend*].

APOLLODORUS [*calling up*] Gently – slowly – mind the eggs.

RUFIO [*calling up*] Easy there – slowly – slowly.

Apollodorus and the bale are deposited safely on the flags in the middle of the platform. Rufio and Cæsar help Apollodorus to cast off the chain from the bale.

RUFIO Haul up.

The chain rises clear of their heads with a rattle. Britannus comes from the lighthouse and helps them to uncord the carpet.

APOLLODORUS [*when the cords are loose*] Stand off, my friends: let Cæsar see. [*He throws the carpet open*].

RUFIO Nothing but a heap of shawls. Where are the pigeons' eggs?

APOLLODORUS Approach, Cæsar; and search for them among the shawls.

RUFIO [*drawing his sword*] Ha, treachery! Keep back, Cæsar: I saw the shawl move: there is something alive there.

BRITANNUS [*drawing his sword*] It is a serpent.

APOLLODORUS Dares Cæsar thrust his hand into the sack where the serpent moves?

RUFIO [*turning on him*] Treacherous dog –

CÆSAR Peace. Put up your swords. Apollodorus: your serpent seems to breathe very regularly. [*He thrusts his hand under the shawls and draws out a bare arm*]. This is a pretty little snake.

RUFIO [*drawing out the other arm*] Let us have the rest of you.

They pull Cleopatra up by the wrists into a sitting position. Britannus, scandalized, sheathes his sword with a drive of protest.

CLEOPATRA [*gasping*] Oh, I'm smothered. Oh, Cæsar, a man stood on me in the boat; and a great sack of something fell upon me out of the sky; and then the boat sank; and

154

	then I was swung up into the air and bumped down.
CÆSAR	[*petting her as she rises and takes refuge on his breast*] Well, never mind: here you are safe and sound at last.
RUFIO	Ay; and now that she *is* here, what are we to do with her?
BRITANNUS	She cannot stay here, Cæsar, without the companionship of some matron.
CLEOPATRA	[*jealously, to Cæsar, who is obviously perplexed*] Arnt you glad to see me?
CÆSAR	Yes, yes; *I* am very glad. But Rufio is very angry; and Britannus is shocked.
CLEOPATRA	[*contemptuously*] You can have their heads cut off, can you not?
CÆSAR	They would not be so useful with their heads cut off as they are now, my sea bird.
RUFIO	[*to Cleopatra*] We shall have to go away presently and cut some of your Egyptians' heads off. How will you like being left here with the chance of being captured by that little brother of yours if we are beaten?
CLEOPATRA	But you mustnt leave me alone. Cæsar: you will not leave me alone, will you?
RUFIO	What! not when the trumpet sounds and all our lives depend on Cæsar's being at the barricade before the Egyptians reach it? Eh?
CLEOPATRA	Let them lose their lives: they are only soldiers.
CÆSAR	[*gravely*] Cleopatra: when that trumpet sounds, we must take every man his life in his hand, and throw it in the face of Death. And of my soldiers who have trusted me there is not one whose hand I shall not hold more sacred than your head. [*Cleopatra is overwhelmed. Her eyes fill with tears*]. Apollodorus: you must take her back to the palace.
APOLLODORUS	Am I a dolphin, Cæsar, to cross the seas with young ladies on my back? My boat is sunk: all yours are either at the barricade or have returned to the city. I will hail one if I can: that is all I can do. [*He goes back to the causeway*].
CLEOPATRA	[*struggling with her tears*] It does not matter. I will not go back. Nobody cares for me.

155

CÆSAR Cleopatra –

CLEOPATRA You want me to be killed.

CÆSAR [*still more gravely*] My poor child: your life matters little here to anyone but yourself. [*She gives way altogether at this, casting herself down on the faggots weeping. Suddenly a great tumult is heard in the distance, bucinas and trumpets sounding through a storm of shouting. Britannus rushes to the parapet and looks along the mole. Cæsar and Rufio turn to one another with quick intelligence*].

CÆSAR Come, Rufio.

CLEOPATRA [*scrambling to her knees and clinging to him*] No, no. Do not leave me, Cæsar. [*He snatches his skirt from her clutch*]. Oh!

BRITANNUS [*from the parapet*] Cæsar: we are cut off. The Egyptians have landed from the west harbor between us and the barricade! ! !

RUFIO [*running to see*] Curses! It is true. We are caught like rats in a trap.

CÆSAR [*ruthfully*] Rufio, Rufio: my men at the barricade are between the sea party and the shore party. I have murdered them.

RUFIO [*coming back from the parapet to Cæsar's right hand*] Ay: that comes of fooling with this girl here.

APOLLODORUS [*coming up quickly from the causeway*] Look over the parapet, Cæsar.

CÆSAR We have looked, my friend. We must defend ourselves here.

APOLLODORUS I have thrown the ladder into the sea. They cannot get in without it.

RUFIO Ay; and we cannot get out. Have you thought of that?

APOLLODORUS Not get out! Why not? You have ships in the east harbor.

BRITANNUS [*hopefully, at the parapet*] The Rhodian galleys are standing in towards us already. [*Cæsar quickly joins Britannus at the parapet*].

RUFIO [*to Apollodorus, impatiently*] And by what road are we to walk to the galleys, pray?

APOLLODORUS [*with gay, defiant rhetoric*] By the road that leads

156

everywhere – the diamond path of the sun and moon. Have you never seen the child's shadow play of The Broken Bridge? "Ducks and geese with ease get over" – eh? [*He throws away his cloak and cap, and binds his sword on his back*].

RUFIO What are you talking about?

APOLLODORUS I will shew you. [*Calling to Britannus*] How far off is the nearest galley?

BRITANNUS Fifty fathom.

CÆSAR No, no: they are further off than they seem in this clear air to your British eyes. Nearly quarter of a mile, Apollodorus.

APOLLODORUS Good. Defend yourselves here until I send you a boat from that galley.

RUFIO Have you wings, perhaps?

APOLLODORUS Water wings, soldier. Behold!

He runs up the steps between Cæsar and Britannus to the coping of the parapet; springs into the air; and plunges head foremost into the sea.

CÆSAR [*like a schoolboy – wildly excited*] Bravo, bravo! [*Throwing off his cloak*] By Jupiter, I will do that too.

RUFIO [*seizing him*] You are mad. You shall not.

CÆSAR Why not? Can I not swim as well as he?

RUFIO [*frantic*] Can an old fool dive and swim like a young one? He is twenty-five and you are fifty.

CÆSAR [*breaking loose from Rufio*] Old! ! !

BRITANNUS [*shocked*] Rufio: you forget yourself.

CÆSAR I will race you to the galley for a week's pay, father Rufio.

CLEOPATRA But me! me! ! me! ! ! what is to become of *me?*

CÆSAR I will carry you on my back to the galley like a dolphin. Rufio: when you see me rise to the surface, throw her in: I will answer for her. And then in with you after her, both of you.

CLEOPATRA No, no, NO. I shall be drowned.

BRITANNUS Cæsar: I am a man and a Briton, not a fish. I must have a boat. I cannot swim.

CLEOPATRA Neither can I.

CÆSAR	[*to Britannus*] Stay here, then, alone, until I recapture the lighthouse: I will not forget you. Now, Rufio.
RUFIO	You have made up your mind to this folly?
CÆSAR	The Egyptians have made it up for me. What else is there to do? And mind where you jump: I do not want to get your fourteen stone in the small of my back as I come up. [*He runs up the steps and stands on the coping*].
BRITANNUS	[*anxiously*] One last word, Cæsar. Do not let yourself be seen in the fashionable part of Alexandria until you have changed your clothes.
CÆSAR	[*calling over the sea*] Ho, Apollodorus: [*he points skyward and quotes the barcarolle*]

The white upon the blue above –

APOLLODORUS	[*swimming in the distance*]

Is purple on the green below –

CÆSAR	[*exultantly*] Aha! [*He plunges into the sea*].
CLEOPATRA	[*running excitedly to the steps*] Oh, let me see. He will be drowned [*Rufio seizes her*] – Ah – ah – ah – ah! [*He pitches her screaming into the sea. Rufio and Britannus roar with laughter*].
RUFIO	[*looking down after her*] He has got her. [*To Britannus*] Hold the fort, Briton. Cæsar will not forget you. [*He springs off*].
BRITANNUS	[*running to the steps to watch them as they swim*] All safe, Rufio?
RUFIO	[*swimming*] All safe.
CÆSAR	[*swimming further off*] Take refuge up there by the beacon; and pile the fuel on the trap door, Britannus.
BRITANNUS	[*calling in reply*] I will first do so, and then commend myself to my country's gods. [*A sound of cheering from the sea. Britannus gives full vent to his excitement*]. The boat has reached him: Hip, hip, hip, hurrah!

ACT 4

Cleopatra's sousing in the east harbor of Alexandria was in October 48 B.C. In March 47 she is passing the afternoon in her boudoir in the palace, among a bevy of her ladies, listening to a slave girl who is playing the harp in the middle of the room. The harpist's master, an old musician, with a lined face, prominent brows, white beard, moustache and eyebrows twisted and horned at the ends, and a consciously keen and pretentious expression, is squatting on the floor close to her on her right, watching her performance. Ftatateeta is in attendance near the door, in front of a group of female slaves. Except the harp player all are seated: Cleopatra in a chair opposite the door on the other side of the room; the rest on the ground. Cleopatra's ladies are all young, the most conspicuous being Charmian and Iras, her favorites. Charmian is a hatchet faced, terra cotta colored little goblin, swift in her movements, and neatly finished at the hands and feet. Iras is a plump, goodnatured creature, rather fatuous, with a profusion of red hair, and a tendency to giggle on the slightest provocation.

CLEOPATRA   Can I –

FTATATEETA   [*insolently, to the player*] Peace, thou! The Queen speaks. [*The player stops*].

CLEOPATRA   [*to the old musician*] I want to learn to play the harp with my own hands. Cæsar loves music. Can you teach me?

MUSICIAN   Assuredly I and no one else can teach the queen. Have I not discovered the lost method of the ancient Egyptians, who could make a pyramid tremble by touching a bass string? All the other teachers are quacks: I have exposed them repeatedly.

CLEOPATRA   Good: you shall teach me. How long will it take?

MUSICIAN   Not very long: only four years. Your Majesty must first become proficient in the philosophy of Pythagoras.

CLEOPATRA   Has she [*indicating the slave*] become proficient in the philosophy of Pythagoras?

MUSICIAN   Oh, she is but a slave. She learns as a dog learns.

CLEOPATRA   Well, then, I will learn as a dog learns; for she plays better than you. You shall give me a lesson every day for a fortnight. [*The musician hastily scrambles to his feet and bows profoundly*]. After that, whenever I strike a false note you shall be flogged; and if I strike so many that there is not time to flog you, you shall be thrown into the Nile to feed the crocodiles. Give the girl a piece of gold; and send them away.

MUSICIAN   [*much taken aback*] But true art will not be thus forced.

FTATATEETA   [*pushing him out*] What is this? Answering the Queen, forsooth. Out with you.

He is pushed out by Ftatateeta, the girl following with her harp, amid the laughter of the ladies and slaves.

CLEOPATRA   Now, can any of you amuse me? Have you any stories or any news?

IRAS   Ftatateeta –

CLEOPATRA   Oh, Ftatateeta, Ftatateeta, always Ftatateeta. Some new tale to set me against her.

IRAS   No: this time Ftatateeta has been virtuous. [*All the*

ladies laugh – not the slaves]. Pothinus has been trying to bribe her to let him speak with you.

CLEOPATRA [*wrathfully*] Ha! you all sell audiences with me, as if I saw whom you please, and not whom I please. I should like to know how much of her gold piece that harp girl will have to give up before she leaves the palace.

IRAS We can easily find out that for you.

The ladies laugh.

CLEOPATRA [*frowning*] You laugh; but take care, take care. I will find out some day how to make myself served as Cæsar is served.

CHARMIAN Old hooknose! [*They laugh again*].

CLEOPATRA [*revolted*] Silence. Charmian: do not you be a silly little Egyptian fool. Do you know why I allow you all to chatter impertinently just as you please, instead of treating you as Ftatateeta would treat you if she were Queen?

CHARMIAN Because you try to imitate Cæsar in everything; and he lets everybody say what they please to him.

CLEOPATRA No; but because I asked him one day why he did so; and he said "Let your women talk; and you will learn something from them." What have I to learn from them? I said. "What they *are*," said he; and oh! you should have seen his eye as he said it. You would have curled up, you shallow things. [*They laugh. She turns fiercely on Iras*]. At whom are you laughing – at me or at Cæsar?

IRAS At Cæsar.

CLEOPATRA If you were not a fool, you would laugh at me; and if you were not a coward you would not be afraid to tell me so. [*Ftatateeta returns*]. Ftatateeta: they tell me that Pothinus has offered you a bribe to admit him to my presence.

FTATATEETA [*protesting*] Now by my father's gods –

CLEOPATRA [*cutting her short despotically*] Have I not told you not to deny things? You would spend the day calling your father's gods to witness to your virtues if I let you. Go take the bribe; and bring in Pothinus. [*Ftatateeta is about to reply*]. Dont answer me. Go.

163

Ftatateeta goes out; and Cleopatra rises and begins to prowl to and fro between her chair and the door, meditating. All rise and stand.

IRAS [*as she reluctantly rises*] Heigho! I wish Cæsar were back in Rome.

CLEOPATRA [*threateningly*] It will be a bad day for you all when he goes. Oh, if I were not ashamed to let him see that I am as cruel at heart as my father, I would make you repent that speech! Why do you wish him away?

CHARMIAN He makes you so terribly prosy and serious and learned and philosophical. It is worse than being religious, at *our* ages. [*The ladies laugh*].

CLEOPATRA Cease that endless cackling, will you. Hold your tongues.

CHARMIAN [*with mock resignation*] Well, well: we must try to live up to Cæsar.

They laugh again. Cleopatra rages silently as she continues to prowl to and fro. Ftatateeta comes back with Pothinus, who halts on the threshold.

FTATATEETA [*at the door*] Pothinus craves the ear of the –

CLEOPATRA There, there: that will do: let him come in. [*She resumes her seat. All sit down except Pothinus, who advances to the middle of the room. Ftatateeta takes her former place*]. Well, Pothinus: what is the latest news from your rebel friends?

POTHINUS [*haughtily*] I am no friend of rebellion. And a prisoner does not receive news.

CLEOPATRA You are no more a prisoner than I am – than Cæsar is. These six months we have been besieged in this palace by my subjects. You are allowed to walk on the beach among the soldiers. Can I go further myself, or can Cæsar?

POTHINUS You are but a child, Cleopatra, and do not understand these matters.

The ladies laugh. Cleopatra looks inscrutably at him.

CHARMIAN I see you do not know the latest news, Pothinus.

POTHINUS What is that?

CHARMIAN That Cleopatra is no longer a child. Shall I tell you

POTHINUS I should prefer to grow wiser without growing older.

CHARMIAN Well, go up to the top of the lighthouse; and get some-body to take you by the hair and throw you into the sea. [*The ladies laugh*].

CLEOPATRA She is right, Pothinus: you will come to the shore with much conceit washed out of you. [*The ladies laugh. Cleopatra rises impatiently*]. Begone, all of you. I will speak with Pothinus alone. Drive them out, Ftata-teeta. [*They run out laughing. Ftatateeta shuts the door on them*]. What are *you* waiting for?

FTATATEETA It is not meet that the Queen remain alone with –

CLEOPATRA [*interrupting her*] Ftatateeta: must I sacrifice you to your father's gods to teach you that *I* am Queen of Egypt, and not you?

FTATATEETA [*indignantly*] You are like the rest of them. You want to be what these Romans call a New Woman. [*She goes out, banging the door*].

CLEOPATRA [*sitting down again*] Now, Pothinus: why did you bribe Ftatateeta to bring you hither?

POTHINUS [*studying her gravely*] Cleopatra: what they tell me is true. You are changed.

CLEOPATRA Do you speak with Cæsar every day for six months: and *you* will be changed.

POTHINUS It is the common talk that you are infatuated with this old man?

CLEOPATRA Infatuated? What does that mean? Made foolish, is it not? Oh no: I wish I were.

POTHINUS You wish you were made foolish! How so?

CLEOPATRA When I was foolish, I did what I liked, except when Ftatateeta beat me; and even then I cheated her and did it by stealth. Now that Cæsar has made me wise, it is no use my liking or disliking: I do what must be done, and have no time to attend to myself. That is not happiness; but it is greatness. If Cæsar were gone, I think I could govern the Egyptians; for what Cæsar is to me, I am to the fools around me.

POTHINUS [*looking hard at her*] Cleopatra: this may be the vanity of youth.

CLEOPATRA No, no: it is not that I am so clever, but that the others are so stupid.

POTHINUS [*musingly*] Truly, that is the great secret.

CLEOPATRA Well, now tell me what you came to say?

POTHINUS [*embarrassed*] I! Nothing.

CLEOPATRA Nothing!

POTHINUS At least – to beg for my liberty: that is all.

CLEOPATRA For that you would have knelt to Cæsar. No, Pothinus: you came with some plan that depended on Cleopatra being a little nursery kitten. Now that Cleopatra is a Queen, the plan is upset.

POTHINUS [*bowing his head submissively*] It is so.

CLEOPATRA [*exultant*] Aha!

POTHINUS [*raising his eyes keenly to hers*] Is Cleopatra then indeed a Queen, and no longer Cæsar's prisoner and slave?

CLEOPATRA Pothinus: we are all Cæsar's slaves – all we in this land of Egypt – whether we will or no. And she who is wise enough to know this will reign when Cæsar departs.

POTHINUS You harp on Cæsar's departure.

CLEOPATRA What if I do?

POTHINUS Does he not love you?

CLEOPATRA Love me! Pothinus: Cæsar loves no one. Who are those we love? Only those whom we do not hate: all people are strangers and enemies to us except those we love. But it is not so with Cæsar. *He* has no hatred in him: he makes friends with everyone as he does with dogs and children. His kindness to me is a wonder: neither mother, father, nor nurse have ever taken so much care for me, or thrown open their thoughts to me so freely.

POTHINUS Well: is not this love?

CLEOPATRA What! when he will do as much for the first girl he meets on his way back to Rome? Ask his slave, Britannus: he has been just as good to him. Nay, ask his very horse! His kindness is not for anything in *me:* it is in his own nature.

166

POTHINUS   But how can you be sure that he does not love you as men love women?

CLEOPATRA   Because I cannot make him jealous. I have tried.

POTHINUS   Hm! Perhaps I should have asked, then, do *you* love *him?*

CLEOPATRA   Can one love a god? Besides, I love another Roman: one whom I saw long before Cæsar – no god, but a man – one who can love and hate – one whom I can hurt and who would hurt me.

POTHINUS   Does Cæsar know this?

CLEOPATRA   Yes.

POTHINUS   And he is not angry?

CLEOPATRA   He promises to send him to Egypt to please me!

POTHINUS   I do not understand this man.

CLEOPATRA   [*with superb contempt*] *You* understand Cæsar! How could you? [*Proudly*] I do – by instinct.

POTHINUS   [*deferentially, after a moment's thought*] Your Majesty caused me to be admitted to-day. What message has the Queen for me?

CLEOPATRA   This. You think that by making my brother king, you will rule in Egypt, because you are his guardian and he is a little silly.

POTHINUS   The Queen is pleased to say so.

CLEOPATRA   The Queen is pleased to say this also. That Cæsar will eat up you, and Achillas, and my brother, as a cat eats up mice; and that he will put on this land of Egypt as a shepherd puts on his garment. And when he has done that, he will return to Rome, and leave Cleopatra here as his viceroy.

POTHINUS   [*breaking out wrathfully*] That he shall never do. We have a thousand men to his ten; and we will drive him and his beggarly legions into the sea.

CLEOPATRA   [*with scorn, getting up to go*] You rant like any common fellow. Go, then, and marshal your thousands; and make haste; for Mithridates of Pergamos is at hand with reinforcements for Cæsar. Cæsar has held you at bay with two legions: we shall see what he will do with twenty.

POTHINUS   Cleopatra –

CLEOPATRA	Enough, enough: Cæsar has spoiled me for talking to weak things like you. [*She goes out. Pothinus, with a gesture of rage, is following, when Ftatateeta enters and stops him*].
POTHINUS	Let me go forth from this hateful place.
FTATATEETA	What angers you?
POTHINUS	The curse of all the gods of Egypt be upon her! She has sold her country to the Roman, that she may buy it back from him with her kisses.
FTATATEETA	Fool: did she not tell you that she would have Cæsar gone?
POTHINUS	You listened?
FTATATEETA	I took care that some honest woman should be at hand whilst you were with her.
POTHINUS	Now by the gods –
FTATATEETA	Enough of your gods! Cæsar's gods are all powerful here. It is no use *you* coming to Cleopatra: you are only an Egyptian. She will not listen to any of her own race: she treats us all as children.
POTHINUS	May she perish for it!
FTATATEETA	[*balefully*] May your tongue wither for that wish! Go! send for Lucius Septimius, the slayer of Pompey. He is a Roman: may be she will listen to him. Begone!
POTHINUS	[*darkly*] I know to whom I must go now.
FTATATEETA	[*suspiciously*] To whom, then?
POTHINUS	To a greater Roman than Lucius. And mark this, mistress. You thought, before Cæsar came, that Egypt should presently be ruled by you and your crew in the name of Cleopatra. I set myself against it –
FTATATEETA	[*interrupting him – wrangling*] Ay; that it might be ruled by you and your crew in the name of Ptolemy.
POTHINUS	Better me, or even you, than a woman with a Roman heart; and that is what Cleopatra is now become. Whilst I live, she shall never rule. So guide yourself accordingly. [*He goes out*].

It is by this time drawing on to dinner time. The table is laid on the roof of the palace; and thither Rufio is now climbing, ushered by a majestic palace official, wand of office in hand, and followed by a slave carrying an inlaid

168

stool. After many stairs they emerge at last into a massive colonnade on the roof. Light curtains are drawn between the columns on the north and east to soften the westering sun. The official leads Rufio to one of these shaded sections. A cord for pulling the curtains apart hangs down between the pillars.

THE OFFICIAL   [*bowing*] The Roman commander will await Cæsar here.

The slave sets down the stool near the southernmost column, and slips out through the curtains.

RUFIO   [*sitting down, a little blown*] Pouf! That was a climb. How high have we come?

THE OFFICIAL   We are on the palace roof, O Beloved of Victory!

RUFIO   Good! the Beloved of Victory has no more stairs to get up.

A second official enters from the opposite end, walking backwards.

2ND OFFICIAL   Cæsar approaches.

Cæsar, fresh from the bath, clad in a new tunic of purple

silk, comes in, beaming and festive, followed by two slaves carrying a light couch, which is hardly more than an elaborately designed bench. They place it near the northmost of the two curtained columns. When this is done they slip out through the curtains; and the two officials, formally bowing, follow them. Rufio rises to receive Cæsar.

CÆSAR [*coming over to him*] Why, Rufio! [*Surveying his dress with an air of admiring astonishment*] A new baldrick! A new golden pommel to your sword! And you have had your hair cut! But not your beard – ? impossible! [*He sniffs at Rufio's beard*]. Yes, perfumed, by Jupiter Olympus!

RUFIO [*growling*] Well: is it to please myself?

CÆSAR [*affectionately*] No, my son Rufio, but to please me – to celebrate my birthday.

RUFIO [*contemptuously*] Your birthday! You always have a birthday when there is a pretty girl to be flattered or an ambassador to be conciliated. We had seven of them in ten months last year.

CÆSAR [*contritely*] It is true, Rufio! I shall never break myself of these petty deceits.

RUFIO Who is to dine with us – besides Cleopatra?

CÆSAR Apollodorus the Sicilian.

RUFIO That popinjay!

CÆSAR Come! the popinjay is an amusing dog – tells a story; sings a song; and saves us the trouble of flattering the Queen. What does she care for old politicians and camp-fed bears like us? No: Apollodorus is good company, Rufio, good company.

RUFIO Well, he can swim a bit and fence a bit: he might be worse, if he only knew how to hold his tongue.

CÆSAR The gods forbid he should ever learn! Oh, this military life! this tedious, brutal life of action! That is the worst of us Romans: we are mere doers and drudgers: a swarm of bees turned into men. Give me a good talker – one with wit and imagination enough to live without continually doing something!

RUFIO Ay! a nice time he would have of it with you when dinner was over! Have you noticed that I am before my time?

CÆSAR Aha! I thought that meant something. What is it?

RUFIO Can we be overheard here?

CÆSAR Our privacy invites eavesdropping. I can remedy that. [*He claps his hands twice. The curtains are drawn, revealing the roof garden with a banqueting table set across in the middle for four persons, one at each end, and two side by side. The side next Cæsar and Rufio is blocked with golden wine vessels and basins. A gorgeous major-domo is superintending the laying of the table by a staff of slaves. The colonnade goes round the garden at both sides to the further end, where a gap in it, like a great gateway, leaves the view open to the sky beyond the western edge of the roof, except in the middle, where a life size image of Ra, seated on a huge plinth, towers up, with hawk head and crown of asp and disk. His altar, which stands at his feet, is a single white stone*]. Now everybody can see us, nobody will think of listening to us. [*He sits down on the bench left by the two slaves*].

RUFIO [*sitting down on his stool*] Pothinus wants to speak to you. I advise you to see him: there is some plotting going on here among the women.

CÆSAR Who is Pothinus?

RUFIO The fellow with hair like squirrel's fur – the little King's bear leader, whom you kept prisoner.

CÆSAR [*annoyed*] And has he not escaped?

171

RUFIO No.

CÆSAR [*rising imperiously*] Why not? You have been guarding this man instead of watching the enemy. Have I not told you always to let prisoners escape unless there are special orders to the contrary? Are there not enough mouths to be fed without him?

RUFIO Yes; and if you would have a little sense and let me cut his throat, you would save his rations. Anyhow, he *wont* escape. Three sentries have told him they would put a pilum through him if they saw him again. What more can they do? He prefers to stay and spy on us. So would I if I had to do with generals subject to fits of clemency.

CÆSAR [*resuming his seat, argued down*] Hm! And so he wants to see me.

RUFIO Ay. I have brought him with me. He is waiting there [*jerking his thumb over his shoulder*] under guard.

CÆSAR And you want me to see him?

RUFIO [*obstinately*] I dont want anything. I daresay you will do what you like. Dont put it on to me.

CÆSAR [*with an air of doing it expressly to indulge Rufio*] Well, well: let us have him.

RUFIO [*calling*] Ho there, guard! Release your man and send him up. [*Beckoning*]. Come along!

Pothinus enters and stops mistrustfully between the two, looking from one to the other.

CÆSAR [*graciously*] Ah, Pothinus! You are welcome. And what is the news this afternoon?

POTHINUS Cæsar: I come to warn you of a danger, and to make you an offer.

CÆSAR Never mind the danger. Make the offer.

RUFIO Never mind the offer. Whats the danger?

POTHINUS Cæsar: you think that Cleopatra is devoted to you.

CÆSAR [*gravely*] My friend: I already know what I think. Come to your offer.

POTHINUS I will deal plainly. I know not by what strange gods you have been enabled to defend a palace and a few yards of beach against a city and an army. Since we cut you off from Lake Mareotis, and you dug wells in the salt sea sand and brought up buckets of fresh water from them, we have known that your gods are irresistible, and that you are a worker of miracles. I no longer threaten you –

RUFIO [*sarcastically*] Very handsome of you, indeed.

POTHINUS So be it: you are the master. Our gods sent the north west winds to keep you in our hands; but you have been too strong for them.

CÆSAR [*gently urging him to come to the point*] Yes, yes, my friend. But what then?

RUFIO Spit it out, man. What have you to say?

POTHINUS I have to say that you have a traitress in your camp. Cleopatra –

MAJOR-DOMO [*at the table, announcing*] The Queen! [*Cæsar and Rufio rise*].

RUFIO [*aside to Pothinus*] You should have spat it out sooner, you fool. Now it is too late.

Cleopatra, in gorgeous raiment, enters in state through the gap in the colonnade, and comes down past the image of Ra and past the table to Cæsar. Her retinue, headed by Ftatateeta, joins the staff at the table. Cæsar gives Cleopatra his seat, which she takes.

CLEOPATRA [*quickly, seeing Pothinus*] What is *he* doing here?

CÆSAR [*seating himself beside her, in the most amiable of tempers*] Just going to tell me something about you. You shall hear it. Proceed, Pothinus.

POTHINUS [*disconcerted*] Cæsar – [*he stammers*].

CÆSAR Well, out with it.

POTHINUS What I have to say is for your ear, not for the Queen's.

CLEOPATRA [*with subdued ferocity*] There are means of making you speak. Take care.

POTHINUS [*defiantly*] Cæsar does not employ those means.

CÆSAR My friend: when a man has anything to tell in this world, the difficulty is not to make him tell it, but to prevent him from telling it too often. Let me celebrate my birthday by setting you free. Farewell: we shall not meet again.

CLEOPATRA [*angrily*] Cæsar: this mercy is foolish.

POTHINUS [*to Cæsar*] Will you not give me a private audience? Your life may depend on it. [*Cæsar rises loftily*].

RUFIO [*aside to Pothinus*] Ass! Now we shall have some heroics.

CÆSAR [*oratorically*] Pothinus –

RUFIO [*interrupting him*] Cæsar: the dinner will spoil if you begin preaching your favourite sermon about life and death.

CLEOPATRA [*priggishly*] Peace, Rufio. I desire to hear Cæsar.

RUFIO [*bluntly*] Your Majesty has heard it before. You repeated it to Apollodorus last week; and he thought it was all your own. [*Cæsar's dignity collapses. Much tickled, he sits down again and looks roguishly at Cleopatra, who is furious. Rufio calls as before*] Ho there, guard! Pass the prisoner out. He is released. [*To Pothinus*] Now off with you. You have lost your chance.

POTHINUS [*his temper overcoming his prudence*] I *will* speak.

CÆSAR [*to Cleopatra*] You see. Torture would not have wrung a word from him.

POTHINUS Cæsar: you have taught Cleopatra the arts by which the Romans govern the world.

CÆSAR Alas! they cannot even govern themselves. What then?

POTHINUS What then? Are you so besotted with her beauty that you do not see that she is impatient to reign in Egypt alone, and that her heart is set on your departure?

CLEOPATRA [*rising*] Liar!

CÆSAR [*shocked*] What! Protestations! Contradictions!

CLEOPATRA [*ashamed, but trembling with suppressed rage*] No. I do not deign to contradict. Let him talk. [*She sits down again*].

POTHINUS From her own lips I have heard it. You are to be her catspaw: you are to tear the crown from her brother's head and set it on her own, delivering us all into her hand – delivering yourself also. And then Cæsar can return to Rome, or depart through the gate of death, which is nearer and surer.

CÆSAR [*calmly*] Well, my friend; and is not this very natural?

POTHINUS [*astonished*] Natural! Then you do not resent treachery?

CÆSAR Resent! O thou foolish Egyptian, what have I to do with resentment? Do I resent the wind when it chills me, or the night when it makes me stumble in the darkness? Shall I resent youth when it turns from age, and ambition when it turns from servitude? To tell me such a story as this is but to tell me that the sun will rise to-morrow.

CLEOPATRA [*unable to contain herself*] But it is false – false. I swear it.

CÆSAR It is true, though you swore it a thousand times, and believed all you swore. [*She is convulsed with emotion. To screen her, he rises and takes Pothinus to Rufio, saying*] Come, Rufio: let us see Pothinus past the guard. I have a word to say to him. [*Aside to them*] We must give the Queen a moment to recover herself. [*Aloud*] Come. [*He takes Pothinus and Rufio out with him, conversing with them meanwhile*]. Tell your friends, Pothinus, that they must not think I am opposed to a reasonable settlement of the country's affairs – [*They pass out of hearing*].

CLEOPATRA [*in a stifled whisper*] Ftatateeta, Ftatateeta.

FTATATEETA [*hurrying to her from the table and petting her*] Peace, child: be comforted –

CLEOPATRA [*interrupting her*] Can they hear us?

FTATATEETA No, dear heart, no.

CLEOPATRA Listen to me. If he leaves the Palace alive, never see my face again.

FTATATEETA He? Poth –

CLEOPATRA [*striking her on the mouth*] Strike his life out as I strike his name from your lips. Dash him down from the wall. Break him on the stones. Kill, kill, *kill* him.

FTATATEETA [*shewing all her teeth*] The dog shall perish.

CLEOPATRA Fail in this, and you go out from before me for ever.

FTATATEETA [*resolutely*] So be it. You shall not see my face until his eyes are darkened.

Cæsar comes back, with Apollodorus, exquisitely dressed, and Rufio.

175

CLEOPATRA [*to Ftatateeta*] Come soon – soon. [*Ftatateeta turns her meaning eyes for a moment on her mistress; then goes grimly away past Ra and out. Cleopatra runs like a gazelle to Cæsar*] So you have come back to me, Cæsar. [*Caressingly*] I thought you were angry. Welcome, Apollodorus. [*She gives him her hand to kiss, with her other arm about Cæsar*].

APOLLODORUS Cleopatra grows more womanly beautiful from week to week.

CLEOPATRA Truth, Apollodorus?

APOLLODORUS Far, far short of the truth! Friend Rufio threw a pearl into the sea: Cæsar fished up a diamond.

CÆSAR Cæsar fished up a touch of rheumatism, my friend. Come: to dinner! to dinner! [*They move towards the table*].

CLEOPATRA [*skipping like a young fawn*] Yes, to dinner. I have ordered *such* a dinner for you, Cæsar!

CÆSAR Ay? What are we to have?

CLEOPATRA Peacocks' brains.

CÆSAR [*as if his mouth watered*] Peacocks' brains, Apollodorus!

APOLLODORUS Not for me. I prefer nightingales' tongues. [*He goes to one of the two covers set side by side*].

CLEOPATRA Roast boar, Rufio!

RUFIO [*gluttonously*] Good! [*He goes to the seat next Apollodorus, on his left*].

CÆSAR [*looking at his seat, which is at the end of the table, to Ra's left hand*] What has become of my leathern cushion?

CLEOPATRA [*at the opposite end*] I have got new ones for you.

MAJOR-DOMO These cushions, Cæsar, are of Maltese gauze, stuffed with rose leaves.

CÆSAR Rose leaves! Am I a caterpillar? [*He throws the cushions away and seats himself on the leather mattress underneath*].

CLEOPATRA What a shame! My new cushions!

MAJOR-DOMO [*at Cæsar's elbow*] What shall we serve to whet Cæsar's appetite?

176

CÆSAR   What have you got?

MAJOR-DOMO   Sea hedgehogs, black and white sea acorns, sea nettles, beccaficoes, purple shellfish –

CÆSAR   Any oysters?

MAJOR-DOMO   Assuredly.

CÆSAR   *British* oysters?

MAJOR-DOMO   [*assenting*] British oysters, Cæsar.

CÆSAR   Oysters, then. [*The Major-Domo signs to a slave at each order; and the slave goes out to execute it*]. I have been in Britain – that western land of romance – the last piece of earth on the edge of the ocean that surrounds the world. I went there in search of its famous pearls. The British pearl was a fable; but in searching for it I found the British oyster.

APOLLODORUS   All posterity will bless you for it. [*To the Major-Domo*] Sea hedgehogs for me.

RUFIO   Is there nothing solid to begin with?

MAJOR-DOMO   Fieldfares with asparagus –

CLEOPATRA   [*interrupting*] Fattened fowls! have some fattened fowls, Rufio.

RUFIO   Ay, that will do.

CLEOPATRA   [*greedily*] Fieldfares for me.

MAJOR-DOMO   Cæsar will deign to choose his wine? Sicilian, Lesbian, Chian –

RUFIO [*contemptuously*] All Greek.

APOLLODORUS Who would drink Roman wine when he could get Greek? Try the Lesbian, Cæsar.

CÆSAR Bring me my barley water.

RUFIO [*with intense disgust*] Ugh! Bring *me* my Falernian. [*The Falernian is presently brought to him*].

CLEOPATRA [*pouting*] It is waste of time giving you dinners, Cæsar. My scullions would not condescend to your diet.

CÆSAR [*relenting*] Well, well: let us try the Lesbian. [*The Major-Domo fills Cæsar's goblet; then Cleopatra's and Apollodorus's*]. But when I return to Rome, I will make laws against these extravagances. I will even get the laws carried out.

CLEOPATRA [*coaxingly*] Never mind. To-day you are to be like other people: idle, luxurious, and kind. [*She stretches her hand to him along the table*].

CÆSAR Well, for once I will sacrifice my comfort – [*kissing her hand*] there! [*He takes a draught of wine*]. Now are you satisfied?

CLEOPATRA And you no longer believe that I long for your departure for Rome?

CÆSAR I no longer believe anything. My brains are asleep. Besides, who knows whether I shall return to Rome?

RUFIO [*alarmed*] How? Eh? What?

CÆSAR What has Rome to shew me that I have not seen already? One year of Rome is like another, except that I grow older, whilst the crowd in the Appian Way is always the same age.

APOLLODORUS It is no better here in Egypt. The old men, when they are tired of life, say "We have seen everything except the source of the Nile."

CÆSAR [*his imagination catching fire*] And why not see that? Cleopatra: will you come with me and track the flood to its cradle in the heart of the regions of mystery? Shall we leave Rome behind us – Rome, that has achieved greatness only to learn how greatness destroys nations of men who are not great! Shall I make you a new kingdom, and build you a holy city there in the great unknown?

CLEOPATRA [*rapturously*] Yes, yes. You shall.

RUFIO Ay: now he will conquer Africa with two legions before we come to the roast boar.

APOLLODORUS Come: no scoffing. This is a noble scheme: in it Cæsar is no longer merely the conquering soldier, but the creative poet-artist. Let us name the holy city, and consecrate it with Lesbian wine.

CÆSAR Cleopatra shall name it herself.

CLEOPATRA It shall be called Cæsar's Gift to his Beloved.

APOLLODORUS No, no. Something vaster than that – something universal, like the starry firmament.

CÆSAR [*prosaically*] Why not simply The Cradle of the Nile?

CLEOPATRA No: the Nile is my ancestor; and he is a god. Oh! I have thought of something. The Nile shall name it himself. Let us call upon him. [*To the Major-Domo*] Send for him. [*The three men stare at one another; but the Major-Domo goes out as if he had received the most matter-of-fact order*]. And [*to the retinue*] away with you all.

The retinue withdraws, making obeisance.

A priest enters, carrying a miniature sphinx with a tiny tripod before it. A morsel of incense is smoking in the tripod. The priest comes to the table and places the image in the middle of it. The light begins to change to the

magenta purple of the Egyptian sunset, as if the god had brought a strange colored shadow with him. The three men are determined not to be impressed; but they feel curious in spite of themselves.

CÆSAR What hocus-pocus is this?

CLEOPATRA You shall see. And it is *not* hocus-pocus. To do it properly, we should kill something to please him; but perhaps he will answer Cæsar without that if we spill some wine to him.

APOLLODORUS [*turning his head to look up over his shoulder at Ra*] Why not appeal to our hawkheaded friend here?

CLEOPATRA [*nervously*] Sh! He will hear you and be angry.

RUFIO [*phlegmatically*] The source of the Nile is out of his district, I expect.

CLEOPATRA No: I will have my city named by nobody but my dear little sphinx, because it was in its arms that Cæsar found me asleep. [*She languishes at Cæsar; then turns curtly to the priest*]. Go. I am a priestess, and have power to take your charge from you. [*The priest makes a reverence and goes out*]. Now let us call on the Nile all together. Perhaps he will rap on the table.

CÆSAR What! table rapping! Are such superstitions still believed in this year 707 of the Republic?

CLEOPATRA It is no superstition: our priests learn lots of things from the tables. Is it not so, Apollodorus?

APOLLODORUS Yes: I profess myself a converted man. When Cleopatra is priestess, Apollodorus is devotee. Propose the conjuration.

CLEOPATRA You must say with me "Send us thy voice, Father Nile."

ALL FOUR [*holding their glasses together before the idol*] Send us thy voice, Father Nile.

The death cry of a man in mortal terror and agony answers them. Appalled, the men set down their glasses, and listen. Silence. The purple deepens in the sky. Cæsar, glancing at Cleopatra, catches her pouring out her wine before the god, with gleaming eyes, and mute assurances of gratitude and worship. Apollodorus springs up and runs to the edge of the roof to peer down and listen.

CÆSAR [*looking piercingly at Cleopatra*] What was that?

CLEOPATRA [*petulantly*] Nothing. They are beating some slave.

CÆSAR Nothing!

RUFIO A man with a knife in him, I'll swear.

CÆSAR [*rising*] A murder!

APOLLODORUS [*at the back, waving his hand for silence*] S-sh! Silence. Did you hear that?

CÆSAR Another cry?

APOLLODORUS [*returning to the table*] No, a thud. Something fell on the beach, I think.

RUFIO [*grimly, as he rises*] Something with bones in it, eh?

CÆSAR [*shuddering*] Hush, hush, Rufio. [*He leaves the table and returns to the colonnade: Rufio following at his left elbow, and Apollodorus at the other side*].

CLEOPATRA [*still in her place at the table*] Will you leave me, Cæsar? Apollodorus: are you going?

APOLLODORUS Faith, dearest Queen, my appetite is gone.

CÆSAR Go down to the courtyard, Apollodorus; and find out what has happened.

Apollodorus nods and goes out, making for the staircase by which Rufio ascended.

CLEOPATRA Your soldiers have killed somebody, perhaps. What does it matter?

The murmur of a crowd rises from the beach below. Cæsar and Rufio look at one another.

CÆSAR This must be seen to. [*He is about to follow Apollodorus when Rufio stops him with a hand on his arm as Ftatateeta comes back by the far end of the roof, with dragging steps, a drowsy satiety in her eyes and in the corners of the bloodhound lips. For a moment Cæsar suspects that she is drunk with wine. Not so Rufio: he knows well the red vintage that has inebriated her*].

RUFIO [*in a low tone*] There is some mischief between those two.

FTATATEETA The Queen looks again on the face of her servant.

Cleopatra looks at her for a moment with an exultant reflection of her murderous expression. Then she flings her arms round her; kisses her repeatedly and savagely; and tears off her jewels and heaps them on her. The two men turn from the spectacle to look at one another. Ftatateeta drags herself sleepily to the altar; kneels before Ra; and remains there in prayer. Cæsar goes to Cleopatra, leaving Rufio in the colonnade.

CÆSAR [*with searching earnestness*] Cleopatra: what has happened?

CLEOPATRA [*in mortal dread of him, but with her utmost cajolery*] Nothing, dearest Cæsar. [*With sickly sweetness, her voice almost failing*] Nothing. I am innocent. [*She approaches him affectionately*]. Dear Cæsar: are you angry with me? Why do you look at me so? I have been here with you all the time. How can I know what has happened?

CÆSAR [*reflectively*] That is true.

CLEOPATRA [*greatly relieved, trying to caress him*] Of course it is true. [*He does not respond to the caress*] You know it is true, Rufio.

The murmur without suddenly swells to a roar and subsides.

RUFIO I shall know presently. [*He makes for the altar in the burly trot that serves him for a stride, and touches Ftatateeta on the shoulder*]. Now, mistress: I shall want you. [*He orders her, with a gesture, to go before him*].

FTATATEETA [*rising and glowering at him*] My place is with the Queen.

CLEOPATRA She has done no harm, Rufio.

CÆSAR [*to Rufio*] Let her stay.

RUFIO [*sitting down on the altar*] Very well. Then my place is here too; and you can see what is the matter for yourself. The city is in a pretty uproar, it seems.

CÆSAR [*with grave displeasure*] Rufio: there is a time for obedience.

RUFIO And there is a time for obstinacy. [*He folds his arms doggedly*].

CÆSAR [*to Cleopatra*] Send her away.

CLEOPATRA [*whining in her eagerness to propitiate him*] Yes, I will.

182

	I will do whatever you ask me, Cæsar, always, because I love you. Ftatateeta: go away.
FTATATEETA	The Queen's word is my will. I shall be at hand for the Queen's call. [*She goes out past Ra, as she came*].
RUFIO	[*following her*] Remember, Cæsar, *your* bodyguard also is within call. [*He follows her out*].
	Cleopatra, presuming upon Cæsar's submission to Rufio, leaves the table and sits down on the bench in the colonnade.
CLEOPATRA	Why do you allow Rufio to treat you so? You should teach him his place.
CÆSAR	Teach him to be my enemy, and to hide his thoughts from me as you are now hiding yours.
CLEOPATRA	[*her fears returning*] Why do you say that, Cæsar? Indeed, indeed, I am not hiding anything. You are wrong to treat me like this. [*She stifles a sob*]. I am only a child; and you turn into stone because you think some one has been killed. I cannot bear it. [*She purposely breaks down and weeps. He looks at her with profound sadness and complete coldness. She looks up to see what effect she is producing. Seeing that he is unmoved, she sits up, pretending to struggle with her emotion and to put it bravely away*]. But there: I know you hate tears: you shall not be troubled with them. I know you are not angry, but only sad; only I am so silly, I cannot help being hurt when you speak coldly. Of course you are quite right: it is dreadful to think of anyone being killed or even hurt; and I hope nothing really serious has – [*her voice dies away under his contemptuous penetration*].
CÆSAR	What has frightened you into this? What have you done? [*A trumpet sounds on the beach below*]. Aha! that sounds like the answer.
CLEOPATRA	[*sinking back trembling on the bench and covering her face with her hands*] I have not betrayed you, Cæsar: I swear it.
CÆSAR	I know that. I have not trusted you. [*He turns from her, and is about to go out when Apollodorus and Britannus drag in Lucius Septimius to him. Rufio follows. Cæsar shudders*]. Again, Pompey's murderer!
RUFIO	The town has gone mad, I think. They are for tearing

the palace down and driving us into the sea straight away. We laid hold of this renegade in clearing them out of the courtyard.

CÆSAR Release him. [*They let go his arms*]. What has offended the citizens, Lucius Septimius?

LUCIUS What did you expect, Cæsar? Pothinus was a favorite of theirs.

CÆSAR What has happened to Pothinus? I set him free, here, not half an hour ago. Did they not pass him out?

LUCIUS Ay, through the gallery arch sixty feet above ground, with three inches of steel in his ribs. He is as dead as Pompey. We are quits now, as to killing – you and I.

CÆSAR [*shocked*] Assassinated! – our prisoner, our guest! [*He turns reproachfully on Rufio*] Rufio –

RUFIO [*emphatically – anticipating the question*] Whoever did it was a wise man and a friend of yours [*Cleopatra is greatly emboldened*]; but none of *us* had a hand in it. So it is no use to frown at me. [*Cæsar turns and looks at Cleopatra*].

CLEOPATRA [*violently – rising*] He was slain by order of the Queen of Egypt. I am not Julius Cæsar the dreamer, who allows every slave to insult him. Rufio has said I did well: now the others shall judge me too. [*She turns to the others*]. This Pothinus sought to make me conspire with him to betray Cæsar to Achillas and Ptolemy. I refused; and he cursed me and came privily to Cæsar to accuse me of his own treachery. I caught him in the act; and he insulted me – *me*, the Queen! to my face. Cæsar would not avenge me: he spoke him fair and set him free. Was I right to avenge myself? Speak, Lucius.

LUCIUS I do not gainsay it. But you will get little thanks from Cæsar for it.

CLEOPATRA Speak, Apollodorus. Was I wrong?

APOLLODORUS I have only one word of blame, most beautiful. You should have called upon me, your knight; and in fair duel I should have slain the slanderer.

CLEOPATRA [*passionately*] I will be judged by your very slave, Cæsar. Britannus: speak. Was I wrong?

BRITANNUS Were treachery, falsehood, and disloyalty left unpunished, society must become like an arena full of wild beasts, tearing one another to pieces. Cæsar is in the wrong.

CÆSAR [*with quiet bitterness*] And so the verdict is against me, it seems.

CLEOPATRA [*vehemently*] Listen to me, Cæsar. If one man in all Alexandria can be found to say that I did wrong, I swear to have myself crucified on the door of the palace by my own slaves.

CÆSAR If one man in all the world can be found, now or forever, to *know* that you did wrong, that man will have either to conquer the world as I have, or be crucified by it. [*The uproar in the streets again reaches them*]. Do you hear? These knockers at your gate are also believers in vengeance and in stabbing. You have slain their leader: it is right that they shall slay you. If you doubt it, ask your four counsellors here. And then in the name of that *right* [*he emphasizes the word with great scorn*] shall I not slay them for murdering their Queen, and be slain in my turn by their countrymen as the invader of their fatherland? Can Rome do less then than slay these slayers, too, to shew the world how Rome avenges her sons and her honor. And so, to the end of history, murder shall breed murder, always in the name of right and honor and peace, until the gods are tired of blood and create a race that can understand. [*Fierce uproar. Cleopatra becomes white with terror*]. Hearken, you who must not be insulted. Go near enough to catch their words: you will find them bitterer than the tongue of Pothinus. [*Loftily, wrapping himself up in an impenetrable dignity*] Let the Queen of Egypt now give her orders for vengeance, and take her measures for defence; for she has renounced Cæsar. [*He turns to go*].

CLEOPATRA [*terrified, running to him and falling on her knees*] You will not desert me, Cæsar. You will defend the palace.

CÆSAR You have taken the powers of life and death upon you. I am only a dreamer.

CLEOPATRA But they will kill me.

CÆSAR And why not?

CLEOPATRA In pity –

CÆSAR   Pity! What! has it come to this so suddenly, that nothing can save you now but pity? Did it save Pothinus?

She rises, wringing her hands, and goes back to the bench in despair. Apollodorus shews his sympathy with her by quietly posting himself behind the bench. The sky has by this time become the most vivid purple, and soon begins to change to a glowing pale orange, against which the colonnade and the great image shew darklier and darklier.

RUFIO   Cæsar: enough of preaching. The enemy is at the gate.

CÆSAR   [*turning on him and giving way to his wrath*] Ay; and what has held him baffled at the gate all these months? Was it my folly, as you deem it, or your wisdom? In this Egyptian Red Sea of blood, whose hand has held all your heads above the waves? [*Turning on Cleopatra*] And yet, when Cæsar says to such an one, "Friend, go free," you, clinging for your little life to my sword, dare steal out and stab him in the back? And you, soldiers and gentlemen, and honest servants as you forget that you are, applaud this assassination, and say, "Cæsar is in the wrong." By the gods, I am tempted to open my hand and let you all sink into the flood.

CLEOPATRA   [*with a ray of cunning hope*] But, Cæsar, if you do, you will perish yourself.

Cæsar's eyes blaze.

RUFIO   [*greatly alarmed*] Now, by great Jove, you filthy little Egyptian rat, that is the very word to make him walk out alone into the city and leave us here to be cut to pieces. [*Desperately, to Cæsar*] Will you desert us because we are a parcel of fools? I mean no harm by killing: I do it as a dog kills a cat, by instinct. We are all dogs at your heels; but we have served you faithfully.

CÆSAR   [*relenting*] Alas, Rufio, my son, my son: as dogs we are like to perish now in the streets.

APOLLODORUS   [*at his post behind Cleopatra's seat*] Cæsar: what you say has an Olympian ring in it: it must be right; for it is fine art. But I am still on the side of Cleopatra. If we must die, she shall not want the devotion of a man's heart nor the strength of a man's arm.

CLEOPATRA   [*sobbing*] But I don't want to die.

CÆSAR   [*sadly*] Oh, ignoble, ignoble!

LUCIUS [*coming forward between Cæsar and Cleopatra*] Hearken to me, Cæsar. It may be ignoble; but I also mean to live as long as I can.

CÆSAR Well, my friend, you are likely to outlive Cæsar. Is it any magic of mine, think you, that has kept your army and this whole city at bay for so long? Yesterday, what quarrel had they with me that they should risk their lives against me? But to-day we have flung them down their hero, murdered; and now every man of them is set upon clearing out this nest of assassins – for such we are and no more. Take courage then; and sharpen your sword. Pompey's head has fallen; and Cæsar's head is ripe.

APOLLODORUS Does Cæsar despair?

CÆSAR [*with infinite pride*] He who has never hoped can never despair. Cæsar, in good or bad fortune, looks his fate in the face.

LUCIUS Look it in the face, then; and it will smile as it always has on Cæsar.

CÆSAR [*with involuntary haughtiness*] Do you presume to encourage me?

LUCIUS I offer you my services. I will change sides if you will have me.

CÆSAR [*suddenly coming down to earth again, and looking sharply at him, divining that there is something behind the offer*] What! At this point?

LUCIUS [*firmly*] At this point.

RUFIO Do you suppose Cæsar is mad, to trust you?

LUCIUS I do not ask him to trust me until he is victorious. I ask for my life, and for a command in Cæsar's army. And since Cæsar is a fair dealer, I will pay in advance.

CÆSAR Pay! How?

LUCIUS With a piece of good news for you.

Cæsar divines the news in a flash.

RUFIO What news?

CÆSAR [*with an elate and buoyant energy which makes Cleopatra sit up and stare*] What news! What news, did you say, my son Rufio? The relief has arrived: what other news remains for us? Is it not so, Lucius Septimius? Mithridates of Pergamos is on the march.

187

LUCIUS He has taken Pelusium.

CÆSAR [*delighted*] Lucius Septimius: you are henceforth my officer. Rufio: the Egyptians must have sent every soldier from the city to prevent Mithridates crossing the Nile. There is nothing in the streets now but mob – mob!

LUCIUS It is so. Mithridates is marching by the great road to Memphis to cross above the Delta. Achillas will fight him there.

CÆSAR [*all audacity*] Achillas shall fight Cæsar there. See, Rufio. [*He runs to the table; snatches a napkin; and draws a plan on it with his finger dipped in wine, whilst Rufio and Lucius Septimius crowd about him to watch, all looking closely, for the light is now almost gone*]. Here is the palace [*pointing to his plan*]: here is the theatre. You [*to Rufio*] take twenty men and pretend to go by *that* street [*pointing it out*]; and whilst they are stoning you, out go the cohorts by this and this. My streets are right, are they, Lucius?

LUCIUS Ay, that is the fig market –

CÆSAR [*too much excited to listen to him*] I saw them the day we arrived. Good! [*He throws the napkin on the table,*

188

and comes down again into the colonnade]. Away, Britannus: tell Petronius that within an hour half our forces must take ship for the western lake. See to my horse and armor. [*Britannus runs out*]. With the rest, *I* shall march round the lake and up the Nile to meet Mithridates. Away, Lucius; and give the word. [*Lucius hurries out after Britannus*]. Apollodorus: lend me your sword and your right arm for this campaign.

APOLLODORUS Ay, and my heart and life to boot.

CÆSAR [*grasping his hand*] I accept both. [*Mighty handshake*]. Are you ready for work?

APOLLODORUS Ready for Art – the Art of War [*he rushes out after Lucius, totally forgetting Cleopatra*].

RUFIO Come! this is something like business.

CÆSAR [*buoyantly*] Is it not, my only son? [*He claps his hands. The slaves hurry in to the table*]. No more of this mawkish revelling: away with all this stuff: shut it out of my sight and be off with you. [*The slaves begin to remove the table; and the curtains are drawn, shutting in the colonnade*]. You understand about the streets, Rufio?

RUFIO Ay, I think I do. I will get through them, at all events.

189

The bucina sounds busily in the courtyard beneath.

CÆSAR Come, then: we must talk to the troops and hearten them. You down to the beach: I to the courtyard [*He makes for the staircase*].

CLEOPATRA [*rising from her seat, where she has been quite neglected all this time, and stretching out her hands timidly to him*] Cæsar.

CÆSAR [*turning*] Eh?

CLEOPATRA Have you forgotten me?

CÆSAR [*indulgently*] I am busy now, my child, busy. When I return your affairs shall be settled. Farewell; and be good and patient.

He goes, preoccupied and quite indifferent. She stands with clenched fists, in speechless rage and humiliation.

RUFIO That game is played and lost, Cleopatra. The woman always gets the worst of it.

CLEOPATRA [*haughtily*] Go. Follow your master.

RUFIO [*in her ear, with rough familiarity*] A word first. Tell your executioner that if Pothinus had been properly killed – in the *throat* – he would not have called out. Your man bungled his work.

CLEOPATRA [*enigmatically*] How do you know it was a man?

RUFIO [*startled, and puzzled*] It was not you: you were with us when it happened. [*She turns her back scornfully on him. He shakes his head, and draws the curtains to go out. It is now a magnificent moonlit night. The table has been removed. Ftatateeta is seen in the light of the moon and stars, again in prayer before the white altar-stone of Ra. Rufio starts; closes the curtains again softly; and says in a low voice to Cleopatra*] Was it she? with her own hand?

CLEOPATRA [*threateningly*] Whoever it was, let my enemies beware of her. Look to it, Rufio, you who dare make the Queen of Egypt a fool before Cæsar.

RUFIO [*looking grimly at her*] I will look to it, Cleopatra. [*He nods in confirmation of the promise, and slips out through the curtains, loosening his sword in its sheath as he goes*].

ROMAN SOLDIERS [*in the courtyard below*] Hail, Cæsar! Hail, hail!

190

Cleopatra listens. The bucina sounds again, followed by several trumpets.

CLEOPATRA   [*wringing her hands and calling*] Ftatateeta. Ftatateeta. It is dark; and I am alone. Come to me. [*Silence*] Ftatateeta. [*Louder*] Ftatateeta. [*Silence. In a panic she snatches the cord and pulls the curtains apart*].

Ftatateeta is lying dead on the altar of Ra, with her throat cut. Her blood deluges the white stone.

ACT 5

*High noon. Festival and military pageant on the es-
planade before the palace. In the east harbor Cæsar's
galley, so gorgeously decorated that it seems to be rigged
with flowers, is alongside the quay, close to the steps
Apollodorus descended when he embarked with the
carpet. A Roman guard is posted there in charge of a
gangway, whence a red floorcloth is laid down the middle
of the esplanade, turning off to the north opposite the
central gate in the palace front, which shuts in the esplanade on the south side. The broad steps of the gate,
crowded with Cleopatra's ladies, all in their gayest
attire, are like a flower garden. The façade is lined by
her guard, officered by the same gallants to whom Bel
Affris announced the coming of Cæsar six months before
in the old palace on the Syrian border. The north side
is lined by Roman soldiers, with the townsfolk on tiptoe
behind them, peering over their heads at the cleared
esplanade, in which the officers stroll about, chatting.
Among these are Belzanor and the Persian; also the
centurion, vinewood cudgel in hand, battle worn, thick-
booted, and much outshone, both socially and decora-
tively, by the Egyptian officers.*

*Apollodorus makes his way through the townsfolk
and calls to the officers from behind the Roman line.*

APOLLODORUS Hullo! May I pass?

CENTURION Pass Apollodorus the Sicilian there! [*The soldiers let him through*].

BELZANOR Is Cæsar at hand?

APOLLODORUS Not yet. He is still in the market place. I could not stand any more of the roaring of the soldiers! After half an hour of the enthusiasm of an army, one feels the need of a little sea air.

PERSIAN Tell us the news. Hath he slain the priests?

APOLLODORUS Not he. They met him in the market place with ashes on their heads and their gods in their hands. They placed the gods at his feet. The only one that was worth looking at was Apis: a miracle of gold and ivory work. By my advice he offered the chief priest two talents for it.

BELZANOR [*appalled*] Apis the all-knowing for two talents! What said the chief Priest?

APOLLODORUS He invoked the mercy of Apis, and asked for five.

BELZANOR There will be famine and tempest in the land for this.

PERSIAN Pooh! Why did not Apis cause Cæsar to be vanquished by Achillas? Any fresh news from the war, Apollodorus?

APOLLODORUS The little King Ptolemy was drowned.

BELZANOR Drowned! How?

APOLLODORUS With the rest of them. Cæsar attacked them from three sides at once and swept them into the Nile. Ptolemy's barge sank.

BELZANOR A marvellous man, this Cæsar! Will he come soon, think you?

APOLLODORUS He was settling the Jewish question when I left.

A flourish of trumpets from the north, and commotion among the townsfolk, announces the approach of Cæsar.

PERSIAN He has made short work of them. Here he comes. [*He hurries to his post in front of the Egyptian lines*].

BELZANOR [*following him*] Ho there! Cæsar comes.

The soldiers stand at attention, and dress their lines. Apollodorus goes to the Egyptian line.

194

CENTURION [*hurrying to the gangway guard*] Attention there! Cæsar comes.

Cæsar arrives in state with Rufio: Britannus following. The soldiers receive him with enthusiastic shouting.

CÆSAR I see my ship awaits me. The hour of Cæsar's farewell to Egypt has arrived. And now, Rufio, what remains to be done before I go?

RUFIO [*at his left hand*] You have not yet appointed a Roman governor for this province.

CÆSAR [*looking whimsically at him, but speaking with perfect gravity*] What say you to Mithridates of Pergamos, my reliever and rescuer, the great son of Eupator?

RUFIO Why, that you will want him elsewhere. Do you forget that you have some three or four armies to conquer on your way home?

CÆSAR Indeed! Well, what say you to yourself?

RUFIO [*incredulously*] I! I a governor! What are you dreaming of? Do you not know that I am only the son of a freedman?

CÆSAR [*affectionately*] Has not Cæsar called you his son? [*Calling to the whole assembly*] Peace awhile there; and hear me.

THE ROMAN
SOLDIERS Hear Cæsar.

CÆSAR Hear the service, quality, rank and name of the Roman governor. By service, Cæsar's shield; by quality, Cæsar's friend; by rank, a Roman soldier. [*The Roman soldiers give a triumphant shout*]. By name, Rufio. [*They shout again*].

RUFIO [*kissing Cæsar's hand*] Ay: I am Cæsar's shield; but of what use shall I be when I am no longer on Cæsar's arm? Well, no matter – [*He becomes husky, and turns away to recover himself*].

CÆSAR Where is that British Islander of mine?

BRITANNUS [*coming forward on Cæsar's right hand*] Here, Cæsar.

CÆSAR Who bade you, pray, thrust yourself into the battle of the Delta, uttering the barbarous cries of your native land, and affirming yourself a match for any four of the Egyptians, to whom you applied unseemly epithets?

BRITANNUS Cæsar: I ask you to excuse the language that escaped me in the heat of the moment.

CÆSAR And how did you, who cannot swim, cross the canal with us when we stormed the camp?

BRITANNUS Cæsar: I clung to the tail of your horse.

CÆSAR These are not the deeds of a slave, Britannicus, but of a free man.

BRITANNUS Cæsar: I was born free.

CÆSAR But they call you Cæsar's slave.

BRITANNUS Only as Cæsar's slave have I found real freedom.

CÆSAR [*moved*] Well said. Ungrateful that I am, I was about to set you free; but now I will not part from you for a million talents. [*He claps him friendly on the shoulder. Britannus, gratified, but a trifle shamefaced, takes his hand and kisses it sheepishly*].

BELZANOR [*to the Persian*] This Roman knows how to make men serve him.

PERSIAN Ay: men too humble to become dangerous rivals to him.

BELZANOR O subtle one! O cynic!

CÆSAR [*seeing Apollodorus in the Egyptian corner, and calling to him*] Apollodorus: I leave the art of Egypt in your charge. Remember: Rome loves art and will encourage it ungrudgingly.

APOLLODORUS I understand, Cæsar. Rome will produce no art itself; but it will buy up and take away whatever the other nations produce.

CÆSAR What! Rome produce no art! Is peace not an art? is war not an art? is government not an art? is civilization not an art? All these we give you in exchange for a few ornaments. You will have the best of the bargain. [*Turning to Rufio*] And now, what else have I to do before I embark? [*Trying to recollect*] There is something I cannot remember: what *can* it be? Well, well: it must remain undone: we must not waste this favorable wind. Farewell, Rufio.

RUFIO Cæsar: I am loth to let you go to Rome without your shield. There are too many daggers there.

CÆSAR It matters not: I shall finish my life's work on my way

back; and then I shall have lived long enough. Besides: I have always disliked the idea of dying: I had
rather be killed. Farewell.

RUFIO [*with a sigh, raising his hands and giving Cæsar up as
incorrigible*] Farewell. [*They shake hands*].

CÆSAR [*waving his hand to Apollodorus*] Farewell, Apollodorus, and my friends, all of you. Aboard!

*The gangway is run out from the quay to the ship. As
Cæsar moves towards it, Cleopatra, cold and tragic,
cunningly dressed in black, without ornaments or decora-
tion of any kind, and thus making a striking figure
among the brilliantly dressed bevy of ladies as she passes
through it, comes from the palace and stands on the
steps. Cæsar does not see her until she speaks.*

CLEOPATRA Has Cleopatra no part in this leavetaking?

CÆSAR [*enlightened*] Ah, I *knew* there was something. [*To
Rufio*] How could you let me forget her, Rufio?
[*Hastening to her*] Had I gone without seeing you, I
should never have forgiven myself. [*He takes her
hands, and brings her into the middle of the esplanade.
She submits stonily*]. Is this mourning for me?

CLEOPATRA No.

CÆSAR [*remorsefully*] Ah, that was thoughtless of me! It is for
your brother.

CLEOPATRA No.

CÆSAR For whom, then?

CLEOPATRA Ask the Roman governor whom you have left us.

CÆSAR Rufio?

CLEOPATRA Yes: Rufio. [*She points at him with deadly scorn*]. He
who is to rule here in Cæsar's name, in Cæsar's way,
according to Cæsar's boasted laws of life.

CÆSAR [*dubiously*] He is to rule as he can, Cleopatra. He has
taken the work upon him, and will do it in his own
way.

CLEOPATRA Not in your way, then?

CÆSAR [*puzzled*] What do you mean by my way?

CLEOPATRA Without punishment. Without revenge. Without
judgment.

CÆSAR [*approvingly*] Ay: that is the right way, the great way,

197

the only possible way in the end. [*To Rufio*] Believe it, Rufio, if you can.

RUFIO Why, I believe it, Cæsar. You have convinced me of it long ago. But look you. You are sailing for Numidia to-day. Now tell me: if you meet a hungry lion there, you will not punish it for wanting to eat you?

CÆSAR [*wondering what he is driving at*] No.

RUFIO Nor revenge upon it the blood of those it has already eaten.

CÆSAR No.

RUFIO Nor judge it for its guiltiness.

CÆSAR No.

RUFIO What, then, will you do to save your life from it?

CÆSAR [*promptly*] Kill it, man, without malice, just as it would kill me. What does this parable of the lion mean?

RUFIO Why, Cleopatra had a tigress that killed men at her bidding. I thought she might bid it kill you some day. Well, had I not been Cæsar's pupil, what pious things might I not have done to that tigress! I might have punished it. I might have revenged Pothinus on it.

CÆSAR [*interjects*] Pothinus!

RUFIO [*continuing*] I might have judged it. But I put all these follies behind me; and, without malice, only cut its throat. And that is why Cleopatra comes to you in mourning.

CLEOPATRA [*vehemently*] He has shed the blood of my servant Ftatateeta. On your head be it as upon his, Cæsar, if you hold him free of it.

CÆSAR [*energetically*] On my head be it, then; for it was well done. Rufio: had you set yourself in the seat of the judge, and with hateful ceremonies and appeals to the gods handed that woman over to some hired executioner to be slain before the people in the name of justice, never again would I have touched your hand without a shudder. But this was natural slaying: I feel no horror at it.

Rufio, satisfied, nods at Cleopatra, mutely inviting her to mark that.

198

CLEOPATRA   [*pettish and childish in her impotence*] No: not when a
            Roman slays an Egyptian. All the world will now see
            how unjust and corrupt Cæsar is.

CÆSAR   [*taking her hands coaxingly*] Come: do not be angry
            with me. I am sorry for that poor Totateeta. [*She
            laughs in spite of herself*]. Aha! you are laughing. Does
            that mean reconciliation?

CLEOPATRA   [*angry with herself for laughing*] No, *no*, NO!! But it is
            so ridiculous to hear you call her Totateeta.

CÆSAR   What! As much a child as ever, Cleopatra! Have I not
            made a woman of you after all?

CLEOPATRA   Oh, it is you who are a great baby: you make me seem
            silly because you will not behave seriously. But you
            have treated me badly; and I do not forgive you.

CÆSAR   Bid me farewell.

CLEOPATRA   I will not.

CÆSAR   [*coaxing*] I will send you a beautiful present from
            Rome.

CLEOPATRA   [*proudly*] Beauty from Rome to Egypt indeed! What
            can Rome give *me* that Egypt cannot give me?

POLLODORUS That is true, Cæsar. If the present is to be really
            beautiful, I shall have to buy it for you in Alexandria.

CÆSAR   You are forgetting the treasures for which Rome is
            most famous, my friend. You cannot buy *them* in
            Alexandria.

POLLODORUS What are they, Cæsar?

CÆSAR   Her sons. Come, Cleopatra: forgive me and bid me
            farewell; and I will send you a man, Roman from head
            to heel and Roman of the noblest; not old and ripe for
            the knife; not lean in the arms and cold in the heart;
            not hiding a bald head under his conqueror's laurels;
            not stooped with the weight of the world on his shoul-
            ders; but brisk and fresh, strong and young, hoping in
            the morning, fighting in the day, and revelling in the
            evening. Will you take such an one in exchange for
            Cæsar?

CLEOPATRA   [*palpitating*] His name, his name?

CÆSAR   Shall it be Mark Antony? [*She throws herself into his
            arms*].

199

RUFIO	You are a bad hand at a bargain, mistress, if you will swop Cæsar for Antony.
CÆSAR	So now you are satisfied.
CLEOPATRA	You will not forget.
CÆSAR	I will not forget. Farewell: I do not think we shall meet again. Farewell. [*He kisses her on the forehead. She is much affected and begins to sniff. He embarks*].
THE ROMAN SOLDIERS	[*as he sets his foot on the gangway*] Hail, Cæsar; and farewell!
	He reaches the ship and returns Rufio's wave of the hand.
APOLLODORUS	[*to Cleopatra*] No tears, dearest Queen: they stab your servant to the heart. He will return some day.
CLEOPATRA	I hope not. But I cant help crying, all the same. [*She waves her handkerchief to Cæsar; and the ship begins to move*].
THE ROMAN SOLDIERS	[*drawing their swords and raising them in the air*] Hail, Cæsar!

NOTES

Notes to
THE DEVIL'S DISCIPLE

General John Burgoyne, who is presented in this play for the first time (as far as I am aware) on the English stage, is not a conventional stage soldier, but as faithful a portrait as it is in the nature of stage portraits to be. His objection to profane swearing is not borrowed from Mr Gilbert's H.M.S. Pinafore: it is taken from the Code of Instructions drawn up by himself for his officers when he introduced Light Horse into the English army. His opinion that English soldiers should be treated as thinking beings was no doubt as unwelcome to the military authorities of his time, when nothing was thought of ordering a soldier a thousand lashes, as it will be to those modern victims of the flagellation neurosis who are so anxious to revive that discredited sport. His military reports are very clever as criticisms, and are humane and enlightened within certain aristocratic limits, best illustrated perhaps by his declaration, which now sounds so curious, that he should blush to ask for promotion on any other ground than that of family influence. As a parliamentary candidate, Burgoyne took our common expression "fighting an election" so very literally that he led his supporters to the poll at Preston in 1768 with a loaded pistol in each hand, and won the seat, though he was fined £1000, and denounced by Junius, for the pistols.

It is only within quite recent years that any general recognition has become possible for the feeling that led Burgoyne, a professed enemy of oppression in India and elsewhere, to accept his American command when so many other officers threw up their commissions rather than serve in a civil war against the Colonies. His biographer De Fonblanque, writing in 1876, evidently regarded his position as indefensible. Nowadays, it is sufficient to say that Burgoyne was an Imperialist. He sympathized with the colonists; but when they proposed as a remedy the disruption of the Empire, he regarded that as a step backward in civilization. As he put it to the House of Commons, "while we remember that we are contending against brothers and fellow subjects, we must also remember that we are contending in this crisis for the fate of the British Empire." Eighty-four years after his defeat, his republican conquerors themselves engaged in a civil war for the integrity of their Union. In 1885 the Whigs who represented the anti-Burgoyne tradition of American Independence in English politics, abandoned Gladstone and made common cause with their political opponents in defence of the Union between England and Ireland. Only the other day England sent 200,000 men into the field south of the equator to fight out the question whether South Africa should develop as a Federation of British Colonies or as an independent Afrikander United States. In all these cases the Unionists who were detached from their parties were called renegades, as Burgoyne was. That, of course, is only one of the unfortunate consequences of the fact that mankind, being for the most part incapable of politics, accepts vituperation as an easy and congenial substitute. Whether Burgoyne or Washington, Lincoln or Davis, Gladstone or Bright, Mr Chamberlain or Mr Leonard

Courtney was in the right will never be settled, because it will never be possible to prove that the government of the victor has been better for mankind than the government of the vanquished would have been. It is true that the victors have no doubt on the point; but to the dramatist, that certainty of theirs is only part of the human comedy. The American Unionist is often a Separatist as to Ireland; the English Unionist often sympathizes with the Polish Home Ruler; and both English and American Unionists are apt to be Disruptionists as regards that Imperial Ancient of Days, the Empire of China. Both are Unionists concerning Canada, but with a difference as to the precise application to it of the Monroe doctrine. As for me, the dramatist, I smile, and lead the conversation back to Burgoyne.

Burgoyne's surrender at Saratoga made him that occasionally necessary part of our British system, a scapegoat. The explanation of his defeat given in the play (p. 72) is founded on a passage quoted by De Fonblanque from Fitzmaurice's Life of Lord Shelburne, as follows: "Lord George Germain, having among other peculiarities a particular dislike to be put out of his way on any occasion, had arranged to call at his office on his way to the country to sign the dispatches; but as those addressed to Howe had not been fair-copied, and he was not disposed to be balked of his projected visit to Kent, they were not signed then and were forgotten on his return home." These were the dispatches instructing Sir William Howe, who was in New York, to effect a junction at Albany with Burgoyne, who had marched from Quebec for that purpose. Burgoyne got as far as Saratoga, where, failing the expected reinforcement, he was hopelessly outnumbered, and his officers picked off, Boer fashion, by the American farmer-sharpshooters. His own collar was pierced by a bullet. The publicity of his defeat, however, was more than compensated at home by the fact that Lord George's trip to Kent had not been interfered with, and that nobody knew about the oversight of the dispatch. The policy of the English Government and Court for the next two years was simply concealment of Germain's neglect. Burgoyne's demand for an inquiry was defeated in the House of Commons by the court party; and when he at last obtained a committee, the king got rid of it by a prorogation. When Burgoyne realized what had happened about the instructions to Howe (the scene in which I have represented him as learning it before Saratoga is not historical: the truth did not dawn on him until many months afterwards) the king actually took advantage of his being a prisoner of war in England on parole, and ordered him to return to America into captivity. Burgoyne immediately resigned all his appointments; and this practically closed his military career, though he was afterwards made Commander of the Forces in Ireland for the purpose of banishing him from parliament.

The episode illustrates the curious perversion of the English sense of honor when the privileges and prestige of the aristocracy are at stake. Mr Frank Harris said, after the disastrous battle of

Modder River, that the English, having lost America a century ago because they preferred George III, were quite prepared to lose South Africa to-day because they preferred aristocratic commanders to successful ones. Horace Walpole, when the parliamentary recess came at a critical period of the War of Independence, said that the Lords could not be expected to lose their pheasant shooting for the sake of America. In the working class, which, like all classes, has its own official aristocracy, there is the same reluctance to discredit an institution or to "do a man out of his job." At bottom, of course, this apparently shameless sacrifice of great public interests to petty personal ones, is simply the preference of the ordinary man for the things he can feel and understand to the things that are beyond his capacity. It is stupidity, not dishonesty.

Burgoyne fell a victim to this stupidity in two ways. Not only was he thrown over, in spite of his high character and distinguished services, to screen a court favorite who had actually been cashiered for cowardice and misconduct in the field fifteen years before; but his peculiar critical temperament and talent, artistic, satirical, rather histrionic, and his fastidious delicacy of sentiment, his fine spirit and humanity, were just the qualities to make him disliked by stupid people because of their dread of ironic criticism. Long after his death, Thackeray, who had an intense sense of human character, but was typically stupid in valuing and interpreting it, instinctively sneered at him and exulted in his defeat. That sneer represents the common English attitude towards the Burgoyne type. Every instance in which the critical genius is defeated, and the stupid genius (for both temperaments have their genius) "muddles through all right," is popular in England. But Burgoyne's failure was not the work of his own temperament, but of the stupid temperament. What man could do under the circumstances he did, and did handsomely and loftily. He fell, and his ideal empire was dismembered, not through his own misconduct, but because Sir George Germain overestimated the importance of his Kentish holiday, and underestimated the difficulty of conquering those remote and inferior creatures, the colonists. And King George and the rest of the nation agreed, on the whole, with Germain. It is a significant point that in America, where Burgoyne was an enemy and an invader, he was admired and praised. The climate there is no doubt more favorable to intellectual vivacity.

I have described Burgoyne's temperament as rather histrionic; and the reader will have observed that the Burgoyne of the Devil's Disciple is a man who plays his part in life, and makes all its points, in the manner of a born high comedian. If he had been killed at Saratoga, with all his comedies unwritten, and his plan for turning As You Like It into a Beggar's Opera unconceived, I should still have painted the same picture of him on the strength of his reply to the articles of capitulation proposed to him by the victorious Gates (an Englishman). Here they are:

PROPOSITION	ANSWER

1. General Burgoyne's army being reduced by repeated defeats, by desertion, sickness, etc., their provisions exhausted, their military horses, tents and baggage taken or destroyed, their retreat cut off, and their camp invested, they can only be allowed to surrender as prisoners of war.

Lieut-General Burgoyne's army, however reduced, will never admit that their retreat is cut off while they have arms in their hands.

2. The officers and soldiers may keep the baggage belonging to them. The Generals of the United States never permit individuals to be pillaged.

Noted.

3. The troops under his Excellency General Burgoyne will be conducted by the most convenient route to New England, marching by easy marches, and sufficiently provided for by the way.

Agreed.

4. The officers will be admited on parole and will be treated with the liberality customary in such cases, so long as they, by proper behaviour, continue to deserve it; but those who are apprehended having broke their parole, as some British officers have done, must expect to be close confined.

There being no officer in this army under, or capable of being under, the description of breaking parole, this article needs no answer.

5. All public stores, artillery, arms, ammunition, carriages, horses, etc., etc., must be delivered to commissaries appointed to receive them.

All public stores may be delivered, arms excepted.

6. These terms being agreed to and signed, the troops under his Excellency's, General Burgoyne's command, may be drawn up in their encampments, where they will be ordered to ground their arms, and may thereupon be marched to the river-side on their way to Bennington.

This article is inadmissible in any extremity. Sooner than this army will consent to ground their arms in their encampments, they will rush on the enemy determined to take no quarter.

And, later on, "If General Gates does not mean to recede from the 6th article, the treaty ends at once: the army will to a man proceed to any act of desperation sooner than submit to that article."

Here you have the man at his Burgoynest. Need I add that he had his own way; and that when the actual ceremony of surrender came, he would have played poor General Gates off the stage, had not that commander risen to the occasion by handing him back his sword.

In connection with the reference to Indians with scalping knives, who, with the troops hired from Germany, made up about half Burgoyne's force, I may cite the case of Jane McCrea, betrothed to one of Burgoyne's officers. A Wyandotte chief attached to Burgoyne's force was bringing her to the British camp as a prisoner of war, when another party of Indians, sent by her betrothed, claimed her. The Wyandotte settled the dispute by killing her and bringing her scalp to Burgoyne. Burgoyne let the deed pass. Possibly he feared that a massacre of whites on the Canadian border by the Wyandottes would follow any attempt at punishment. But his own proclamations had threatened just what the savage chief executed.

Brudenell is also a real person. At least, an artillery chaplain BRUDENELL of that name distinguished himself at Saratoga by reading the burial service over Major Fraser under fire, and by a quite readable adventure, chronicled, with exaggerations, by Burgoyne, concerning Lady Harriet Acland. Others have narrated how Lady Harriet's husband killed himself in a duel, by falling with his head against a pebble; and how Lady Harriet then married the warrior chaplain. All this, however, is a tissue of romantic lies, though it has been repeated in print as authentic history from generation to generation, even to the first edition of this book. As a matter of fact, Major Acland died in his bed of a cold shortly after his return to England; and Lady Harriet remained a widow until her death in 1815.

The rest of the Devil's Disciple may have actually occurred, like most stories invented by dramatists; but I cannot produce any documents. Major Swindon's name is invented; but the man, of course, is real. There are dozens of him extant to this day.

Notes to
CÆSAR AND CLEOPATRA

For the sake of conciseness in a hurried situation I have made Cleopatra recommend rum. This, I am afraid, is an anachronism: the only real one in the play. To balance it, I give a couple of the remedies she actually believed in. They are quoted by Galen from Cleopatra's book on Cosmetic.

"For bald patches, powder red sulphuret of arsenic and take it up with oak gum, as much as it will bear. Put on a rag and apply, having soaped the place well first. I have mixed the above with a foam of nitre, and it worked well."

Several other receipts follow, ending with: "The following is the best of all, acting for fallen hairs, when applied with oil or pomatum; acts also for falling off of eyelashes or for people getting bald all over. It is wonderful. Of domestic mice burnt, one part; of vine rag burnt, one part; of horse's teeth burnt, one part; of bear's grease one; of deer's marrow one; of reed bark one. To be pounded when dry, and mixed with plenty of honey til it gets the consistency of honey; then the bear's grease and marrow to be mixed (when melted), the medicine to be put in a brass flask, and the bald part rubbed til it sprouts."

Concerning these ingredients, my fellow-dramatist Gilbert Murray, who, as a Professor of Greek, has applied to classical antiquity the methods of high scholarship (my own method is pure divination), writes to me as follows: "Some of this I dont understand, and possibly Galen did not, as he quotes your heroine's own language. Foam of nitre is, I think, something like soapsuds. Reed bark is an odd expression. It might mean the outside membrane of a reed: I do not know what it ought to be called. In the burnt mice receipt I take it that you first mixed the solid powders with honey, and then added the grease. I expect Cleopatra preferred it because in most of the others you have to lacerate the skin, prick it, or rub it till it bleeds. I do not know what vine rag is. I translate literally."

The only way to write a play which shall convey to the general public an impression of antiquity is to make the characters speak blank verse and abstain from reference to steam, telegraphy, or any of the material conditions of their existence. The more ignorant men are, the more convinced are they that their little parish and their little chapel is an apex to which civilization and philosophy has painfully struggled up the pyramid of time from a desert of savagery. Savagery, they think, became barbarism; barbarism became ancient civilization; ancient civilization became Pauline Christianity; Pauline Christianity became Roman Catholicism; Roman Catholicism became the Dark Ages; and the Dark Ages were finally enlightened by the Protestant instincts of the English race. The whole process is summed up as Progress with a capital P. And any elderly gentleman of Progressive temperament will testify that the improvement since he was a boy is enormous.

Now if we count the generations of Progressive elderly gentlemen since, say, Plato, and add together the successive enormous improvements to which each of them has testified, it will strike us at once as an unaccountable fact that the world, instead of having been improved in 67 generations out of all recognition, presents, on the whole, a rather less dignified appearance in Ibsen's Enemy of the People than in Plato's Republic. And in truth, the period of time covered by history is far too short to allow of any perceptible progress in the popular sense of Evolution of the Human Species. The notion that there has been any such Progress since Cæsar's time (less than 20 centuries) is too absurd for discussion. All the savagery, barbarism, dark ages and the rest of it of which we have any record as existing in the past, exists at the present moment. A British carpenter or stonemason may point out that he gets twice as much money for his labor as his father did in the same trade, and that his suburban house, with its bath, its cottage piano, its drawingroom suite, and its album of photographs, would have shamed the plainness of his grandmother's. But the descendants of feudal barons, living in squalid lodgings on a salary of fifteen shillings a week instead of in castles on princely revenues, do not congratulate the world on the change. Such changes, in fact, are not to the point. It has been known, as far back as our records go, that man running wild in the woods is different from man kennelled in a city slum; that a dog seems to understand a shepherd better than a hewer of wood and drawer of water can understand an astronomer; and that breeding, gentle nurture and luxurious food and shelter will produce a kind of man with whom the common laborer is socially incompatible. The same thing is true of horses and dogs. Now there is clearly room for great changes in the world by increasing the percentage of individuals who are carefully bred and gently nurtured, even to finally making the most of every man and woman born. But that possibility existed in the days of the Hittites as much as it does to-day. It does not give the slightest real support to the common assumption that the civilized contemporaries of the Hittites were unlike their civilized descendants today.

This would appear the tritest commonplace if it were not that the ordinary citizen's ignorance of the past combines with his idealization of the present to mislead and flatter him. Our latest book on the new railway across Asia describes the dulness of the Siberian farmer and the vulgar pursepride of the Siberian man of business without the least consciousness that the string of contemptuous instances given might have been saved by writing simply "Farmers and provincial plutocrats in Siberia are exactly what they are in England." The latest professor descanting on the civilization of the Western Empire in the fifth century feels bound to assume, in the teeth of his own researches, that the Christian was one sort of animal and the Pagan another. It might as well be assumed, as indeed it generally is assumed by implication, that a murder committed with a poisoned arrow is different from a murder committed with a Mauser rifle. All such notions are illusions. Go back to the first syllable of recorded time, and there you will find your Christian and your Pagan, your yokel and your poet, helot and hero, Don Quixote and Sancho, Tamino and Papageno, Newton and bushman unable to count eleven, all alive and contemporaneous, and all convinced that they are the heirs of all the ages and the privileged recipients of THE truth (all others damnable heresies), just as you have them to-day, flourishing in countries each of which is the bravest and best that ever sprang at Heaven's command from out the azure main.

Again, there is the illusion of "increased command over Nature," meaning that cotton is cheap and that ten miles of country road on a bicycle have replaced four on foot. But even if man's increased command over Nature included any increased command over himself (the only sort of command relevant to his evolution into a higher being), the fact remains that it is only by running away from the increased command over Nature to country places where Nature is still in primitive command over Man that he can recover from the effects of the smoke, the stench, the foul air, the overcrowding, the racket, the ugliness, the dirt which the cheap cotton costs us. If manufacturing activity means Progress, the town must be more advanced than the country; and the field laborers and village artizans of to-day must be much less changed from the servants of Job than the proletariat of modern London from the proletariat of Cæsar's Rome. Yet the cockney proletarian is so inferior to the village laborer that it is only by steady recruiting from the country that London is kept alive. This does not seem as if the change since Job's time were Progress in the popular sense: quite the reverse. The common stock of discoveries in physics has accumulated a little: that is all.

One more illustration. Is the Englishman prepared to admit that the American is his superior as a human being? I ask this question because the scarcity of labor in America relatively to the demand for it has led to a development of machinery there, and a consequent "increase of command over Nature" which makes many of our English methods appear almost medieval to the up-to-date Chicagoan. This means that the American has an advantage over the Englishman of exactly the same nature that the Englishman has over the contemporaries of Cicero. Is the Englishman prepared to draw the same conclusion in both cases? I think not. The American, of course, will draw it cheerfully; but I must then ask him whether, since a modern Negro has a greater "command over Nature" than Washington had, we are also to accept the conclusion, involved in his former one, that humanity has progressed from Washington to the *fin de siècle* Negro.

Finally, I would point out that if life is crowned by its success and devotion in industrial organization and ingenuity, we had better worship the ant and the bee (as moralists urge us to do

211

in our childhood), and humble ourselves before the arrogance of the birds of Aristophanes.

My reason then for ignoring the popular conception of Progress in Cæsar and Cleopatra is that there is no reason to suppose that any Progress has taken place since their time. But even if I shared the popular delusion, I do not see that I could have made any essential difference in the play. I can only imitate humanity as I know it. Nobody knows whether Shakespear thought that ancient Athenian joiners, weavers, or bellows menders were any different from Elizabethan ones; but it is quite certain that he could not have made them so, unless, indeed, he had played the literary man and made Quince say, not "Is all our company here?" but "Bottom: was not that Socrates that passed us at the Piræus with Glaucon and Polemarchus on his way to the house of Kephalus?" And so on.

CLEOPATRA

Cleopatra was only sixteen when Cæsar went to Egypt; but in Egypt sixteen is a riper age than it is in England. The childishness I have ascribed to her, as far as it is childishness of character and not lack of experience, is not a matter of years. It may be observed in our own climate at the present day in many women of fifty. It is a mistake to suppose that the difference between wisdom and folly has anything to do with the difference between physical age and physical youth. Some women are younger at seventy than most women at seventeen.

It must be borne in mind, too, that Cleopatra was a queen, and was therefore not the typical Greek-cultured, educated Egyptian lady of her time. To represent her by any such type would be as absurd as to represent George IV by a type founded on the attainments of Sir Isaac Newton. It is true that an ordinarily well educated Alexandrian girl of her time would no more have believed bogey stories about the Romans than the daughter of a modern Oxford professor would believe them about the Germans (though, by the way, it is possible to talk great nonsense at Oxford about foreigners when we are at war with them). But I do not feel bound to believe that Cleopatra was well educated. Her father, the illustrious Flute Blower, was not at all a parent of the Oxford professor type. And Cleopatra was a chip of the old block.

BRITANNUS

I find among those who have read this play in manuscript a strong conviction that an ancient Briton could not possibly have been like a modern one. I see no reason to adopt this curious view. It is true that the Roman and Norman conquests must have for a time disturbed the normal British type produced by the climate. But Britannus, born before these events, represents the unadulterated Briton who fought Cæsar and impressed

212

Roman observers much as we should expect the ancestors of Mr Podsnap to impress the cultivated Italians of their time.

I am told that it is not scientific to treat national character as a product of climate. This only shews the wide difference between common knowledge and the intellectual game called science. We have men of exactly the same stock, and speaking the same language, growing in Great Britain, in Ireland, and in America. The result is three of the most distinctly marked nationalities under the sun. Racial characteristics are quite another matter. The difference between a Jew and a Gentile has nothing to do with the difference between an Englishman and a German. The characteristics of Britannus are local characteristics, not race characteristics. In an ancient Briton they would, I take it, be exaggerated, since modern Britain, disforested, drained, urbanified and consequently cosmopolized, is presumably less characteristically British than Cæsar's Britain.

And again I ask does anyone who, in the light of a competent knowledge of his own age, has studied history from contemporary documents, believe that 67 generations of promiscuous marriage have made any appreciable difference in the human fauna of these isles? Certainly I do not.

As to Cæsar himself, I have purposely avoided the usual anachronism of going to Cæsar's books, and concluding that the style is the man. That is only true of authors who have the specific literary genius, and have practised long enough to attain complete self-expression in letters. It is not true even on these conditions in an age when literature is conceived as a game of style, and not as a vehicle of self-expression by the author. Now Cæsar was an amateur stylist writing books of travel and campaign histories in a style so impersonal that the authenticity of the later volumes is disputed. They reveal some of his qualities just as the Voyage of a Naturalist Round the World reveals some of Darwin's, without expressing his private personality. An Englishman reading them would say that Cæsar was a man of great common sense and good taste, meaning thereby a man without originality or moral courage.

In exhibiting Cæsar as a much more various person than the historian of the Gallic wars, I hope I have not been too much imposed on by the dramatic illusion to which all great men owe part of their reputation and some the whole of it. I admit that reputations gained in war are specially questionable. Able civilians taking up the profession of arms, like Cæsar and Cromwell, in middle age, have snatched all its laurels from opponent commanders bred to it, apparently because capable persons engaged in military pursuits are so scarce that the existence of two of them at the same time in the same hemisphere is extremely rare. The capacity of any conqueror is therefore more likely than not to be an illusion produced by the incapacity of his adversary. At all events, Cæsar might have won his battles without being wiser than Charles XII or Nelson or Joan of Arc, who were, like most modern "self-made" millionaires, half-witted geniuses, enjoying the worship accorded by all races to certain forms of insanity. But Cæsar's victories were only advertisements for an eminence that would never have become popular without them. Cæsar is greater off the battle field than on it. Nelson off his quarterdeck was so quaintly out of the question that when his head was injured at the battle of the Nile, and his conduct became for some years openly scandalous, the difference was not important enough to be noticed. It may, however, be said that peace hath her illusory reputations no less than war. And it is certainly true that in civil life mere capacity for work—the power of killing a dozen secretaries under you, so to speak, as a life-or-death courier kills horses—enables men with common ideas and superstitions to distance all competitors in the strife of political ambition. It was this power of work that astonished Cicero as the most prodigious of Cæsar's gifts, as it astonished later observers in Napoleon before it wore him out. How if Cæsar were nothing but a Nelson and a Gladstone combined! a prodigy of vitality without any special quality of mind! nay, with ideas that were worn out before he was born, as Nelson's and Gladstone's were! I have considered that possibility too, and rejected it. I cannot cite all the stories about Cæsar which seem to me to shew that he was genuinely original; but let me at least point out that I have been careful to attribute nothing but originality to him. Originality gives a man an air of frankness, generosity, and magnanimity by enabling him to estimate the value of truth, money, or success in any particular instance quite independently of convention and moral generalization. He therefore will not, in the ordinary Treasury bench fashion, tell a lie which everybody knows to be a lie (and consequently expects him as a matter of good taste to tell). His lies are not found out: they pass for candors. He understands the paradox of money, and gives it away when he can get most for it: in other words, when its value is least, which is just when a common man tries hardest to get it. He knows that the real moment of success is not the moment apparent to the crowd. Hence, in order to produce an impression of complete disinterestedness and magnanimity, he has only to act with entire selfishness; and this is perhaps the only sense in which a man can be said to be *naturally* great. It is in this sense that I have represented Cæsar as great. Having virtue, he has no need of goodness. He is neither forgiving, frank, nor generous, because a man who is too great to resent has nothing to forgive; a man who says things that other people are afraid to say need be no more frank than Bismarck was; and there is no generosity in giving things you do not want to people of whom you intend to make use. This distinction between virtue and goodness is not understood in England: hence the poverty of our drama in heroes. Our stage attempts at them are mere goody-goodies.

Goodness, in its popular British sense of self-denial, implies that man is vicious by nature, and that supreme goodness is supreme martyrdom. Not sharing that pious opinion, I have not given countenance to it in any of my plays. In this I follow the precedent of the ancient myths, which represent the hero as vanquishing his enemies, not in fair fight, but with enchanted sword, superequine horse and magical invulnerability, the possession of which, from the vulgar moralistic point of view, robs his exploits of any merit whatever.

As to Cæsar's sense of humor, there is no more reason to assume that he lacked it than to assume that he was deaf or blind. It is said that on the occasion of his assassination by a conspiracy of moralists (it is always your moralist who makes assassination a duty, on the scaffold or off it), he defended himself until the good Brutus struck him, when he exclaimed "What! you too, Brutus!" and disdained further fight. If this be true, he must have been an incorrigible comedian. But even if we waive this story, or accept the traditional sentimental interpretation of it, there is still abundant evidence of his lightheartedness and adventurousness. Indeed it is clear from his whole history that what has been called his ambition was an instinct for exploration. He had much more of Columbus and Franklin in him than of Henry V.

However, nobody need deny Cæsar a share, at least, of the qualities I have attributed to him. All men, much more Julius Cæsars, possess all qualities in some degree. The really interesting question is whether I am right in assuming that the way to produce an impression of greatness is by exhibiting a man, not as mortifying his nature by doing his duty, in the manner which our system of putting little men into great positions (not having enough great men in our influential families to go round) forces us to inculcate, but as simply doing what he naturally wants to do. For this raises the question whether our world has not been wrong in its moral theory for the last 2,500 years or so. It must be a constant puzzle to many of us that the Christian era, so excellent in its intentions, should have been practically such a very discreditable episode in the history of the race. I doubt if this is altogether due to the vulgar and sanguinary sensationalism of our religious legends, with their substitution of gross physical torments and public executions for the passion of humanity. Islam, substituting voluptuousness for torment (a merely superficial difference, it is true) has done no better. It may have been the failure of Christianity to emancipate itself from expiatory theories of moral responsibility, guilt, innocence, reward, punishment, and the rest of it, that baffled its intention of changing the world. But these are bound up in all philosophies of creation as opposed to cosmism. They may therefore be regarded as the price we pay for popular religion.